Marketing the City

OTHER TITLES FROM E & FN SPON

Caring for our Built Heritage
A survey of conservation schemes carried out by County Councils in England and Wales
T. Haskell

European Directory of Property Developers, Investors and Financiers 1993
2nd Edition
Building Economics Bureau

Industrial and Business Space Development
Implementation and Urban Renewal
S. Morley, C. Marsh, A. McIntosh and H. Martinos

Industrial Property Markets in Western Europe
Edited by B. Wood and R. Williams

International Real Estate Valuation, Investment and Development
V.J. Nurcombe

Microcomputers in Property
A surveyor's guide to Lotus 1-2-3 and dBASE IV
T.J. Dixon, O. Bevan and S. Hargitay

The Multilingual Dictionary of Real Estate
L. van Breughel, R.H. Williams and B. Wood

National Taxation for Property Management and Valuation
A. MacLeary

Property Development
3rd Edition
D. Cadman and L. Austin-Crowe
Edited by R. Topping and M. Avis

Property Investment and the Capital Markets
G.R. Brown

Property Valuation
The five methods
D. Scarrett

Rebuilding the City
Property-led urban regeneration
Edited by P. Healey, D. Usher, S. Davoudi, S. Tavsanoglu and M. O'Toole

Risk, Uncertainty and Decision-making in Property Development
P.J. Byrne and D. Cadman

Transport, the Environment and Sustainable Development
D. Banister and K. Button

UK Directory of Property Developers, Investors and Financiers 1993
7th Edition
Building Economics Bureau

Urban Regeneration, Property Investment and Development
J. Berry, W. Deddis and W. McGreal

Effective Speaking
Communication in speech
C. Turk

Effective Writing
Improving scientific, technical and business communication
2nd Edition
C. Turk and J. Kirkman

Write in Style
A guide to good English
R. Palmer

Journals
Journal of Property Research (formerly Land Development Studies)
Editors: B.D. MacGregor, D. Hartzell and M. Miles

Planning Perspectives
An international journal of planning, history and the environment
Editors: G.E. Cherry and A.R. Sutcliffe

For more information on these and other titles please ccontact:
The Promotion Department, E & FN Spon, 2–6 Boundary Row, London, SE1 8HN.
Telephone 071-865 0066.

Marketing the City

The role of flagship developments in urban regeneration

Hedley Smyth

Civil Engineering and Building Division
Oxford Brookes University
UK

The research on which this book is based was initiated by the British Urban Regeneration Association and sponsored by J Sainsbury plc.

E & FN SPON
An Imprint of Chapman & Hall

London · Glasgow · New York · Tokyo · Melbourne · Madras

Published by E & FN Spon, an imprint of Chapman & Hall, 2–6 Boundary
Road, London SE1 8HN, UK

Chapman & Hall, 2–6 Boundary Row, London SE1 8HN, UK

Blackie Academic & Professional, Wester Cleddens Road, Bishopriggs, Glasgow
G64 2NZ, UK

Chapman & Hall Inc., One Penn Plaza, 41st Floor, New York NY10119, USA

Chapman & Hall Japan, Thomson Publishing Japan, Hirakawacho Nemoto
Building, 6F, 1–7–11 Hirakawa-chom, Chiyoda-ku, Tokyo 102, Japan

Chapman & Hall Australia, Thomas Nelson Australia, 102 Dodds Street, South
Melbourne, Victoria 3205, Australia

Chapman & Hall India, R. Seshadri, 32 Second Main Road, CIT East, Madras
600 035, India

First edition 1994

© 1994 British Urban Regeneration Association

Typeset in 10/12 Times by Florencetype Ltd, Kewstoke, Avon
Printed in Great Britain by St Edmundsbury Press Ltd, Bury St Edmunds, Suffolk

ISBN 0 419 18610 7

A catalogue record for this book is available from the British Library

Library of Congress Cataloging-in-Publication data

Smyth, Hedley.
    Marketing the city : the role of flagship developments in urban
regeneration / Hedley Smyth. – 1st ed.
        p. cm.
    Includes index.
    ISBN 0–419–18610–7 (alk. paper)
    1. Urban renewal – England. I. Title.
HT178.G72E547   1994
307.3′416′0941–dc20

I dedicate this book to Sue with love

They will rebuild the ancient ruins
and restore the places long devastated;
they will renew the ruined cities
that have been devastated for generations.

Isaiah 61:14

Contents

Preface

The research has its origins in a discussion between Hartley Booth MP, former chair of the British Urban Regeneration Association (BURA), and Bob Dalziel, a director of architects Geoffrey Reid Associates. Establishing the nature of 'good practice' in urban regeneration is a thorny problem. People tend to impose their own criteria according to what it is they are trying to prove or what it is they think they would like to hear. The views of Prince Charles concerning the built environment and urban regeneration in particular are a far cry from the financial criteria of the governments of the 1980s, which stressed 'value for money' and 'additionality'.

This prompted us to suggest that it may be more helpful to respect the integrity of those trying to promote an area or indeed a city through an urban regeneration scheme, rather than to impose other people's views or invent our own. That respect demands that each scheme is evaluated according to the aims and objectives of the project initiators.

It was also suggested that so-called flagship developments would be a prime target to test out the approach in a practical piece of research. Flagship developments were at the forefront of testing concepts for 'marketing the city'. They were also an important part of the armoury for regenerating areas and employment during the 1980s. Many were privately led, yet many were still initiated by local public agencies, and a large number were undertaken as partnerships between the public and private sectors. This occurred during a period when urban regeneration projects were being property-led in policy terms. Central government was 'reducing' intervention and endeavouring to contain the efforts of local government, while local government was trying to recreate ways of intervening in the local economy and property markets. Flagship developments have been an entrepreneurial solution for many authorities and a way of creating development opportunities for the private sector.

In the aftermath of a property boom, within recessive conditions and a changing political milieu it is, I believe, appropriate and relevant to evaluate flagships, both as developments and as vehicles for regenerating urban areas, promoting the city and therefore regenerating local and regional economies. This evaluation is aimed primarily at practitioners and policy makers and those responsible for policy implementation, whether in the public or private sectors. The evaluation also draws extensively on recent academic research and theoretical reappraisal, for the developments and urban policies of the last decade have prompted a reappraisal of the types of development that are preferable, the thrust for future policy making and the kind of cities that people would like to see, and live in and work in for the next century. There is far from agreement as to what this means; indeed many of the ideas are in competition with each other. However, it is important that decision makers benefit from the range of views and kinds of discussions that have taken place and continue to do so. Furthermore, I hope that consideration of the issues raised will contribute to those discussions.

The choice of project case studies reflects a broad range of circumstances. Geographically, they include examples from the more prosperous South, at least before the main effects of the current recession began to bite hard, from the West Midlands and from the North-East. The city locations – Bristol, Birmingham and Newcastle – have different histories and different economic and social circumstances, and the local outworking of the processes of urban degeneration have been varied too. The flagship developments chosen are the Watershed Complex, Bristol, the International Convention Centre, the Hyatt Hotel, the National Indoor Arena and Brindley Place in Birmingham, the Theatre Village and Chinatown, Newcastle and the Byker Wall, also in Newcastle. The concentration of schemes in Birmingham was deliberate for it begs the question 'how many flagships can be developed on the back of each other?' The Byker Wall is not strictly a flagship; however, it was felt important to choose a large residential scheme and one that had a longer time span than many other projects, and, of course, it has acted as an important role model. The choice of the flagship case studies was made because they also exhibit a range of features. They include primarily area-based approaches as well as development-based approaches where it was then intended that the developments would have an impact upon the adjacent areas. The area characteristics include a dockside scheme for Bristol, former industrial land in Birmingham, an area of former retail and warehouse functions and a residential area. The building types include uses for the arts, retailing, business tourism, hotel, leisure and sports, offices and residential. New build and refurbishment flagship projects are included. The orientation of the schemes covers the range from an international outlook to a predominantly local one. Finally, the types of organizations undertaking the projects, the 'initiators', cover public, private and partnership ventures, and voluntary and interest group organizations. The seven case studies therefore embody a wide and rich range of experiences. Reference to other flagship projects in Britain and in the United States helps to highlight the particularities of each case study as well as draw out the common features and threads in the development and policy process. There are lessons to be learnt from each flagship case study, as well as general lessons for both flagship developments and urban regeneration.

The task of doing the research has been exciting and challenging. I wish to credit the following organizations for their support of the research. I particularly thank BURA for commissioning the project, J Sainsbury plc for supporting the work financially and Geoffrey Reid Associates for the opportunity to undertake the research while I was Joint Director of their R&D unit.

I have tried to present the material in a way that most adequately makes sense of the phenomena I researched. While every effort has been made to ensure the accuracy of opinions, information and data, neither the author nor publisher can accept liability for inaccuracies and for use made of the information in this book. It is hoped that the sum of the research will stimulate discussion and further analysis, and contribute towards improving the quality and appropriateness of urban regeneration for the whole of society.

Hedley Smyth
Division of Civil Engineering and Building
Oxford Brookes University
June 1993

Acknowledgements

I have received a great deal of help from a large number of people. I would like to thank Hartley Booth, MP for Finchley, for his enthusiasm for the work in getting the research going, Gerald Cary-Elwes of BURA, J Sainsbury plc for their assistance, and Professor Martin Symes, British Gas Chair of Urban Renewal, School of Architecture, University of Manchester, for his help and comments. My colleagues at Geoffrey Reid Associates gave support and I wish to single out Bob Dalziel for the discussions we have had over a whole range of issues, as these helped me to crystallize my thoughts.

I particularly wish to thank those who were directly or indirectly involved with the case studies:

Neil Barker, former chair of Northumbria RIBA
Gordon Campbell, General Manager, Hyatt Regency Hotel, Birmingham
Alan Chatham, Director, Brindleyplace plc
Martin Heighton, Director of Leisure Services, City of Bristol District Council
Michelle Hodson, former Neighbourhood Manager, Shield Field Housing
John Hume, Economic and Development Division, Development Department, Newcastle City Council
Ian Hegginbotton, Policy Team, Planning Department, Newcastle City Council
Paul Keenan, Principal Housing Needs Officer, Housing Department, City of Newcastle
Luqman Khan, Property Information Officer, Economic Development Unit, Birmingham City Council
Chris Mills, Housing Renewal Officer, Housing Department, City of Newcastle
Roger Mortimer, former Director of, and a Consultant to, the JT Group
Dick Penny, Chief Executive, Watershed Media Centre
Nigel Perry, former City Planning Officer and employee of architects Fairhursts

ACKNOWLEDGEMENTS

Peter Smith, former Executive Director, Westgate Trust
Paul Swan, Managing Director, Spectrum Communications Ltd
Mike Turnbull, former Area Housing Officer for Byker, Housing Manager, Cruddas Park
John Vergette, Chair of Percy Thomas Partnership
Councillor Bernard Zissman, former Chair of the Birmingham City Council International Sub-Committee and former Mayor of Birmingham

I also wish to thank those who have discussed the issues of urban regeneration with me and drawn my attention to useful sources:

David Byrne, Department of Sociology, Durham University
Stuart Cameron, Department of Town and Country Planning, University of Newcastle
Rose Gilroy, Department of Town and Country Planning, University of Newcastle
Professor David Harvey, Halford Mackinder Chair of Geography, University of Oxford
Professor Patsy Healey, Department of Town and Country Planning, University of Newcastle
Kevin Robins, Centre for Urban and Regional Development Studies, University of Newcastle.
Fred Robinson, Department of Sociology, Durham University
Sue Wilkinson, Centre for Urban and Regional Development Studies, University of Newcastle.
Barry Wood, Department of Town and Country Planning, University of Newcastle

City visions and flagship developments

1.1 VISIONS FOR THE CITY

Change is inherent to our society. The scale and rate of change accelerated throughout the 1980s and by the turn of the decade it was more than apparent that many of these changes were to be of lasting significance. The demise of the Eastern Bloc was the most dramatic series of events. The process and the promise of further upheaval will continue. As the dominant culture of the West moves towards the millennium, the psychology of the next years will mould expectations about what is to come and the visions people would wish to see.

What sort of cities do we wish to see in the next century? How do we get from here to there? Harnessing our experiences of the recent past in order to shape the processes that will mould and reform our urban environment is central to achieving our expectations. Renewing the existing fabric and regenerating the areas of decline and dereliction is one of the greatest challenges for the well-being of society. This challenge embraces not only the physical form but those affected by the degeneration. Yet this raises two vital questions. The first concerns the extent of the gap between our visions for our cities and the constraints of achieving these in the changing social, political and economic circumstances of the next few years. The second question must address what the nature of our vision is for future cities, and we must immediately recognize that our visions do, and will, vary considerably. Our visions tend to be formed from an amalgam of ideas. These ideas emanate from current interests and concerns, such as:

- an attractive, safe and healthy environment;
- a city without homelessness;
- a city in which citizens and organizations contribute rather than take out;
- adequate housing and income for everybody;

- opportunities to pursue business interests, development or other activities;
- good communications and infrastructure;
- a place of cultural excellence.

Each of these ideas has implications for implementation. From where will these ideas be resourced? Who will decide upon and implement the initiatives and projects required to realize the visions? Some of the ideas are in conflict with each other and will either be excluded through the policy process or lose out in competition for resources in the market-place.

Certainly there has been no clear vision of the future for our urban environment since the 1960s. Perhaps the vision was not always entirely clear, but there was a shared sense of a goal, a 'rational' end, which was being negotiated and fought over constantly in the efforts to determine the future. Yet a renewed sense of vision, an overall 'urban project' is needed for future development to be purposeful (Harvey, 1989a), whether from a partisan viewpoint or for broader social and economic well-being. For a vision to emerge that is implementable, it must be shared in the broadest terms by key constituents of society – local people, a selection of interest groups, politicians, developers and business. A vision requires more than just acceptance, the lowest common denominator of legitimacy; it needs active support and a high degree of involvement.

1.2 MARKETING THE CITY

Having such a vision is a long way off, yet its formation has already started. Its formation has been arising out of the most innovative element of recent urban development, that is, the process of **marketing the city**. Developing a coherent marketing strategy for any city is still remote and, indeed, there may be some serious restraints on achieving such a goal conceptually and through the implementation stages in a meaningful way. The purpose of marketing a city is to create strategies to promote an area or the entire city for certain activities and in some cases to 'sell' parts of the city for living, consuming and productive activities.

Successful developments start with a market strategy for that development, yet their promotion frequently demands a market context beyond the boundary of the site, or indeed of the area. The city strategy is the next logical step, which in turn begins to raise issues about competing interests as to what sort of city we need, what sort of urban regeneration and development is needed. In other words, the process of marketing the city begs the question as to what sort of cities we wish to see. What concepts, ideas, assumptions and processes are being brought together in marketing strategies? Assuming these can be implemented, how are these strategies going to shape our cities, and do they form part of a vision in which we wish to share? The negotiation process has already started in practice with concepts being tentatively tested, the results of which will filter through our thinking and practice into the next century.

A few qualifications will demonstrate the significance of these negotiations. Firstly, marketing is a process, because the application of marketing concepts to the city is both recent and immature. Many concepts are not easily transferable from products and services, and, in addition, their appropriateness is still being evaluated by advocates. Marketing the city is therefore still at an experimental stage and the process has unfolded in a gradual and frequently *ad hoc* way. Secondly, although a shared vision may involve a marketing approach, it must contain different strategies for different cities because each is unique. A shared vision may exclude marketing or include a few elements, for the vision may arise from else-where, perhaps as a challenge to a marketing approach. Other influences are being debated (cf. Coleman, 1990; Harvey, 1989a; Healey, 1992; Rogers and Fisher, 1991; Wilson, 1991); however, what is happening 'on the ground' is influencing the envisioning process, as shown in Figure 1.1.

It is a process in its early and formative stages without a clear end in sight. The form it will take will be influenced by the events of the next years and may fail to emerge. At this stage it is impossible to make a prediction, yet the process has begun.

1.3 MARKETING AND FLAGSHIP DEVELOPMENTS

This book is contributing to the envisioning process because it seeks to evaluate the phenomenon of the last decade that has done much to assert marketing as a city concept, that is, the flagship development.

In some respects, flagship developments have already lost part of their policy appeal and the recession has served to undermine many of the underpinning economic assumptions. New policy approaches are being tried and tested, yet these have been born out of the experience of flagship developments and hence are part of the process and debate. Therefore, it is necessary to focus on issues raised by flagship developments, for it is from projects like these that our grand visions and future policies will flow.

The purpose of this research is to evaluate those projects that have come to be known as flagship developments. The subject appears to be a definable area, yet the very purpose of a flagship is to 'mark out 'change' for a city' (Bianchini, Dawson and Evans, 1990, p.11; see also Bianchini, Dawson and Evans, 1992). The change envisaged extends beyond the physical boundaries of the flagship and contributes to the development and

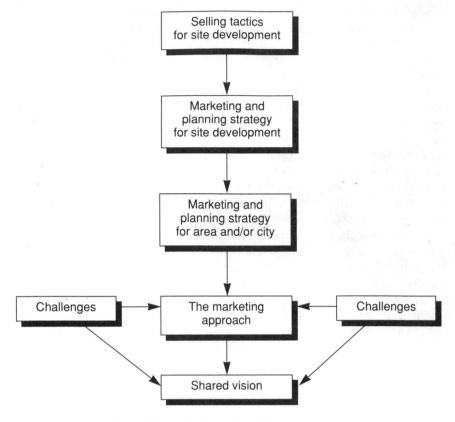

Figure 1.1 Marketing and negotiating a city vision

the economic and policy base of the area and city. Immediately the sphere of research grows, raising larger development issues both for implementing flagship projects and for future policies that will shape the urban form beyond the millennium. The sphere of research grows **because** the flagship is part of the 'selling' of an area and marketing the city. It is from both the projects themselves and the broader implications that we can learn important lessons for future policy and development.

1.4 DEFINITION

Firstly, it is necessary to define a flagship development. They have been cited as being significant, high profile developments that play an influential and catalytic role in urban regeneration, which can be justified if they attract other investment (Bianchini, Dawson and Evans, 1990, 1992). A more detailed categorization will be provided at a later stage, it being sufficient to state at this point that a flagship comprises the following elements:

- a development in its own right, which may or may not be self-sustaining;
- a marshalling point for further investment;
- a marketing tool for an area or city.

The general thrust is not entirely new. There is a long history of local public and private sector developments, which were intended to have a broader remit than the immediate function for the development. There are new 'twists' in the particular concept of the flagship. Their role within urban regeneration during the 1980s has been of enormous significance, arising from the proactive development of flagships, the *post hoc* labelling of projects and also the reduction of overall central government spending on urban regeneration within central city areas.[1] Their most prominent role, however, has been in the tentative exploration and development of marketing concepts for a project and, indeed, for a city.

1.5 ORIGINS

The specific concept of the flagship development originates from the United States, Baltimore providing the inspiration for many projects and a role model for some. Baltimore had been experiencing long-term decline and its poor image was a product of divestment, deprivation and the social unrest of the 1960s. In 1970 a city fair was held, which successfully united a number of disparate neighbourhoods and interest groups. Within two years the fair was attracting nearly two million visitors. Civic pride was being restored. The recession, commencing in 1973, ushered in a further wave of redundancies. It was decided to institutionalize and further commercialize the fair. The construction of the Maryland Science Center, the National Arena, Convention Center, a marina, hotels, and a variety of leisure and retail facilities was the result. Baltimore reached the coveted front cover of *Time* magazine as the 'renaissance city', the Inner Harbor area became an international tourist destination and the flagship project was born (Harvey, 1991).

The onset of the 1990s was not painting such a rosy picture for Baltimore. Many of the poorest neighbourhoods had been largely shut off from the new growth, the trickle-down effect through the economy being limited. The recession in general was affecting both retailing and tourism and there was a vast oversupply of commercial property development. The proposition was mooted that the whole development thrust had exacerbated conditions in the poor neighbourhoods by diverting resources away from housing into an overheated property market (Harvey, 1989a).

1.6 HYPOTHESIS

There is a long tradition of Britain emulating the United States, and the development of flagships is no exception. The question this raises is whether Britain has adopted the better practices and learnt from being followers rather than pioneers. Indeed, have flagship development initiators thought through the implications of their projects in a thorough way in the short and long term? Or have projects been conceived as a reaction to circumstances, as a 'good idea'? Have they been implemented with energy and enthusiasm, but without the structures and support necessary for successful implementation and continuing management? There is a hypothesis to be tested:

Is it not the case that flagship developments are an expensive means to effectively promote urban regeneration, that is, economic growth and social well-being, within an area?

This hypothesis appears at first sight to tie down the subject. Yet on further consideration it becomes more difficult. Embedded within the question is the need to address the broader role of urban policy. A supplementary question illustrates this: is a flagship development a fundamental tool for unlocking latent demand within a local economy? If it is, then its significance is very broad and, I would suggest, has not therefore been fully taken on board in Britain, even – or especially – within recessive conditions. If it categorically is not, then are we simply looking at a 'sign'? Such an effort to create some sign of life in a local economy may prove very expensive. Or perhaps we should treat it culturally as a legitimate 'experience' in terms of both the activities that the flagship accommodates and as a visual contribution to urban regeneration. As such it becomes part of a process, which is an end in itself, because achieving a steady-state goal is impossible. The minute a goal is achieved it becomes the subject of change in a dynamic economy.

1.7 CULTURAL CONTEXT

The cultural context places flagships in the arena of 'postmodern culture'. Flagships can be seen as both an important expression of that culture, even more so when the planning and architecture is postmodern, and an important contributor to that ferment. In an urban context this is experiential, Jonathan Raban's *Soft City* (quoted in BBC, 1992; Harvey, 1989a) being used as a benchmark for the perception of the period as postmodern:

Cities, unlike villages and small towns, are plastic by nature. We would mould them in our images: they, in their turn, shape us by the resistance they offer when we try to impose our own personal form on them. In this sense, it seems to me that living in a city is an art, and we need the vocabulary of art, of style, to describe the peculiar relation between man and material that exists in the continual creative play of urban living. The city as we imagine it, the soft city of illusion, myth, aspiration, nightmare, is as real, maybe more real, than the hard city one can locate in maps and statistics, in monographs on urban sociology and demography and architecture. (Raban, p. 9–10)

The implications tend to polarize our thinking. At one pole, our thinking moves in the realm of pure imagination or grand visions, the implementation being incidental; at this pole the 'good idea' cannot be evaluated unless implemented and the implementation contributes to the wider goals of the 'vision'. Or, at the other pole, our thinking becomes concerned merely with the immediate experience of the completed project, rendering both the private aims or public policies ephemeral and the investment short-lived in functional and physical terms. This may imply, as Daniel Bell (1978) proposed, that the organization of space has 'become the primary aesthetic problem of mid-twentieth century culture' (quoted in Harvey, 1989a, p.78). Maintaining the aesthetic momentum has tremendous cost implications, especially when harnessed with fashion, as well as posing problems for long-term economic stability. Here we are looking at the possible content of a marketing strategy for the city, whether by design or by default. Perhaps the experience described by Raban means that the environment is no more than packaging for the soft city of experience. Perhaps it is a separate 'product' in its own right and one that can help organize our lives more efficiently. This again raises the question posed of Baltimore: are the benefits real, lasting? If there are no lasting benefits and no identifiable economic opportunity costs, then we are left with the proposition of Bourdieu (1984): 'the most successful ideological effects are those which have no words' (quoted in Harvey, 1989a, p.78). The function of a flagship is reduced to inducing social stability, assuming the generated experience is sustainable for enough people over a long period and is targeted towards those who are potentially the harbingers of disruption. Perhaps the analysis should take a step back: what are the markets and what is the purpose of marketing the city?

While each of the issues raised is interesting and needs to be addressed, in themselves they are part of a melting pot of ideas. Understanding the development options, the needs to be met and evaluating the promotion efforts is just beginning, for many of the concepts behind flagships were developed in the confusion of a heady period of optimism. The ferment was useful because it was creative. It was not enough because ferment in itself is a constraint because of the confusion. The paradox posed is that the postmodern culture is apocalyptic in its literary sense: symbolism paints a picture, each successive picture creating another layer covering a larger scale, which is laid down on its predecessor within the same time-frame. From the ferment is distilled in prophetic and revelatory ways new goals with new policies, a new purpose, a new set of commonly held values and an attendant philosophy. Both the vision and process are needed. Both the goals and the detailed implementation are necessary.

The aim is for this research to make a positive and constructive contribution to this process. In between the 'grand visions' and the 'ephemeral experience' rest the initiators of each flagship. It is they who are responsible for the policy formulation, project implementation from design, through construction, to the projects full functioning as an entity and as a draw for further investment. It is intended to respect the intentions of the initiators, and analyse the project management and how it is perceived as a completed flagship. The purpose is to draw out practical lessons and to both inform and envision future urban regeneration. How this will be addressed is described in the outline.

1.8 OUTLINE

Chapter 2 reviews the context for urban regeneration policy. This describes the thrust of inner city policy and practice over recent years and how marketing emerged as a key tool of management practice. An analysis is provided of the limits of transferring marketing concepts into a city context, which demonstrates that flagship developments became the most fertile ground for testing their application to policy and practice in the future. In Chapter 3, the research approach is described in detail. The purpose is to evaluate flagship projects on the basis of the original aims and intentions of the project initiators. This provides lessons based upon each project and some general pointers. In itself this does not permit a 'compare and contrast' exercise, therefore the findings are put under the scrutiny of a marketing analysis in Chapter 4. General lessons can be derived from the divergent project types and project management because such an approach encompasses the different market positions adopted by each project.

Chapter 5 addresses the project management necessary for bringing together the resources and support for a successful flagship development. This leads to consideration of a project's impact upon the urban form in Chapter 6, so completing the basis for the case study analysis.

The case studies are:

- The Watershed Complex, the Floating Harbour, Bristol
- International Convention Centre, Birmingham
- Hyatt Regency Hotel, Birmingham
- Brindley Place, including the National Indoor Arena, Birmingham

- Theatre Village and Chinatown, Newcastle upon Tyne
- Byker Wall, Newcastle upon Tyne.

They cover a wide range of project type in terms of size, content and function as well as geographical distribution. The Watershed Complex in Bristol is part of the regeneration of Bristol Docks, which was one of the first dock regeneration schemes and perceived as successful. The Watershed is generally thought of as a public sector scheme, although it is in fact a private development, containing retail operations, as well as having a strong voluntary sector involvement and user input, albeit supported from public as well as private funds.

The International Convention Centre is a public sector development, operated as a private company within the National Exhibition Centre management structure, NEC Ltd. It is the largest case example and has been targeted towards rejuvenating the area and economy through business tourism plus the attraction of inward investment. The Hyatt Hotel was conceptually and is physically linked to the International Convention Centre. Its development was undertaken with a mixture of private and public sector funding as a joint venture partnership.

The Brindley Place scheme is located adjacent to the International Convention Centre. It has been developer-led, with the sale of public land funding the National Indoor Arena. The Arena also involved some public funding and is owned and operated through the NEC management on behalf of the local authority. The Arena is mainly used as an indoor sports venue, although its multiple uses also include concerts, exhibitions, and conventions, which are facilitated by its proximity to the International Convention Centre. The remainder of Brindley Place is a purely private development. It started as primarily a development for speciality shopping and leisure attractions. Having undergone a number of conceptual transformations, it has emerged as a more traditional retail and office scheme, although development has yet to get under way.

The reason for including a number of projects in Birmingham is to explore the relationship between them. In particular, there is the opportunity to assess how many flagships can be developed adjacent to each other and whether the logic for regeneration becomes purely dependent upon the configuration rather than the market for inward investment and consumption. There is an important issue to be investigated about the relationship of marketing as a management tool and the economics of the city market-place.

The Theatre Village and Chinatown is an area located in the centre of Newcastle close to the central business and shopping areas. The economic history of the area was based upon retailing and warehousing. The aim has been to generate arts-based development, harnessing an existing core of arts activities as a base for further development. In contrast to some other high profile development in and around the city, the Metro Centre being the most well known and successful, the Theatre Village concept largely failed during the 1980s. Although some improvements in arts facilities were made in addition to retail, restaurant and residential development, these occurred despite the Theatre Village concept. The flagship was run through a trust under The Newcastle Initiative, which was set up by the CBI, the industry interest and lobby organization.

There are three reasons for the selection of Byker as a project. Firstly, there was a wish to include a major housing scheme because of the innovative architecture and social approach to development. Secondly, although it strictly predates flagships, it has been an important role model and certainly would have been labelled a flagship if it had commenced during the 1980s. Thirdly, many of the projects are still quite recent, rendering analysis dependent more upon recent perception than long-term data, and Byker provides a longer time horizon. As a public sector development it is important to analyse the issues faced when adopting innovative approaches. Innovation can be an important part for some marketing strategies and will undoubtedly feature in future policy initiatives.

The case studies therefore cover a wide range of operations: arts and leisure, business tourism, retail, office and residential development. The urban regeneration projects are located, with the exception of Byker Wall, in the inner city. Each area has had a contrasting history, ranging from an international port, through manufacturing, to retail and distribution. Each area reflects the heritage and strategic economic history of the city in which it is located and the cities occupy important positions within contrasting regional economies. The North-East has experienced long-term regional decline, in contrast to Birmingham and the West Midlands, whose experience of decline is much more recent. Bristol, on the other hand, is located in the south and has a more prosperous recent history, showing a flexibility towards adapting quickly to changing economic circumstances. Each of these case studies is very different, covering a spectrum of activities and, as the book will demonstrate, reflecting different explicit and implicit marketing positions.

The implications of flagships for urban regeneration are drawn out of the case study work in Chapter 14. Their impact upon the urban form is considered, and the impact upon the surrounding areas in terms of the culture, the functions and who stands to gain and lose from these types of development is analysed. The section concludes with an analysis of their role in the economy and the coherence of the marketing and management of the projects.

The final chapter, 'Future development and city visions', draws together some of the threads and focuses some of the implications for practice and policy.

Context for urban policy and marketing the city

2

2.1 BACKGROUND

By the late 1960s the concentration of redundant industry and dereliction in the central urban areas had become widely noticed. If not entirely new, the extent and scale of the divestment became known in the public domain as the problem of 'inner cities'.

During the 1970s the inescapable conclusion was reached that the inner city problem was as much social as it was economic. Concurrently, the economy was restructuring and divestment accelerated. The pattern was repeated across a number of developed economies, although the history and life cycle of British industry had concentrated the problem spatially. The severity of the problems led the Labour Government to produce a White Paper in 1977, which identified the causes as lying outside the inner cities, yet their policies were addressed within the areas (HMSO, 1977). This was a turning point. The policies of the 1980s remained focused upon areas, and chose to ignore the causes in favour of addressing what was thought to be achievable.

Inner city policy was evolving in a climate of fiscal austerity at both central and local government levels. National governments were no longer agents that would control and stimulate activity. This gave rise to a wave of private and public decentralization of cost and supply factors, the central tiers being responsible for overall financial control as well as the fostering of guiding principles. The emergent conviction in a number of spheres was that the private sector was better equipped to supply the needs through the market. Inner city policy was no exception.

For the inner city to be regenerated the environment had to be re-created. It was therefore the property development sector that was to lead the way. Another shift had taken place. The area policy focus had become directed towards property-led urban regeneration. It assumed that the solution for urban regeneration rested with 'supply side' blockages of various types – land ownership, especially in the public sector; conflicts between local government and the private sector, and between between local government and central government; lack of entrepreneurial initiative; and a private sector that was too constrained by the poor image of the inner city to identify clearly the positive investment opportunities (Healey, 1990). The policies of the 1980s were designed to facilitate the supply side and encourage property development, the main impetus arriving in 1987 with the Conservative Government's announcement of a major programme for recycling underused and derelict land.

2.2 IMPACT

The impact of these initiatives has to be seen in two ways. Undoubtedly a great deal has been achieved. Major developments have taken place through the Urban Development Corporations, such as Trafford Park in Manchester and London Docklands, or on underused public land, such as Broadgate in London. Attitudes changed. On the one hand, the advocates for the local populations, who had tried to protect the employment history, were forced to concede that the past would not return under any circumstances. On the other hand, the developers contemplated more imaginative developments in the location and scale and had some success in attracting tenants.

The second way of considering the impact is to look at what remains. Derelict land, one significant indicator, had increased in area. In 1974 there were over 43 000 hectares in England, rising to 45 000 hectares in 1982, and falling to just over 40 000 by 1988, over 14 000 having been reclaimed during the latter period (Department of the Environment, 1989). The distribution of this is uneven between urban and rural areas and also within urban areas, a high proportion being located in the inner city. The recession in the development market has put a halt to new schemes coming on stream to attack the balance of dereliction. The recession has created an oversupply of space in general and in city and most inner city areas. The property-led urban regeneration has had some successes, but it has not provided a solution to the problem of urban regeneration, even during the property boom of the mid- and late-1980s.

2.3 MARKETING

Marketing as a discipline of management experienced rapid growth in the 1970s and 1980s. It would be inaccurate to say that there is a coherent body of management theory (Drucker, 1955, 1986) or even competing theories, unlike economics or politics. However, there are principles, and these are being applied in an increasingly systematic way across all organizations. Management practice emerged in the public sector and railway organizations.

Marketing draws upon a broad spectrum of concepts from economics, sociology and psychology, as well as from politics and biology. It has become more dominant in management practice or, as Drucker (1986, p. 63) rather technically puts it, 'increasingly a marketing decision becomes a systems decision'. If we start with the notion that the aim of marketing is to create the strategy for selling, then satisfying a customer requires the production of a good or the delivery of a service to be of high quality, at an affordable price and readily available. The level of output to meet demand has marketing implications, as does the after sales service, because it is important to keep a customer.

As the mass markets of the 1960s and 1970s increasingly fragmented into segments and niches during the 1980s, the demands placed upon marketing functions were stretched. The increasing prominence of the private sector in all areas of life served to further influence the population and, specifically, all areas of management with some marketing principles. Advertising has probably had the greatest influence. This is for two reasons. Firstly, there has been greater continuity of selling through advertising. Many producers increased their advertising expenditure in the economic downturn of the late 1970s and early 1980s, although this trend is not being repeated in the current recession. Secondly, advertising was used more extensively by the property sector in the development boom of the late 1980s. Prior to that Barratt Homes had pioneered television coverage in the early 1980s. Throughout the period, the Economic Development Units of local authorities and the Urban Development Corporations and agencies were developing a broader range of advertising and promotion techniques.

Indeed, so successful were some campaigns that for many marketing became synonymous with promotion. Promotion includes advertising and public relations. This emphasis has been picked up across academic comment under the heading of 'civic boosterism' (see, for example, Barnekov, Boyle and Rich, 1988; Hambleton, 1990; Harvey, 1989a,b; Robins and Wilkinson, 1990; Squires, 1991; Wilkinson, 1992; cf. Ashworth and Voogd, 1990). The concept of civic boosterism will not be used extensively in the book because it is necessary to get behind the notion to address the **means** by which an area or city is having its civic pride and image boosted. In other words, there is a need to unpack the strategic issues, the tactics and the implementation of the sales process. What the notion clearly conveys is the desired **outcome**, that is the improved perception of the city through generating confidence internally and a place for inward investment. While the latter may not flow from the promotion, the more fundamental critique is that a great deal of civic boosterism was founded upon rhetoric alone or the claims being made far exceeding what could be delivered from the activities and projects, such as flagship developments, which were in the pipeline. The problem with this type of promotion, or indeed any sales exercise of this type, is that expectations are being raised to the level of fiction. The reality – delivering the goods or meeting the promises – will fall far short and the customer will become dissatisfied, perhaps cynical, resentful or even revengeful; so may the onlooker and in the urban context there are many – whole neighbourhoods where people live and work.

What we have seen in the application of marketing concepts to the city during the 1980s is largely an effort to help unblock the supply side. In other words, the hype has been applied in a general way with little or no understanding of the demand side. While it has hit certain targets, it has largely failed to meet demand because it has soon been seen to make exaggerated claims and create unrealistic expectations. Ironically, it did feed back to influence key decisions makers and players whereby they ended up beginning to believe their own rhetoric – a widespread social and political characteristic of the late 1980s in many levels of society.

The resultant supply-side emphasis helped fuel the oversupply of development in the property market. Development decisions, including those for some flagships, were made on the basis of false confidence. This was a long way short of the marketing principle of creating and satisfying a customer. Marketing is aimed at the demand side with a view to creating an **exchange** by linking the demand to supply. The marketing mission is to understand needs and how these can be translated into demand. Real demand cannot be created because that is a broader economic issue; however, effective demand can be identified through innovation, latent market need, persuasion, product substitution and trade-offs. Additionally, supplying the product competitively will secure market share from the suppliers viewpoint. Most developments are unique, if not in design and construction, then in location, therefore an element of product development and possibly innovation are a feature of flagship projects.

This summarizes the way in which marketing has been applied to urban regeneration and the city in practice. However, there are also methodological problems in transferring marketing concepts to an area or to the city. A city is not a product or a service. There are a number of reasons for this. The first concerns change and homogeneity. All products change. They deteriorate during consumption. In the case of food and many services, consumption involves their destruction in order to extract the usefulness. Most products suffer wear and tear. A service may have changes built into it, such as the stages of design and management in architecture or an accumulation of an investment in a managed unit trust. However, the city is dynamic. Change is both frequent and in many ways unpredictable. The city is not a homogeneous place because the activities are diverse and the control of these is also highly fragmented. Many decisions affecting the city will be made away from the locality, increasingly on a global scale. Of course, there are regular patterns of activity – living at home, travelling, work and recreation – yet the maintenance of these patterns is a product of the decisions about consumption and investment which constitute the uncertainty. In areas of urban degeneration these decisions will have accelerated or come to an end if the area is derelict. The heterogeneity is therefore twofold, involving both the urban land uses and the diverse organizations responsible for decisions. One organization does not control the marketing environment. The second aspect is the population in the area or city. Although Harvey (1989a) notes the trend towards converting more and more facets of life into commodities, it remains difficult, if not impossible, to package areas into a discrete 'product'. This is because people live and work in those areas. While there is a contract between employer and employee which ascribes certain functions and understandings about behaviour and activities, a mechanism for achieving this has yet to be found in the urban realm. For many, such a mechanism would be unacceptable and therefore only implementable by force. This is not to say that the way in which the built environment is developed does not have an influence on behaviour. It does, but it does not determine behaviour (see for example Altman and Chemers, 1984). People visiting an area, especially for consumption and recreation, cannot be subject to a contract or shared understanding, further undermining the application of the concept of the city as a discrete 'product' or 'service'.

However, it is people and their activities that give meaning and use to the built environment. It is this richness of human activity and need that gives rise to general features and characteristics that can be subjected to some guiding principles of marketing. Any principle must be judged on its ability to permit, indeed encourage, rather than constrain, activity and diversity. An appropriate concept is **market position**, which neither denies existing activities, nor rules out any activity. However, it will, if applied with integrity, have as its principle the aim of encouraging certain generic types of activity. These can be very diverse, yet many will benefit from each other. The book will return to the concept of **market position** as a prime means to explore the extent and coherence of marketing flagships and hence the city.

The other methodological issue occurs on the demand side. Those being 'sold' to are in fact 'buying' something else. They may buy or rent a house, buy from shops, buy or rent a building for their administrative or commercial activities. Although the city or location in one sense is intrinsic to any of these purchases it is not the 'product'. It is not even strictly analogous to the packaging because it is not discarded for use. In fact, it becomes more important during product usage. It is the **context** for other activities and one that is assuming greater importance.

Although there are clear difficulties with the application of marketing concepts to the city, this does not mean that project initiators or local agencies need to fall back upon the promotional devices of 'civic booster-ism'. These are empty promises and bankrupt, yet have been part of the experimentation of marketing the city. There has been a certain irony to the experimentation. The greatest thrust has come from the public sector, using concepts that have been perceived as belonging to the private sector. This may not seem too surprising given the greater penetration of the private sector into public services and increased interdependency, yet there is a parallel for marketing the city with the growth of the practice of management in the public sector. It is the public sector that has most coherently tested out the potential and limits for marketing the city in an era of property-led urban regeneration, where private sector interests were being encouraged to lead regeneration through the development process. Thus, the public sector has unwittingly being contributing most towards any vision of the city.

2.4 PROCESS

The desire to see the private sector lead urban regeneration did not in practice materialize in a clear-cut way. Public agencies were integrally involved. Landowners and developers tend to be led by short-term market forces. Unless there is an immediate payback or the expectation of one the private sector will not act. Even where development does take place, the landowner and developer interests are seldom both satisfied within the market (BURA, 1991a). Urban regeneration is a long-term activity, and therefore, undertaking 'unprofitable' developments may be necessary in order to stimulate the market to profitable levels (BURA, 1991a). This has been the function of some flagship developments. The private sector may not always be the initiator and frequently not the only player in the process of urban regeneration. Flagship developments perform a selling function for their location and can contribute towards the broader marketing of the city. A project initiator can undertake the marketing and selling for an area, but a public authority is best placed to link it to a broader city-wide marketing approach.

The urban area to be regenerated will have come to the end of its useful life. This life cycle has parallels with the product life cycle, but the comparison cannot be pushed too far, for an area is not a product and it may not be the built form that is worn out, but the activities within them that cannot be sustained. Particular patterns of investment will have been laid down at different times, each 'layer' leaving its historical mark on the urban form and culture for the area, city or region (Massey, 1984). It has been argued that one of the characteristics of the 1980s was that cities were no longer portrayed as centres of production, but of consumption (Bianchini, Dawson and Evans, 1990, 1992). This is true in part. Certainly retail, leisure, hotels and other consumption-dominated activities were in expansion during the 1980s and provided an important development platform for many urban regeneration projects. However, the restructuring of financial services, particularly in London, and the growth in media and arts activities offer other diverse characteristics to the layers laid down in the 1980s.

The reliance upon attracting national and multinational production and command functions as the engines for local economic development has been eroded. There has been growing concern over local economies based upon large investments, which in a global economy of footloose industry could be withdrawn with devastating affect on the locale. Similarly, the 1980s witnessed some concern for town shopping areas which were wholly at the mercy of multiple retail chains that had no allegiance to the local economy:

> A town centre in which it is no longer possible to buy a pint of milk, a tin of paint, a fishing rod, a ball of wool, a bicycle tyre, or get a pair of shoes mended – and there are many such towns in Britain – will be in serious trouble in the future, when mobile companies and populations start relocating again and look for self-reliant towns and cities that exhibit an economic and cultural dynamic and its associated 'quality of life' (Worpole, 1991, p. 145).

Therefore, the process of urban regeneration has involved a range of public and private agencies, and the economic activities in which they have been involved has been varied.

2.5 IMPLICATIONS

The implication is that an economy with a diverse base is more dynamic and hence more profitable overall. Accompanied by adequate infrastructure, a diverse base not only protects the local population from the extremes of recession and external decision making, but also attracts and keeps inward investment (Worpole, 1991). This raises the concerns of planners for diversity and facilitation of urban life upon a human scale that Jacobs iterated in the 1960s (Jacobs, 1965). The issue is not to be underrated, for one of Jacobs' central propositions is that the city is the generator of wealth (Jacobs, 1972), and therefore in any 'system' its health and dynamic comes from diversity.[2] Urban regeneration can stimulate diversity, although it is important to match labour market skills and maybe retrain the local population to achieve diversity. The identification and creation of diversity can be a tenet of a marketing strategy and therefore will include planning policies.

Part of the diversity created by urban regeneration has been in the arts sector. Worpole comments that urban and cultural policies were inseparable, therefore the arts and cultural industries have an important role to play in urban renewal (Worpole, 1991). Whether this will continue to be the case remains to be seen. Certainly these sectors have been important contributors to urban regeneration, particularly in many flagship projects across Britain during the 1980s. This will be apparent in the case studies.

If Jacobs is correct about diversity, then innovative flagship developments and flagships that engender innovation in their wake will help sustain the city economy. If the biological analogy is also correct (see note 2), then it is to be expected that the evolutionary process will give rise to new industries and new ways of working where the upheaval has been greatest, in other words via urban regeneration. Innovation may be a condition for continuing to attract and keep inward investment. Such innovation is disparate and cannot be organized, it is argued, by central organizations, and therefore local government can and has adopted this role (Mayer, 1989).

To be facilitative in this way, local government cannot stand back from the process. It helps to create the market for property development and investment in activities. Its role will help determine what activities are encouraged or restrained. It has to engage fully in development and, indeed, that is what the private sector has required in order to:

- ensure profitable regeneration through the market;
- create innovation;
- sustain the momentum in the long term;
- secure comparative competitive advantage for the area and city.

This has had two effects upon local government. The first is the move away from managerialism towards marketing and entrepreneurialism. The second, as a result of the entrepreneurialism, has been for associations and partnerships with a broader base of organizations to give rise to a greater emphasis upon local **governance** (Harvey, 1989b). Government implies some direct relation to the population through a democratic process or dictatorship, **governance** being an indirect relation, at least at times and for certain places. This can be termed 'covering'. A covering is sustainable where a local society shares a core of absolute values,[3] but where values are predominantly relative, or eclipsed by the pursuit of experience as an end in itself, the ability to call the representatives to account is difficult. Society is currently based upon relative values. Yet, governance tends to be more task-orientated in that there is a need to focus the activities of the various groups and a spatial focus is frequently favoured, the flagship project offering just that. The irony is that the focus on place may draw attention away from the people and existing activities within the place and surrounding area, with consultation, lobbying and accountability being difficult to effect. This will only further encourage the use of marketing in a supply-side fashion rather, than meeting real needs or effective demand.

2.6 FLAGSHIP DEVELOPMENTS

Flagship developments have been an important part of the commercial and policy thrust during the 1980s. They are a product of the policy background. They have arisen out of, and contributed towards, the impact of those policies. This has occurred through a policy thrust to encourage private sector initiatives in property-led regeneration. The practice has been less clear cut with public agencies playing major roles, particularly at local government level. The implications for the policy and practice of flagship developments is the subject of the case study analysis in later chapters. The broader implications for the economy and governance have already been posted. Encouraging diversity of activities has certainly been a product of recent development, if not always an intention. The entrepreneurial role of local government, particularly in partnerships, has raised issues concerning the nature of governance and accountability.

The emphasis of marketing in management has begun to influence the way in which the city is portrayed and considered. Policy has embraced marketing at the area and city levels. The flagship development has been part of such thinking and more importantly has become a vehicle for the development and testing of marketing strategies for an area and for a project. It is at this project level where the experimentation with marketing concepts has been most active and concerted, although less visible than the boosterism. It is therefore through analysing the role of flagship developments that the greatest understanding of the limits and potential for marketing the city can begin to be determined.

These issues will be returned to in the light of the case studies, but first it is necessary to set out the approach to the case work.

Research approach | 3

3.1 DEFINITION

A flagship may be defined as:

- a development in its own right, which may or may not be self-sustaining;
- a marshalling point for further investment;
- a marketing tool for an area or city.

Elaborating, this means that the prime purpose of a flagship is to create a development that is more than the entity in its own right. Therefore, it may not be necessary for the development to be self-sustaining. The meaning of this will vary. Certainly self-sustaining would mean covering the costs of implementation, project management and construction, and could include operational costs. Profitability provides a broader meaning.

Marshalling further investment could take one of two functional forms – catalytic generation of further capital investment in administration, services and production, or acting as poles of attraction for consumption, including household formation and living accommodation. These are in practice often entwined.

The nature of the marketing for an area or city may vary. The physical presence of a development can be seen as sufficient in itself. In essence, the flagship is acting as a large advertising hording for the area, the implied message being that this is the place for others to spend or to invest. The development may be proactively promoted to spread the message beyond the visual presence of the development on the ground or letting agents particulars. The prime purpose of such marketing is to draw attention to the development and area outside the city, in order to stimulate further investment.

The marketing may be more extensive than that, frequently being a jigsaw piece in a larger marketing approach for the city. The aim would be to:

- advertise the city as having a competitive edge for inward investors;

- create demand for inward investment;
- offer the surrounding area as one of the potential locations within the city and its hinterland.

This last aim raises one of the other prominent policy trends that emerged during the 1980s, that of the 'image of the city' and the role of the 'image' in being competitive in securing investment on a national and international scale (Harvey, 1989a,b; Robins and Wilkinson, 1990; Wilkinson, 1992).

3.2 METHOD OF EVALUATION

Evaluation of a flagship project raises questions concerning which criteria should be used. The selection of criteria will tend to reflect what it is the researcher and client wish to know. What anyone wishes to know is a reflection of what is seen as important, hence reflecting values they hold. Escaping values has been attempted repeatedly,[4] the current general thinking being that this has failed and will always do so. Indeed, if there is a common thread running through current thinking it is that the difference between values is to be recognized and celebrated. Yet this is not without its problems. Firstly, any research, or indeed opinion, can be lightly dismissed as being 'valid' but not mine or not that of the organization or milieu in which I operate'. Secondly, there are conflicts and sometimes contradictions between different values, rendering it impossible for the parties to act upon their values within the same time, place and circumstances. This leads to power struggles where one or other set of values comes to dominate.

It is not the intention of this research to impose a set of criteria for the purpose of evaluation. The Conservative Governments' criteria of 'additionality', whereby public money must attract additional private sector investment, preferably on a minimum of a one-to-one ratio, is clearly different from the approach that, say, Prince Charles or his followers would advocate as successful regeneration. Other organizations have adopted open-ended criteria, for example BURA (1991b), where the interpretation of each criterion is left with the value system of each committee member.[5] Others have sought to evaluate flagships based upon their contribution to the most disadvantaged (for example, Loftman and Nevin, 1992) even though this may not have been an original aim. Inventing or developing another set of criteria is in danger of simply adding to the confusion.

Respecting the integrity of those who have thought of, lobbied for and developed a flagship is important. The aim is therefore to take the criteria of the initiators of the flagship and evaluate the success of the project on those terms. This evaluation has a twofold content:

- the success of the flagship as an entity;
- the success in meeting the broader promotional and investment goals.

All development initiators are not interested in both these facets. In addition, for many projects there are more than one initiator and so there may be a number of criteria, sometimes competing, sometimes in contradiction. The clarity, definition or the glossing over of the criteria will vary from project to project. A number of key points can be raised about the **aims** and **objectives** of each project:

- extent of clarity and definition;
- extent of understanding and cooperation between the parties;
- extent of understanding between the policy formulators and the implementors;
- extent of change in macro- and micro-economic and social conditions during implementation;
- post-rationalization of aims and objectives.

This makes the task of evaluating projects in terms of the aims and objectives of the initiators more difficult. Indeed, the research requires that the data is interpreted according to the weight each initiator has within the project, the degree of coordination, and the significance of changes taking place during the project completion. Added to this, many of the projects are quite recent, so 'hard' data is lacking in some cases; the 'soft' data of the initiators' perception of success therefore comes to the fore. It has been impossible to interview every party and capture every piece of data, hence a degree of selectivity has been in play. Every effort has been made to ensure that the views of those interviewed have been interpreted with integrity and to their own satisfaction.[6]

How is it possible to analyse the threads from a disparate set of case studies? The first step is to undertake a compare and contrast exercise for the identification of 'good' policy and practice and for improvements. This requires commonality in reference. A marketing matrix is proposed in order to provide a framework for understanding and, hence, analysis. Marketing matrices are used in theory and practice as a 'top-down' tool, the evaluation ultimately coming from sales. A 'bottom-up' approach is required in this context, because local populations, to whom there is some direct or indirect accountability,[7] are involved with change in their area and in the city. The structure and detail of the marketing matrix will be described in Chapter 4. While the choice of matrix is being imposed, it does permit each projects' characteristics to be respected; indeed, this is necessary for the tool of analysis to work.

The case study work brings to light a series of issues requiring further synthesis, which do not fall neatly within the marketing matrix. At this point it will not be the projects that are being evaluated, but the more general lessons for urban regeneration and the stimulation of development. The analysis of these issues will be informed not only by the preceding research, but also by other flagships and the current debates on urban development.

3.3 PROJECT CLASSIFICATION

Developments have been classified in many ways according to what authors believe to be important. It is worth noting some of these classifications prior to setting out the marketing matrix, itself a form of classification. Each is helpful and provides a useful background for the matrix.

A review has recently been undertaken by Healey of models of the development process (Healey, 1991). She reviews ten different models, classifying them according to:

- theoretical assumptions;
- economic processes;
- event sequence;
- agency.

This is a valuable review for development in general. For flagships in particular a narrower context is necessary. There are over two hundred urban regeneration initiatives, which essentially have three classifications by **vehicle**:

- area initiatives;
- project initiatives;
- enabling initiatives.

In practice, these are frequently overlapping. Area initiatives provide a policy vehicle for flagships, for example Urban Development Corporation (UDC) flagships or City Challenge finance subscribed to an area. A project initiative relies on the project alone. An enabling initiative does not involve a project *per se*, but is aimed at providing the policy and economic vehicle for projects to arise out of the initiative (Fox and Healey, 1991).

Projects also can be classified by:

- geographical location;
- building or development type;
- initiator.

There are strong regional variations. Most flagships are in large towns and cities and located in areas that require substantial regeneration.[8] There are fewer schemes in the wealthiest regions, particularly the London region, but these are among the largest, for example Broadgate and Canary Wharf. Northern cities have tended to have many more, yet smaller scale projects. There is a range of development types, offices, retailing and leisure being more prevalent than housing, and within the developments there is a range of building configurations and functions.

The character of the initiator or initiators is of great importance. Although government policies of the 1980s stressed leadership by the private sector, the public sector was inextricably involved, public–private partnerships being the main initiator (Harvey, 1989b). There are further complexities. Partnerships have indeed been popular, but there have been a variety of forms. These range from informal associations, through complex legal agreements that structure the deals, to joint ventures and consortia of equal equity. The experimentation with hybrid structures and organizations, as the research will demonstrate, has been extensive and what the spread or share of risk is between the parties is an important issue. In addition, the public sector has been active on its own. The voluntary sector has also been involved in some schemes. The case work illustrates this range. In addition, local people have also been responsible for initiating developments, for example the Eldonians self-help housing scheme in Liverpool. A categorization by **initiators** is as follows:

- private
- public
- voluntary
- popular
- hybrid forms.

Perhaps the most interesting categorization is the one developed by Harvey (1989c), which looks at alternative strategies for urban **governance**, within which flagships can be identified according to their **function**:

- exploitation of international competitive advantage of resource base, location and investment for the production of goods and services;
- exploitation of competitive advantage as a location of consumption;
- acquisition and development of key control and command functions.

This scheme is the most interesting because it embraces the latent or effective demand within the 'range' of the project and identifies the supply-side activity necessary to capture the function through development. The role of the flagship project within the first category would be to capture large-scale footloose global investments. To do this, the flagship may be for that type of user, such as a major office development, or a development of another use that enhances the competitiveness of and helps promote the area, such as infrastructure or a concert hall, respectively. For many cities the congestion costs do not offset the distinctive advantages of the location (Harvey, 1989b) and urban regeneration may reduce congestion through new infrastructure provision and spatial distribution of functions. These functions are routine in character. New York's World Financial Center or

London Docklands Canary Wharf, both developed by Olympia and York, contain examples of the function and character. Many recent developments provide tertiary, rather than production, facilities because of the market need to accelerate the turnover of capital through increased efficiency in administration (Smyth, 1985) and more instantaneous consumption, such as spectacles and arts activities (Harvey, 1989a).

Consumption-orientated **governance** endeavours to stimulate and create a range of retail, leisure and cultural activities and will encourage housing development, refurbishment and gentrification. The tourist related developments in Bradford, Liverpool and Stoke-on-Trent are examples of consumption-orientated projects in Britain. The process of regeneration in general and gentrification specifically is divided into phases – pioneers moving into an area, using their own initiative and effort to improve the area, early followers, who learn of the emergent opportunities, and finally the general awareness that brings in larger scale investors, who displace many of those who were pioneers (Berry, 1985).

Key control and command functions embrace finance, government, research and information gathering and processing, including the media. Broadgate in London and the two Olympia and York schemes mentioned above are also examples of such flagships. Once again there is an overlap between functions in practice, but the classification is a very useful aid.

The more immediate **purpose** of flagships may be:

- primarily a promotional tool;
- primarily a commercial development;
- self-help;
- combinations.

These **functions** and **purposes** begin to raise some of the elements that appear in the marketing matrix, for a matrix is a classification tool that can be used by any flagship initiator to formulate the aims and objectives, as well as being a tool of research analysis. It is the introduction of a marketing framework to which we now turn.

Marketing framework | 4

4.1 MARKETING

This chapter develops some marketing concepts. The previous discussions
have focused upon marketing in practice, namely 'civic boosterism', and
problems of transferability of marketing to the city. This chapter uses
marketing concepts as a tool for analysis. In this way it becomes possible to
analyse the extent and coherence of marketing concepts for and in
practice.

The starting point is to use the concept of **market position** in the form of
a matrix. This is an appropriate concept because it provides few constraints
and, hence, overcomes the transferability problem. Neither does the
matrix – and any market position within it – deny existing activity in an
area. Indeed, it is important that project initiators understand the spatial
and organizational characteristics of the area *vis-à-vis* their own resources.
This requires an audit (Ashworth and Voogd, 1990), but the present
analysis will not begin with that because the aims and objectives of the
initiators are taken as given. Nor does the market position exclude any
type of new activity, yet endeavours to encourage **generic** types of activities
that will be mutually reinforcing. It also permits a flexible approach to
urban regeneration. Three scales of operation have already been
identified:

- the project
- the area
- the city.

There are very close interrelationships between them and, indeed, de-
pendency too, especially between a flagship project and an area. Used with
integrity, that is to say with sensitivity to the nature of the urban context
and the people within it, the application of the concept of **market position**
becomes useful as a guideline for both analysis and practice on the appropriate scale of operation.

4.2 FLAGSHIPS AND MARKETING

A flagship development project **is** about marketing the area or the city. The development as an entity in itself is important, yet it is the wider promotional value that makes the flagship distinctive. It is clear that the greater the investment in an area, the greater the rent that can flow, providing, of course, that the overall level of economic activity permits this (Smyth, 1985). Assuming a flagship is attracting investment and consumption over and above the level that would be achieved by 'pure' economic mechanisms, a development acts as its own advertising by being there. This is passive promotion. Marketing is **proactive**, asking strategic questions about how to sell the area or city. Sales is the **active** part of implementing the strategy. So, for the purposes of the analysis, the following definitions of behaviour are used:

- promotion: proactive, active and passive
- marketing: proactive
- sales: active.

Marketing is a key part of any successful 'promotion', yet is frequently misunderstood. This is for a number of reasons. The first is that sales is still considered somewhat 'dirty' and therefore many involved with selling are given the 'status' associated with marketing. Secondly, it is a cross-cutting discipline involving serving, including market research, customer needs and psychology; economics, including budgeting, profitability and financial control; and personnel, including team working and motivation. This leads to a lack of understanding among some and perceptions of encroaching on the domain of others. Thirdly, the thinking of many decision makers is pragmatic and reactive, being subject to frequent change, and usually being driven by financial concerns rather than by anything else.

A consequence of this latter pragmatic management approach is that many marketing initiatives are reduced to slogans, announcing a service or market orientation, and the product or service does not match the promise. The hope is always that the demand will itself make it possible for the organization to deliver the promise. This is particularly true of a service, the gearing up being reactive to demand or at worst following on from the income generated by initial sales. In the latter case the initial customers do not get what they want and in the former case the customers suffer the mistakes and shortcomings from this 'learning on the job' approach. The result is 'hype' – posturing and image boosting without substance. There are clear parallels with the 'civic boosterism' style of promotion.

Delivering the product or service is important for customer satisfaction, and through that for repeat orders or referrals. The precise definition of marketing remains elusive, but Levitt's proposition – 'the marketing view of the business process: that the purpose of a business is to create and keep a customer' (1983, p.7) – is appropriate, showing the necessary proactive and creative input. It is this process that cities have begun to embrace in general and exploited through flagships in particular over the last decade. Many corporate organizations exhibit shortcomings in the delivery of the marketing promise, so it should come as no surprise that cities too, and their flagship initiators, have frequently fallen short. The shortcomings have been exacerbated by problems of transferring concepts to the urban realm in which people live and work.

4.3 MARKET STRATEGY

Like any other activity, marketing needs resources and support. If the primary purpose is promotion, then the physical presence of a flagship is insufficient. The marketing role needs to be taken seriously. Concerning the remit of the project aims and objectives, marketing strategy will involve a number of stages, as follows:

- relate to other corporate or agency plans where appropriate
- establish market position
- identify market segments
- select sales targets.

Many organizations will go straight to the stage of selecting targets, running the risks of choosing targets on an intuitive and ill-informed basis. Developing offices and production facilities or flagships that enticed inward investors to a city has been a repeated formula. Yet it is not necessarily the one most suited to the competitiveness of the area in terms of the criteria outlined by Harvey (1989c): exploitation of international competitive advantage for the production of goods and services, exploitation of competitive advantage as a location of consumption, and acquisition and development of key control and command functions. Nor may such an approach attract or stimulate the diversity of economic activities advocated by Jacobs (1972). There are choices about the sorts of economy and social configuration that are perceived both as desirable **and** realizable within the cultural organization and structure a city exhibits. Similarly, there are issues concerning the geographical outlook that a city may have. The choices made concerning activities could be generated within the local economy, or it may be that an international outlook is needed to attract footloose industry or consumers. How will the existing economy complement, relate to or be separate from the new activities that are being targeted? What is most appropriate in the circumstances?

Thus, it must be assumed that it is impossible to attract each and every type of activity. Indeed, given the history and current resources of a city, certain competitive advantages will be easier to create or sustain than others. Deciding where a flagship is broadly going to compete in the market will determine the **market position**. A flagship development ideally should adopt a **position** of competitive advantage in the market. Any market position will embrace a range of potential activities. The selection of those activities should be suspended until the next strategic stage.

4.4 MARKET POSITION

Establishing a market position for a flagship, an area or a city is arguably the most effective concept to utilize. There are a number of ways of establishing the market position for intended or planned urban regeneration. The framework to be used in this analysis is a marketing matrix. A matrix has two axes; the vertical axis concerns the **dominant culture**, and includes the following aspects:

- economic base and diversity;
- technological and infrastructure provision;
- social composition, including labour market size, skills and potential;
- use of free time and patterns of consumption.

Culture is therefore taken in its broadest meaning. Three principal or dominant cultures can be identified, which determine the approach to the aspects listed. Two qualifications are necessary before describing these. Firstly, they are 'ideal types' and therefore provide guidelines, not absolutes, which will in practice reflect an emphasis for a flagship. Secondly, these market positions need not reflect the overall 'position' of the area historically, nor that of the city. Indeed, it may be part of a strategy of diversification to select contrasting positions to the past or for different areas of the city. However, any change in emphasis or longer term repositioning will require more resources in order to implement the plans successfully.

4.4.1 Routinized culture

A culture can be **routinized**, where activities tend to be procedural, perhaps bureaucratic, and solutions are standardized, drawing upon tried and tested practices. Change tends to proceed by refining what has gone before and will therefore be incremental or evolutionary. A perception of stability, security and low risk will tend to pervade, as far as a fast changing world will permit. A routinized culture would typically involve mass production of standardized goods, routinized office work, a high level presence of multiples for consumption goods and standardized leisure, and housing produced mostly by volume housebuilders using standard house types. One qualification is necessary. Many of those employers that fall into the routinized category are footloose and the local impact can therefore be dramatic if multiples or branch plants close, especially where the investments are large. This latter feature can undermine the potential stability of encouraging routinized activities. Although many labour skills are transferable between organizations, not every organization will require the same skills. There is a high level of risk with routinized investment, especially in a fast changing economy when one divestment may not be replaced by new investment.

4.4.2 Service culture

A culture may be based upon **service** provision. Activities will tend to be analytical, concerned with problem solving, drawing upon generic skills for application to specific circumstances. Change will be incremental and subject to waves of upheaval. A perception of relative stability with challenges and some excitement will pervade. The reality may be more dramatic due to change in the 'external' environment and losing a competitive advantage is not always outweighed by inertia, especially where key personnel are as footloose as the investment of the organization. A service culture will translate into personal services, an analytical problem solving commercial sector, production of differentiated goods, and a diverse choice in consumption, leisure and housing opportunities. The current debate that claims there has been a shift from a 'Fordist economy', which is routinized, to one based upon flexible accumulation, which is more service-based (see for example Harvey, 1989a, pt. II), would suggest that the service culture is the most dominant at present, but the debate remains unresolved. While there may be a higher degree of specialist skills in the workforce, a greater propensity for adaptation will be present, and this can increase economic stability in a growing economy. In recessive conditions there may be no particular advantage. This is especially the case in the current recession where 'professional' and highly qualified and experienced white collar employees are being made redundant. It has been a feature of the last decade that many city authorities in both the United States and Britain have encouraged the service sector (Barnekov, Boyle and Rich, 1988), much of which does fall within the service culture category.

4.4.3 Innovative culture

A culture can be based upon **innovation**. Developing new practices and inventiveness characterize activities derived from experimentation and, therefore, trial and error. Exploration will be based as much upon belief and intuition as upon any 'scientific' procedure. Innovation is a management issue and the objectives should be clear. Innovative approaches are not to be valued because of their technical or technological importance.

Nor is such an approach engendered, or to be used, as a vehicle for particular ideologies and causes, such as political movements or lifestyles, which is not to say that such predilections should not form the main thrust or an integral part of an innovative approach. It is the innovation that is the primary focus and the purpose is to assess the contribution that an innovative approach will make to the culture; that is, to the economic and technical base, to the social composition and to consumption. In marketing parlance this means satisfying the customer, hence the need to take on board ideologies and causes in order to assess their capacity and scope in contributing towards urban regeneration specifically and the city's economic and social well-being generally.

Change is the driving force and flexible social practices the norm. Therefore a high degree of risk will be associated with an innovative culture. Project initiators and city authorities must be prepared for 'failure'. The great majority of innovative ideas will not make sense. There is clearly a financial tension with innovative approaches, because it will usually be argued that these approaches are costly. However, this is not the appropriate question because the real issue is what will happen if innovation is **not** pursued. Cities will fail to create new competitive advantages and will lose their competitive edge (cf. Drucker, 1986). This innovative culture would embody pioneering industry and services such as fundamental research and small batch product development and production. A high degree of niche markets in shopping, leisure and housing plus divergent and experimental lifestyles, not necessarily for 'minorities', would be expected.

4.4.4 Culture and geographical orientation

Two points have to be made about the dominant culture. The culture can be addressed at two levels. The first is the flagship development as an entity. The assessment at this level depends upon the functions carried out within the development and hence the **building type**. The second concerns the area being regenerated. It is this latter aspect with which we are more concerned for the matrix, and hence for evaluation. It raises the issue of scale and begins to address the horizontal axis of the matrix, that of **geographical orientation**. The geographical orientation concerns the attitude or outlook of the project initiators. How far is it intended that the project will have an influence? How far should the sales reach? To put it another way, how extensive is the market from where investment and consumption will be attracted? The orientation may concern the spatial scope of the urban regeneration, in other words the areas surrounding the flagship. In this case the orientation is **local**. The orientation may be seeking to stimulate activities by attracting inward investment and consumption on a broad scale, thus giving a **regional** or **national** orientation.

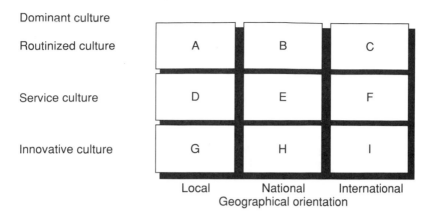

Figure 4.1 Establishing market positions

Finally, the outlook may be **international**, where integration into a network of decision making and activity is more obvious.

4.5 MARKETING MATRIX

The following variables have been introduced and are summarized as follows:

- Dominant culture:
  - routinized
  - service
  - innovative
- Orientation:
  - local
  - national
  - international.

These can be incorporated along two axes to form a matrix of nine market positions for flagship urban regeneration, as shown in Figure 4.1.

Each of the nine positions in the matrix is different. Therefore, the aims and objectives with which a flagship promoter will commence will also be different. Successful outcomes cannot be evaluated upon a common basis. Success should reflect the original aims and objectives and, thus, engender the culture being fostered. How this can be achieved for each position will be addressed in Chapter 5. A number of points concerning the matrix need to be made, to qualify the picture in practice. The complications affect the strategic risk for any chosen market position.

In any area or city there are likely to be aspects of each of the three

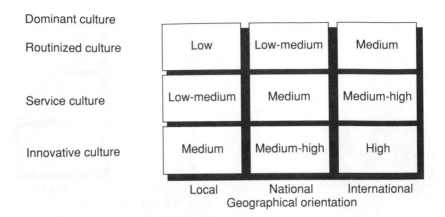

Figure 4.2 Market position risk profile

cultures and orientations. Indeed, it is necessary for that to be the case. These make a 'city' more difficult to understand than a product in marketing terms. However, the point here is which types of activity would best benefit those based in the city, in terms of both economic activity and social well-being. In stating this, there may be economic and political judgements to be made between functions yielding a competitive advantage and those of social well-being, where there is incongruence.[9] Therefore the matrix should be applied **to** the aims and objectives of the flagship project for the benefits to be generated **for** the immediate area and possibly for the city region as a whole. It is not always possible to determine where follow-on investments will take place, although consumption is more easy to control than office or production activities. There may also be a trade-offs between short-term gains and long-term stability. The more innovative the project and the greater the geographical orientation, the more risky the venture. This produces a risk profile, as shown in Figure 4.2.

A matrix is a 'neutral' tool, therefore it passes no judgement upon the overall performance of an economy at any time or on any scale. Although we are dealing with a tool to maximize potential, it does not address economic cycles. Flagships are concerned with the harnessing and creation of growth. What is possible depends on either capturing a share of a stagnant or contracting base or creating the conditions for growth within the scope for demand in the economy. This recognizes that oversupply is a feature of the market-place and that flagship developments are not immune to this. A marketing matrix is therefore a reflection of the effective and latent demand. It thus contributes to the notion that the built environment is a reflection, although not a replica, of the dominant culture. Although the activities will slowly change within developments and the uses may change, marked by refurbishment, each layer of development is an indirect and partial historical record of the cultural moment that gave rise to the development (Clark, 1985; see also Harvey, 1989c, cf. Massey, 1984). It is these layers that give a 'sense of place' and identity specific to the time as well as place. It is social activity and economic growth that lend the integrity to the place.[10] One of the issues faced by flagship developments, where the means with which to promote the area, and create or attract growth are limited, is an increased reliance on spectacles. The origins of the Baltimore flagships is evidence of that (Harvey, 1989b), as is the street theatre of Covent Garden in London or some of the major pop concerts and laser shows used to promote London Docklands, or the features of the buildings and environment itself. In this definition of 'spectacle', the built environment does take the role of spectacle in the sense of an experience, a destination to view in its own right (Clark, 1985). This induces and reduces the flagship to a large advertisement hoarding or billboard, enhancing the promotional impact, but undermining the integrity beyond buildings as 'media', buildings as 'hype' that can be disposed of once the campaign is complete.

The raising of some of the marketing issues from the positioning matrix brings the discussion closer to the next level of decision making, concerned with identifying market segments within each market position.

4.6 SEGMENTING MARKET POSITIONS

A market segment can be defined as a sector or subset that is more specific than any market position, yet is not so specific as to identify a potential 'buyer', in other words consumers and occupiers. This does not mean taking single characteristics, such as residents, workers, shoppers and tourists (Ashworth and Voogd, 1990), but combinations of these coupled with gender, age, family and income profiles, living patterns and expectations. In the urban context it is even more complicated than this, for two reasons. Firstly, each development itself changes the nature of the 'product', and therefore, secondly, affects the nature of demand among those in the market, perhaps even redefining the segments.

It is useful to quote two authors, Jacobs (1965) and Harvey (1989b), whose rather different views help to focus on the segments within the market positions:

> So long as we are content to believe that city diversity represents accident and chaos, of course its erratic generation appears to represent a mystery. However, the conditions that generate city diversity are quite easy to discover by observing places in which diversity flourishes and studying the economic reasons why it can flourish in these places. Although the results are intricate and the ingredients producing them may vary enormously, this complexity is based on

tangible economic relationships which, in principle, are much simpler than the intricate urban mixtures they make possible. (Jacobs, 1965, p. 162)

Part of what we have seen in the last two decades is the attempt to build a physical and social imagery of cities suited for that competitive purpose. The production of an urban image of this sort also has internal political and social consequences. . . . It particularly does so when an urban terrain is opened for display, fashion and the 'presentation of self' in a surrounding of spectacle and play. If everyone, from punks and rap artists to the 'yuppies' and the *haute bourgeoisie* can participate in the production of an urban image through their production of social space, then all can at least feel some sense of belonging to that place. The orchestrated production of an urban image can, if successful, also help create a sense of social solidarity, civic pride and loyalty to place and even allow the urban image to provide a mental refuge in a world that capital treats as more and more place-less. Urban entrepreneurialism . . . here meshes with a search for local identity and, as such, opens up a range of mechanisms for social control. Bread and circuses was the famous Roman formula that now stands to be reinvented and revived. (Harvey, 1989b, p.14)

Jacobs raises the desirability for diversity in our cities. The proposition is that economic diversity, conditioned in particular urban ways, induces social well-being. She says that the creation of diversity can be observed and understood. Four conditions are identified for observing the process. These are the **district**, which must serve more than one primary function, the **block** or **street**, which should be short, the **built form**, which must vary in size, age and economic use, and finally a **dense concentration of people**, which should include residents. Each of these can be measured. In the case of flagships, these would be established from neighbouring areas and transposed. Clearly, there are problems where large tracts of previously single-use land are being regenerated or where the surrounding areas do not conform to the desired diversity. An ideal measure would have to be established in these cases.

Jacobs clearly has in mind the neighbourhood scale. Masterplanning at that level can follow such guidelines. However, the far more powerful point that is implicit in her statement, and is applicable regardless of scale, is that an environment can be economically and socially understood in this way. Principles can therefore be applied to create such conditions. Having established the market position, the content can be established, if not exactly, then in outline. Jacobs, of course, is implying that diversity is the key. However, a project initiator or authority may seek a single user or one type of user for an area – a single segment – but the greater the diversity, the more market segments there are to be identified and accommodated.

In contrast, Harvey raises the issues for social control. Harvey is concerned with a larger scale. The issues may initially reside within a neighbourhood, the threats to the social order spilling out to affect the image of the city and the performance of the local and national economy. The issues are more strategic than those of Jacobs. Both share the perception that it is necessary to start from understanding the economic realm and how this will affect people within an area, but whereas Jacobs' concern is for serving the population and the economy, Harvey's analysis highlights the control of the population in order to serve the economy.

What these two passages bring to light is the way in which there can be a number of objectives within each market position. This simply means that the segments that can be served within each position cannot be determined automatically. Each segment can focus on different activities and produce a varying built form. The function that each segment performs for the area and the city can vary. As both passages clearly demonstrate, these functions cannot be treated in an orthodox marketing sense, for we are not dealing with people who express their preferences through purchase, but a population that is based within and around an area of regeneration.

This extra dimension complicates the process. It affects the risk, since a local population generally expresses its wishes periodically through the ballot box. Other agencies of regeneration, such as Urban Development Corporations (UDCs), are not accountable through the ballot box and public–private partnerships fall into the category of **governance** rather than government. In addition, the decision making for a scheme that will fundamentally affect an area and the city, where the orientation is national or international, cannot usually incorporate the views of the population through the ballot box due to the timing and range of issues a local election addresses.

Jacobs provides a means of minimizing risks for the local population through the creation of economic diversity, albeit in this context within one market position. A number of segments can be targeted. The implication of this is that the innovative and service positions should be favoured, for the more routinized the activities, the larger the scale of activity or the greater the tendency for identical functions to run in parallel or be serialized. A similar statement can be made for the orientation. The tendency for the scale of activities to grow can be depicted as follows:

Scale of activity

Innovative culture → Routinized culture
Local orientation   → International orientation

This scale of activity does not necessarily imply that a project is large or small overall, although generally the greater the number of smaller activities, the more demanding will be the management of the project implemen-

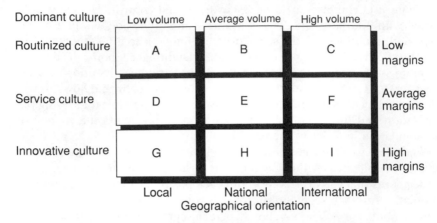

Figure 4.3 Market position, scale of activity and their impact upon profit margins

tation, especially in marketing terms. Coupled with this is an issue of cost and profit. The innovative–local positions will tend to yield activities that are high in profit margin (or low in cost) and low in volume; the routinized–international operations will involve low profit margin and high volume. The overall aim is to achieve a similar mass of profit through trading profits off against volume or scale of activity (see Figure 4.3).

Again, this cannot be read as an automatic process because of the risk factors. It is a guiding principle and can be used in conjunction with the market position risk profile (see Figure 4.2), providing the stage of the economic cycle is also taken into account. This takes the analysis back to the quote from Harvey, whose main focus is upon the consequences of economic activity for the population. Larger scale activity brings with it more risk to the locale, because routinized–international investment tends to create a larger number of jobs, but at lower wages and salaries on average, with an inherent risk of activities relocating again at some future date. Conversely, the innovative–local approach tends to yield fewer but higher paid jobs which may not carry a great deal of security.

This cost–benefit approach raises the classic dilemma between the numerically low-risk option, which induces large-scale consequences when 'failure' does ensue, and the high-risk option where failures may only create ripples. Adding economic cycles to this analysis, the higher risk options are exacerbated, while the lower risk ones are more likely to ride out recessions, although in both cases there will be social as well as economic costs.

The process of segmenting the market within the market position has to take all these factors into consideration. Following Guiltinan and Paul (1988), the 'buyers' – in our case the occupiers in the area to be regenerated – will vary in their decision making process. It is essential to determine a basis for segmenting the market, whether it is a market that is **consumer**-based or an **organizational** market. For most flagship projects, and indeed, for development as a whole, the **organizational** basis is more appropriate. The consumer characteristics of bulk buying are not present, except perhaps in volume housebuilding, although even here every location and plot is different. Therefore mass market advertising is inappropriate. The organizational characteristics include high levels of personal contact with decision makers, frequently involving a number of individuals within each organization. These decision makers will typically limit the number of locations for their search as they will wish to receive preferential treatment from the project initiators.

What is therefore sought is the matching of the needs for the area and city with the demand in the market. The immediate need for the area is regeneration. The position is established in economic terms and the segments must reflect the economic aims and the social needs of the population, even though it has been shown that there are difficulties with this. Social need is particularly difficult when an international orientation is adopted, and frequently both the risk and scale factors affect the population's perception of the benefits and the likelihood and timing of delivering these. How that is to be satisfied is an ideological and political issue – cost, profit, social well-being, social control – and helps to define the function. For example, local authorities have provided facilities locally at their cost, in the expectation that inward investment will enhance the local tax base. That option is no longer available with the replacement of a commercial property rating system with a uniform business rate, controlled by central government. Leisure and cultural facilities, which are generally non-profit-making, may be a function that will be viewed less favourably as flagship developments in the future.

The matching of the local need with demand is usually done by offering the 'product' on the market and seeing what the demand is. 'Speculative' development is no different to the production of most other products, for the development is produced ahead of sale or letting (Smyth, 1985). Even where a prelet exists, the character of the development and building type is established.

Thus, the process of segmenting the market may well require functional building types, the selection of these by size and quality being key determinants. Flexibility can be achieved by securing prelets ahead of development, so that the preferential treatment identified by Guiltinan and Paul (1988) can be maximized. Some building types can accommodate users within the different dominant cultures, such as speculative office developments. This adds further flexibility.

The precise users cannot always be identified, indeed that is the **sales** function. The size and functional requirements can usually be established for each building type. For example, the service culture would embrace such functions as small batch production and just-in-time deliveries for goods. There has been a trend since the 1970s towards serving smaller market segments according to consumer profiles and producer needs. This contrasts with the more routinized mass markets that dominated the 1960s. The switches towards a more flexible approach to new product development, production, distribution and retailing have also resulted in a shift to more flexible working practices. Some of the trends have included the decentralization of authority to branch plants and subsidiaries, with the 'centre' or parent organization setting financial targets, the removal of demarcation practices and the greater use of subcontracting. These are some of the functions that could be attracted within the service sector. Smaller plants with on-site offices and low bay warehousing were typical requirements for the 1980s.

However, this is looking in hindsight. What are the implications for future segments? If flexible production practices, to stick to the same example, have run their course then a switch back to mass markets could be in store. This would draw on the experiences of flexible working practices, yet develop new markets through investments and resultant cost reductions. The return of many large corporations to their 'core' businesses in the last few years could be pointed to as a precondition for such a trend. If this is the forecast, then a routinized culture and buildings for mass production, distribution and retailing will be favoured for future flagships and other developments. Larger plants and owner-occupied high bay mechanized warehousing will be demanded.

On the other hand, it may be thought that flexible practices have a way to go, although a further leap in attitude and investment is necessary to realize the possibilities. Taking subcontracting as an example, this can be extended through telecommuting and networking to new developments that link the workplace close to home, to higher education establishments or to the market. Small plants, more 'informal' distribution with minimal storage requirements and small offices could be favoured, but with the maximum flexibility available, implying that each small unit is part of a larger managed development. Perhaps these types of facilities would be more akin to the innovative culture.

Although the matrix cannot take into account economic cycles, it is not a static concept. Segments do move market positions over time. The tendency is for yesterday's innovations to be tomorrow's routinized products and services. Innovations, following the product life cycle, tend to be modified, with resultant enhancements in application and reductions in cost. The service culture usually undertakes this process, drawing upon generic skills until such time as a 'flow line' delivery of product and service can be established. Organizations may follow their product by changing market position, or in the case of drug companies, once the brand patent expires, the generic producers take over, and new brands emerging from research and development take their place for those companies. One of the case studies shows this type of move in the case of flagships.

A flagship development may involve a number of segments, and the inward investment that is to be subsequently attracted will almost certainly do so. This increases the diversity of the local economy, minimizing risk, while promoting a coherent position in the market for the area and possibly for the city.

4.7 SALES TARGETS

The next step is to identify the targets within each segment. There are two ways of undertaking this task: select the entire **market segment**, which leads to blanket coverage, or identify **selective demand** (Guiltinan and Paul, 1988). Organizations will only 'buy' buildings or relocate periodically, and most leisure and retail consumption is periodic. Therefore, markets tend to be selective. They may also be selective in geographical terms. The orientation may exclude potential occupiers and consumers where local or national orientations have been chosen. Conversely, an international orientation does not necessarily mean coverage of the whole globe. There will be selectivity according to where it is thought the main market segments are already located.

The aim is to target particular organizations directly or provide information to them so that they may respond. In drawing up the lists of organizations and locations a number of questions need to be addressed concerning **market opportunities** and **market requirements**.

In analysing market opportunities, each segment will be examined in relation to the following questions:

- What is the size of the market?
- What are the economic prospects for the market?
- Are competitive locations providing the desired level of benefits?
- Are the needs of the segment largely unmet?
- Are there occupiers and consumers who do not have the willingness or the ability to relocate or spend, respectively?
- Is the image of areas and cities strongly established – branded – or is there a good deal of scope for extending locational choices?

In analysing market requirements, it is necessary to establish, within the market position, whether the benefits can be delivered:

- Can the flagship deliver the required benefits to attract subsequent investment and consumption?
- Are the costs of meeting the opportunities in each segment going to be exceeded by the return in economic and social terms?

- What scope is there, if necessary, for switching segments or moving market position in the future?
- Will the flagship, area and city be competitive in the market and for how long?

The final step is to undertake the sales effort for each target, through the promotional channels. This is part of the project management and will be addressed in Chapter 5. Before proceeding to that stage, a few concluding remarks can be made on the wider implications of applying marketing frameworks to an urban context.

4.8 BEYOND THE IMMEDIATE MARKET HORIZON

The main thrust of this chapter has been to continually focus down, starting with strategic marketing and ending with the sales process expressed through the building types. Looking outwards again is useful to expose some of the implicit features in the marketing process in an urban context.

Firstly, there is often a shift in scale for promotion, almost by sleight of hand, from the area for regeneration to the city level. The flagship tends to address both the site on which it sits as an entity in its own right and the surrounding area into which it is hoped to attract the subsequent investment 'in its wake'. However, the initiators of the flagship, especially where there is direct local authority involvement, do frequently consider the whole regeneration project as part of a wider city strategy, either intentionally, through policy development, or by default. This is often closely linked to the orientation, and therefore market position. Promotion at the city level can also be linked closely to large-scale projects and those that are more routinized. It is, of course, possible for a flagship project to be strategic for the city, while keeping the orientation local, in other words confined to that city. Segmentation should take this into account by both preserving the integrity of the area circumstances of the project and, regardless of orientation, ensuring that the marketing strategy and sales effort for the project is not compromised by city-wide hype and image making that goes well beyond what the project can deliver.

Secondly, the focus on the city can be extended to review the market position of the city **in** the economy. This does require a shift in orientation to at least the national scale. One of the recent trends in the international economy may have been the beginnings of greater stratification of cities (Mayer, 1989). The strata follow the functions in order of importance identified by Harvey, concerning control and command functions, places of consumption and competitive advantage for investment (Harvey, 1989c). The irony is that inner city decline has thrown up opportunities for cities to capture such functions. It is a long-term business, which appears to be engendering particular crises among private developers performing that function 'on behalf of' the city or even the nation. Canary Wharf in London Docklands is the most conspicuous example. The functional role of a flagship development can, as in this example, extend well beyond the commercial benefits of development into urban **governance**, especially where the private sector is performing a strategic role for the city. During recession, these strategic roles are put at risk. For large projects, the time from formulation of the policy or project to its completion is likely to extend well beyond a single economic cycle, so recessive conditions are likely to arise during project implementation. Should the agents of government not be playing a financial role for projects of such strategic scale? Should they not also be assisting the developers in establishing the market position and segments for the proposed development? On the other hand, in some public–private partnerships it has been stated that the private sector takes limited or no risk, the profitability of the flagship project being underwritten with public finance (Harvey, 1989a). Is this a reasonable strategy for a city or government to adopt with public money?

The larger the project, the larger the risk. The financial consequences of that risk are seldom addressed[11] or were only beginning to be addressed in the recession of the late 1980s and early 1990s. Large private sector schemes create indebtedness, which has been absorbed by the banks. This in turn puts constraints on others. In Baltimore, flagships have put financial stress on the savings and loan institutions, which has impacted upon the poorest inhabitants in their efforts to secure homes, the very people whom it was claimed the flagships would help (Harvey, 1989a). In Britain the property debt of banks is constraining and will constrain, through a resultant restricted investment in other sectors, economic recovery. These matters begin to raise some of the questions as to whether there are 'winners' and 'losers' in flagship development. This subject will be looked at in more depth in Chapter 6. The point at this stage of the analysis is that the choice of market position, segment and, indeed, size of the flagship and its constituent parts may need to take these wider issues into account.

4.9 APPLYING THE MARKETING FRAMEWORK

The aim of this chapter has been to show the way in which a marketing framework can be used for two purposes. Firstly, it can be used to increase the certainty of success for a flagship and the effectiveness of urban regeneration. It is a complex process, involving many additional factors that have to be addressed and understood in the urban context. In the decision making process, it cannot be claimed that there is a statistical or 'scientific' basis; however, it is certainly the case that decisions, no matter how subjective they may be, have been based upon full consideration of the economic and social factors. This does not mean that all flagships have to have been using a marketing approach to be considered successful. Nor does it mean that a well-considered project will not fail. The Baltimore case arose by a collision of ideas and opportunities in a particular set of circumstances, and some of the largest spectacles that result in the city becoming a place of ephemeral experience are not consciously planned (Clark, 1985; Harvey, 1989c). Yet phases of development have been planned and the net result at best appears to be mixed. It can only be said that the risks are minimized and chances of success increased through the use of a marketing framework in practice.

Secondly, the purpose is to provide an analytical framework for evaluating the case studies. Given the complexity, especially concerning local populations, it is hard to see how a purely private sector scheme can address all issues. Perhaps this is one reason that has driven local authorities to be so active in flagship developments during the 1980s, even if this was unconsciously motivated at times. This does not mean that the private sector cannot undertake a successful scheme that achieves social benefits. Nor does it mean that social factors, or indeed economic factors, have to be incorporated. The approach adopted by this research is to take the aims and objectives of each flagship initiator and evaluate each project on those terms. However, when it comes to comparing and contrasting schemes, the marketing matrix comes to the fore. At this stage of the analysis all factors have to be considered, and it is suggested that in cases when factors have been excluded in practice there should be 'good' reasons for so doing; a point that will be returned to in the case analyses and in Chapter 14, which addresses the implications of flagships for urban development.

The next task of the analysis is to set out the resources and skills that need to be mobilized to realize a successful project and show how these differ for each market position. This is the subject of Chapter 5.

Project management 5

5.1 POLICY ANALYSIS

Having the appropriate skills and resources for implementing a project is important for achieving the original the aims and objectives. The marketing strategy, and the matrix in particular, provide the policy or part of a broader policy strategy. Policy analysis, whether it is for practitioners or applied to research, comprises distinct stages.

Figure 5.1 shows how policy progresses chronologically. This does not necessarily suggest that policy is hierarchical, although most frequently it is. The 'top-down' model of policy formulation means that the aims, objectives and the criteria for the project implementation are largely established by the initiators. These may be moderated by statutory requirements and through other interested parties, but essentially the policy, and hence the project, is imposed upon the area, city and the population.

This is not to say that such policy is formed in a vacuum. The initiators,

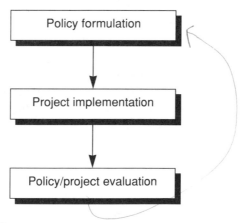

Figure 5.1 Principal policy stages

in forming their aims and objectives, may be influenced by a number of matters, such as:

- their values
- their past experience
- other similar policies and projects
- advice from organizations with which they work
- advice from users
- political pressures
- other interested parties
- lobby and pressure groups
- the local population.

A largely top-down approach will probably give priority in the order shown above.

However, in the policy process, there is usually a 'bottom-up' element as well. This will emanate from a number of sources, such as:

- feedback from past experience in policy and practice;
- reinterpretation of the aims and objectives by those responsible for implementation;
- changing circumstances during implementation compromising the aims and objectives;
- demands for change from political, lobby and pressure groups;
- empowerment of the local population.

The influence of bottom-up policy making will vary according to:

- the extent to which the initiators seek to embrace external influences;
- the extent to which external influence from the local population can be brought to bear on the initiators;
- the rate of cultural change during the project implementation;
- the extent to which the initiators undertake or control the implementation process.

The process is, therefore, about managing change and the political repercussions concerning the project and the wider cultural context.

Applying this three-stage analysis to the marketing matrix requires each market position to be scrutinized for each policy stage. The skills and resources will therefore relate to every stage within each market position.

5.2 PRINCIPAL ELEMENTS

In any policy there are a number of elements. There is the object or operation itself, in this case the flagship. There are three other elements – cost, people and marketing. The cost concerns all financial matters and provides the means with which to undertake the flagship development.

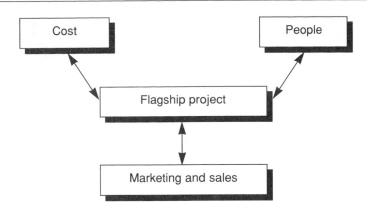

Figure 5.2 Principal operating elements

People covers all contacts and personnel matters. It is people in whom the skills are embodied. Marketing covers all aspects of strategy, sales and public relations, in other words, the means for matching demand to the flagship development and the area to be regenerated. These elements are shown in Figure 5.2.

5.3 MARKET POSITIONS

Each market position needs to be considered under each of the three principal policy stages. In doing this, it is necessary to be clear how the matrix can be applied. Firstly, there is the flagship as an entity in itself. Secondly, there is the surrounding investment and consumption that is to be attracted. Finally, there is the combination – the overall policy aim of successful urban regeneration – that makes a contribution to economic and social well-being for the area. The skills and resources will tend to be focused upon the flagship development itself, with the working assumption and expectation that the investment and consumption will follow in its wake.

Generally, this will not provide any conflict concerning market position. However, there may be exceptions on occasions, for one of two reasons. A flagship development may occupy a different market position compared to the subsequent targeted investment. To illustrate the point, certain prominent yet varied arts and leisure programmes may be provided as a flagship development with the sole intention of helping to secure standardized office employment. This would bring a flagship of a service culture alongside routinized activities. It would make greater sense for the arts and leisure facilities also to be routinized, unless there are very specific local reasons for not so doing.

Another case would be where a flagship development of one market position had been developed, yet the inward investment was of another position. This is the more likely outcome. This may be the result of decisions made by key and probably large investors coming into the area, or may be caused by a change in circumstances in the letting or investment markets during implementation that shifted the market position. In these cases the flagship development will not be having the maximum promotional effect. It will be lending 'confidence' to the market and will act as a large advertising hoarding or billboard within the area, but that will be the extent of its contribution to regeneration.

The resources, skills and support needed at each stage of a project will vary according to market position. The cultural variable is also a strong determinant of resources and their management. The geographical orientation is less influential in configuration, but affects the level of detail and the number of organizations and people involved. The management of the resources is the key to realizing the marketing strategy. This is not to suggest that 'managerialism' or its 'corporatist' parent are being either suggested or advocated. It is simply to state that a strategy remains a concept until resources are mobilized. Nor is it to suggest that marketing strategies cannot be mobilized in managerialist or corporatist ways. They can, but no more or less so than any other approach to government or indeed to any business.

5.4 RESOURCES, SKILLS AND SUPPORT

The mobilization and management of resources will be analysed by considering each market position in turn. There are nine market positions in the matrix, each of which has three policy stages. Each stage requires an analysis of the principal elements. Although there is a core set of requirements, it is the variations that matter because they will induce the different market characteristics where used effectively. As the analysis proceeds, each of the market positions will be summarized in a corresponding figure, and a brief description of each one will be given, the main attention being turned towards the variations and the reasons for these. There is greater variation according to the dominant culture in comparison to the geographical orientation. The analysis will therefore be grouped according to culture.

5.4.1 Routinized culture

The overall management emphasis for flagships that are promoting a routinized culture will be upon moving the development process down the management hierarchy. The detailed implementation will be dependent on sets of procedures, mechanisms and practices that are taken for granted and require minimal explanation or 'hands-on' management. Overall control or supervision will come from 'above', with the management structures acting as the main forms of control and discipline. Those responsible for implementation will be able to have authority because of the procedural nature of the work and through delegation, which will be used down the management line. Where there are a number of initiators and external advisors, the reporting procedures will replace the internal management control.

Therefore, routinized flagship developments also tend to require routinized management of the project in a top-down fashion. Considerably more emphasis will be given to the project as an entity in itself for routinized projects, because it will be expected that the inward investment and consumption can be drawn in using a procedural approach to promotion.

A-type project

The **A-type** market position concerns the **routinized–local** flagship. The guidelines are set out in Figure 5.3.

Focusing upon the stage of **policy formulation**, the three elements appear in the column with the pertinent points listed below. The idea or concept will tend to emanate from elsewhere, being refined and developed according to experience and the local context. Ideas for projects will evolve in an evolutionary or incremental fashion. The key decisions will therefore focus upon whether to have a flagship project and what idea or model to adopt. The more detailed analysis of policy will be developed by senior management with middle management, in an endeavour to create a smooth handover. This will not require many organizations or people for a flagship that is orientated towards the area and city. Decision making and reporting will tend to be handled along fairly 'autocratic' lines. Although the stimulus for undertaking a locally orientated project may have arisen from local demands and pressures, the policy process will tend to be predominantly top-down.

Cost will be the key criterion because this will be potentially the most variable and unknown factor. There will be considerable emphasis on cost control for two reasons: firstly, those involved are more likely to affect their career progression or public standing through the control of cost, and, secondly, organizations will be similarly motivated, private initiators being concerned about profit and shareholder perceptions, and public authorities about accountability and public scrutiny. Budgets will be defined in detail and fixed in many cases.

This type of project will be the least proactively promoted and the closest to the approach of 'being there'. The flagship as an advertising hoarding or billboard is most relevant where the market is local. However, there is

Flagship type: *Routinized–Local*

Policy formulation	Project implementation	Policy/project evaluation
People: 1. Whose idea? 　– importing external 　model or idea 　– executive or 　senior management 　level	People: 1. Internal 　– management 　delegated 　– procedural 　systems	People: 　– middle manage- 　ment with report 　back to senior 　management 　– procedural at 　department level
2. Formulating policy/ 　criteria 　– senior and middle 　management levels 　– detailed sub-goals 　established 　– formulated for 　'autocratic' control 　(individual or 　committee) or 　delegation to 　subordinates/ 　community group	2. External 　– professional and 　construction 　services may be in- 　house or contracted 　out 　– procedural 　contracts and 　may be an 　uncomplicated 　product/project	
Cost: 　– the key criterion 　– profit maxi- 　mization, cost 　minimization 　–defined and fixed 　budget	Cost: 　– high level of 　monitoring, unless 　let as fixed price 　contract	Cost: 　– relating capital and 　revenue expenditure 　to direct income, 　indirect income/ 　promotional benefits
Marketing and sales: 　– executives, senior 　management levels 　– 'sells itself', track 　record or via 　community 　– clear objectives as 　part of well defined 　criteria	Marketing and sales: 　– executives, senior 　management 　– external agents 　notified and may be 　involved with lettings	Marketing and sales: 　– 'common sense' 　evaluation 　– measured, if 　quantifiable 　– impact on organi- 　zation and area

Figure 5.3 *A-type* market position

more substance than this. The project, and hence the surrounding area, will 'sell itself' through the local network of contacts and agencies within the city. Public relations will mainly serve to reinforce this process by ensuring that the key people in the initiating organizations talk about the project at meetings and events involving those in positions of influence. The local community may form a key part of the network, especially for projects with a strong social orientation or where small and 'family' businesses and start-ups are being fostered. Track record may also be important, either regarding other similar schemes within the locale or citing examples or successful schemes elsewhere.

At the stage of **project implementation**, the initiators may not be heavily involved. The delegation of management is a key principle. Management may be contracted out; in the case of the public sector, this may involve the appointment of a private sector developer. In effect the developer becomes one of the initiators, although their aims and objectives will primarily revolve around profit, which becomes the incentive for cost control. The public initiators can control the policy by selecting the developer through a tender package which includes a scheme design. Other constraints can be imposed through the contract and through planning procedures. More direct control can be secured through a partnership arrangement, which would normally be linked to the provision of some finance or land.

The selection of an independent developer or partner and their teams would certainly involve the land, tender or package prices, yet their approach to the market is also relevant. A developer that is more routinized in organization and develops a standard 'product' is more likely to be suited to a routinized scheme. The team employed by the developer should be similarly orientated, concentrating upon strong delivery (Coxe *et al.*, 1987). In the case of developers, their market position is not defined by geographical orientation, but by value orientation. Value orientation can be corporate or social (Smyth, 1991). These orientations are not to do with any intrinsic desire to make profits or not: it is assumed that a developer will always seek to do so. They are about emphasis, and therefore which niche market the developer chooses to exploit as a means of making profit. A corporate orientation is almost solely about the maximization of profit, while a social orientation may imply social or philanthropic concerns yet may not necessarily require that. It can simply arise out of a awareness that social markets can yield a good rate of return. The value orientation could come into play when a local authority wishes to promote a development that has partnership or social housing, where a 'per cent' for art policy is encouraged or where high profile design is required. All of these could equally be secured through strict planning criteria and the use of Section 106 (formerly 52) agreements to ensure that certain facilities are provided 'in exchange' for planning permission. This latter approach is procedural, and can be pursued through a corporate developer.

In-house teams for design and construction could equally be used because the requirements are standard and, in principle, there are economies of scale and an absence of the learning curve in such an approach. However, throughout the 1980s, cost criteria have overridden these theoretical benefits. It was found that savings could be achieved through putting out to tender and that there were sufficient routinized firms with a strong delivery that were able to tackle such work. Added to this, many of the theoretical economies were not achieved in-house. It appears that this approach of decentralization and privatization is continuing into the 1990s as a means for achieving greater economic flexibility by reducing in-house costs and taking advantage of low tender prices driven by overcapacity in the construction industry during recessive conditions.

In general, cost criteria will always be most dominant in a routinized market position. Therefore, cost will be closely monitored at every step during the implementation stage. Promotion of the project will continue throughout implementation in much the same way as in the policy formulation stage. Letting agents will have been brought in by this time, although in recessive conditions prelets may have been required to commence construction. Where the flagship as an entity does not seek tenants, lettings through agents' sales efforts will come into play for the inward investment into the surrounding area. Promotion will reflect the risk factor. Overall, the risk is low for this type of project. From the developer viewpoint the risk is low within a corporate orientation and low-to-medium for a project with a high social content. The scope for bargaining will be similar for both because of the routinized nature of operations (Smyth, 1991).

The **evaluation** of the entity will be undertaken after completion. There may be several ways in which the project is assessed. Initial perceptions will be formed in the light of lettings, throughput of people or some indicator of rates of utilization, depending upon the project functions and building types. Financial data may be unavailable, but opinions may be widely canvassed among those involved, both those in positions of influence and those on the ground. The media and political interests may supply unsolicited opinions, but as data becomes available the evaluation will tend to switch away from qualitative assessments towards quantitative ones.

Evaluation will also involve the wider policy aims and objectives. This will be particularly important where there is public involvement. It will tend to be undertaken by middle management, reporting back to senior levels. Cost will form the most important element, and an assessment of value for money or profitability will be made. In the case of public policy, the evaluation will closely consider the success of attracting further investment and consumption, regardless of any problems arising on the flagship development. An evaluation is important, because a routinized project is easily repeated and the likely smaller scale of a locally orientated scheme will render funding more feasible for future projects.

Evaluating the success of the marketing strategy and sales efforts should also be undertaken. This would be carried out in a 'common-sense' way, depending more on observation than on any detailed research and analysis. Available data will be used as supplementary and support material. It will include evaluation of the organizations that stand to benefit from the regeneration, and hence the impact upon the area. The top-down nature of this kind of development will mean that the benefits for local people will tend to be the last factor considered, although this does not necessarily mean that the social impact is less important. It is a reflection of cause and effect that is built into this proposition.

B-type project

The **B-type** project occupies a **routinized–national** market position. The initiators will have a regional or national outlook. Just as an international orientation does not include the entire globe, so a national orientation need not encapsulate the entire nation. Many of the features of the routinized–national flagships are shared with the previous position (see Figure 5.4). The differences will be highlighted.

During **policy formulation**, there may be a larger number of organizations involved in addition to the executive and senior management functions of the initiator. Therefore the idea could arise from a wider constituency, possibly interorganizationally, as in the case of partnership schemes. An intraorganizational formulation of the aims and objectives could arise, perhaps confined to local organizations, but more likely to embrace organizations from outside the area, not only in the development sectors, but also from the public and voluntary sectors. This will tend to limit bottom-up contributions other than well-organized groups that put forward defined demands.

Well-defined criteria for achieving the aims and objectives will be established through delegation to senior management. The detailed sub-goals, which will probably be less explicit than those for the locally orientated projects, will be developed through all participants and advisors, through groups and committees. Ratification will remain at executive levels.

Cost will again be dominant, but may be less certain at this stage, particularly where a nationally orientated scheme is designed to be large. Larger scale schemes may incur additional costs for the whole area for infrastructure provision. As a result, the budget may be highly defined, but it may not be finite.

Marketing and sales efforts will differ in three possible respects. Firstly, there will be greater responsibility upon the executive levels to promote the scheme through their networks. Secondly, the flagship development is much more likely to be linked with, or be an element within, a broader development strategy. Thirdly, external agents may be appointed to assist

Flagship type: *Routinized–National*

Policy formulation	Project implementation	Policy/project evaluation
People: 1. Whose idea? – importing external model or idea – executive or senior management level – perhaps intraorganizational 2. Formulating policy/criteria – senior management level – well-defined criteria – outline sub-goals – formulated through groups or committees – executive decision making	People: 1. Internal – senior management control – procedural management delegated 2. External – professional services in-house or contracted out – construction services contracted out	People: – senior management at department level with report back to executive – may be contracted out to consultants in part or wholly – media
Cost: – the key criterion – profit maximization, cost minimization –defined budget	Cost: – high level of monitoring – opportunity to let as fixed price could be more limited, but may be let out as fixed-price packages	Cost: – precise accountancy and cost–benefit analysis procedures used
Marketing and sales: – executive level – 'sells itself' locally via track record – may link into wider development strategy – external agents assist in promotion	Marketing and sales: – executives, senior management – external promotion, letting and other agencies	Marketing and sales: – evaluation using well-defined criteria: • as a project • as part of wider development strategy • raising profile of organization/area • attracting additional rent/asset value or investment in area • impact on population

Figure 5.4 *B-type* market position

with promotion – planning public relations, advertising and letting or sales effort aimed at their national targets.

During the **implementation** stage, senior management will play a more direct or controlling role. The actions following from the formulated policy and the controlling input from senior management will be implemented down the hierarchy in a procedural fashion. The construction of the project will be contracted out. Cost control will be of considerable concern, particularly for the construction phase because it is here that price uncertainty could arise, with costs escalating as the flagship concept is firmed up and during the contract period. Some cost increases may be inevitable in the precontract stage. However, cost concerns can lead to compromising the market position and hence the aims and objectives.

In the construction phase it is unlikely to be possible to control costs through a fixed price. If the initiator is a public sector organization, the costs of development, which would include the construction phase, could be handed to the developer. Where rental income will not be present, a large contractor may take on the development role, using their working capital to fund the project in return for a lump sum payment at the end or at agreed stages. Public authorities are only likely to receive the desired quality of development under this system if the specification is closely scrutinized and 'cost in use' criteria are closely examined by the flagship operators. Furthermore, the quality of work achieved on site is more likely to be of a high standard if the contractor negotiates their development role, rather than being appointed through open bids, where the contractor is absorbing greater risk than that arising purely from construction.

Greater cost certainty can be provided by letting the project in fixed-price packages. The contractor may be undertaking some work directly. In many cases, the contractor is operating purely in a management contracting role, thus helping to control cost and quality for the client in a defined programme. The initiator can act as project manager instead of the contractor. A project manager could be appointed, although the tendency in these cases is to put more emphasis upon cost than quality, inputs rather than output. In practice, cost control is frequently less than successful for the initiator. The project manager can lack the expertise or the resources to control cost because inadequate time or understanding is given to the overseeing of progress and work under the construction contracts.

Active sales and promotion will begin in earnest at this stage, letting agents being involved on a national basis where commercial space is being provided. Other promotional bodies will be involved for other types of facilities, for example the finalizing and promotion of an opening and the initial programme for arts facilities.

The **evaluation** of the policy and project will address the same sorts of issues, but in a more concerted way. Both senior management and middle management will be involved, reporting to the executive levels. Data will be used extensively, and research and analysis will be undertaken. The evaluation may be contracted out by a public authority, perhaps to accountants and management consultancy organizations. The media may become directly involved in the evaluation process, not just as a source of data and information as in the case of locally orientated projects, but because the flagship and subsequent regeneration will themselves be newsworthy items in many instances. Media evaluation will tend to become inextricably linked to the policy evaluation, framing the agenda for evaluation and lending weight to the political perceptions of schemes. The reactions of the local business community and population will be evaluated where the bottom-up element is weak.

Cost will be top of the agenda for evaluation, not simply in statistical terms, but usually in a cost–benefit equation. The benefits will, of course, embrace the extent to which social and economic well-being has been encouraged into the area and city through regeneration and more general inward investment and consumption. The evaluation of the promotion, using well-defined criteria, will play a key part in this and will focus on the issues of the development:

- as a project;
- as part of a wider development strategy;
- as raising the profile of key organizations and the area;
- as attracting additional rent, asset value and investment to the area;
- with regard to its impact on the population.

These criteria should closely reflect the original aims and objectives, with cost being the prominent measure to assess the impact of the project.

C-type project

The **C-type** project occupies the **routinized–international** position and is described in outline in Figure 5.5.

In the **policy formulation** stage, the same types of organization could be involved, the scale of the project and intensity of the involvement being the two most likely distinguishing features. For a public sector flagship project, central government is likely to have a role, and international governments and agencies, such as the European Commission, could be involved via grant provision. This level of involvement demands that the executive levels of management are involved with the policy formulation. This will include any developer, for they will need to be involved at this stage even where they were not responsible for the original idea. Their selection at this stage does not emanate from any intrinsic risk associated with the market position, but is associated with the risk derived from the scale of project that the market position could induce.

Policy formulation	Project implementation	Policy/project evaluation
People: 1. Whose idea? – importing external model or idea – executive levels and intraorganizational 2. Formulating policy/ criteria – executive and senior management, intraorganizational – well-defined overall goals – outline criteria and sub-goals formulated through groups and committees – intraorganizational steering group and organizational executive decision making	People: 1. Internal – steering group decision making/ monitoring – executive control – senior management of day to day procedure 2. External – professional and construction services contracted out – project management may be contracted out	People: – steering group and executives – may be contracted out to consultants – media
Cost: – important criterion – profit maximization, cost control –defined budget	Cost: – high level of monitoring	Cost: – relating capital and revenue expenditure to direct income, indirect income/promotional benefits
Marketing and sales: – intraorganizational and executive levels – use of external agents and central government	Marketing and sales: – intraorganizational executive levels – external agents and central government	Marketing and sales: – Overall evaluation using well-defined goals • as a project • as part of wider development strategy • raising profile of organization/area • attracting additional rent/asset value or investment in area • impact on population – evaluation of above at level of each organization using well-defined criteria

Figure 5.5 *C-type* market position

An additional layer of policy criteria would ideally be introduced for such a flagship. This layer will require well-defined overall goals, with outline criteria and sub-goals being addressed under these. The structures for policy formulation will be more complex, involving intraorganizational steering groups with working groups and committees operating under their overall control. This structure will continue throughout, with representative executives and senior management from each organization being responsible for implementing the project through their own organizations. The process will be top-down.

Cost remains key, profit maximization being the main aim. Budgets will be defined and controlled, but the degree of certainty over the duration of the implementation stage cannot be determined.

Promotion will follow a similar pattern to that for the nationally orientated scheme, but will also include intraorganizational promotion and may well involve central government.

The main differences at the **implementation** stage will be the definite contracting out of professional services, especially the design team. There is a greater likelihood that a project manager will be appointed, not so much to control cost, but rather to coordinate the design teams, other consultants and construction, and to monitor costs.

The **project and policy evaluation** will be undertaken at the steering group level, although the work may be subcontracted out to consultants. The objectives are likely to be twofold – those concerned with the overall regeneration and those relating to each initiator represented on the steering group. Capital and revenue costs will be addressed. Costs will therefore be related to direct and indirect income, as well as the wider benefits for the area that have come about as a result of the regeneration.

5.4.2 Service culture

The overall management emphasis for flagships that are promoting a service culture will be upon analysis. Whereas the routinized culture stresses delivery, the service culture emphasizes problem solving. The management structure will tend to be flatter, and teamwork and coordination will be fostered. This will not only be the case in delivering the service or undertaking the operations by users and customers of the completed project, but will also apply to the creation of the flagship in the first place.

The flagship as an entity in itself will receive attention, but the way in which the policy process is set up will give far greater significance to the subsequent inward investment and consumption in the surrounding area. How this will be achieved in practice will vary from project to project; indeed, the relationship between the flagship and anticipated regeneration may be one of the problems to be solved. It will not be possible in most cases to determine the mix of uses, but the promotion may be more targeted to specific uses and users, so permitting an overall concept or masterplan to be created for the area, into which subsequent activities can be slotted as they become known.

This approach cuts across the policy emphasis of property-led urban regeneration, which places great store on the market to determine out-comes. It has been seen in London Docklands, for example, that some early commercial developments were demolished to make way for larger and different developments as confidence and values rose during the property boom of the late 1980s. The interesting point about a flagship development, even though it has frequently been part of a property-led strategy, is that its very presence sets the tone for further development. In other words, the flagship helps to form the market, and hence influence the market position of investment and consumption in its wake. A flagship is therefore prescriptive for the area, but it is not descriptive because it cannot determine the nature of subsequent investment and activity.

The service culture is the most conducive to a bottom-up policy process. In certain circumstances, the prime motive may be the wish to serve the local population or business. In extreme cases, this could be where there has been the threat of social instability or where civil disorder has occurred. Clearly, it is better to respect the local population and involve them in the process before there is any potential of disorder. Indeed, where disorder is potentially present, neglect and lack of respect are also present.

D-type project

The **D-type** market position is the locally-orientated project promoting a service culture. The people involved at the policy **formulation** stage will be concerned with setting out the aims and objectives of the flagship. These are shown in Figure 5.6 for the D-type **service–local** project.

The idea for a flagship development is likely to come from elsewhere – another flagship, another development or another area or country – or from local needs and demands. The issue will be to adapt the idea to the particular aims and objectives and to the local environmental and cultural context. This will be carried out at executive and senior management levels.

The policy criteria will be well defined, including sub-goals, but there will be recognition that these criteria can change during the policy process. Therefore, it is important to build consensus among all those involved at an early stage in order to ensure that the aims are shared and that change can be accommodated as the project unfolds. This consensus should include the dominant views of the local population.

For routinized projects, cost criteria were paramount. For service

Flagship type: *Service–Local*

Policy formulation	Project implementation	Policy/project evaluation

People:
1. Whose idea?
  – adapting external model or idea
  – executive or senior management level
 	
2. Formulating policy/ criteria
  . – well-defined criteria, subject to change
  – outline sub-goals
  – 'consensus'-based control
	People:
	1. Internal
	  – managed by project team, accountable to executive
	  – procedural systems, allowing some flexibility for managing change
	
	2. External
	  – either integrated with project team or set up parallel project team
		People:
		  – project team management with report back to senior management

Cost:
  – important criterion
  – profit maxi-mization, cost minimization
  –defined budget
	Cost:
	  – close monitoring of spend to budget
	  – contracts may be let on fixed price
	  – construction element may be highly standardized
		Cost:
		  – cost–benefit analysis relating capital and revenue expenditure to direct income, indirect income/perceived promotional benefits

Marketing and sales:
  – executive, senior management levels
  – strong personal commitment
  – general objectives as moderated by corporate or government politics
	Marketing and sales:
	  – executives, senior management
	  – external promo-tion, involvement of external agencies harnessing the personal commit-ment
		Marketing and sales:
		  – 'broad brush' evaluation of 'political', social, and economic benefits
		  – measured, if quantifiable
		  –impact on organiza-tion and area

Figure 5.6 *D-type* market position

projects cost will be a vital factor; however, it may not be the only vital factor, nor the dominant one, especially during the policy formulation stage.

Marketing is the third factor concerning policy formulation. It will be undertaken by executives and senior management, requiring a strong personal commitment to a project with a local orientation. The marketing objectives will necessarily be general at this stage because corporate and local political pressure may change the means and form for the sales effort.

During the **project implementation** stage, a management team, accountable to the executive would be set up, if there is not already a department or team to tackle the project. It will be the team that undertakes the main analysis, addressing the key problems with the remaining work being delegated via procedural systems. The design and construction can be undertaken in-house or externally and integrated.

In all flagships promoting a service culture, the selection or self-selection of a developer is important. The developer needs to be analytical and adaptive as far as the organizational culture is concerned. There will be scope for bargaining and negotiating scheme content, ranging from a medium-to-high scope for a socially-orientated scheme to high for a corporate approach (Smyth, 1991). The risk is dependent upon the scale of project, and the locally orientated scheme will tend to be smaller scale. The risk is highest for the social approach because of the lower rate of return, the extent of effective demand, and whether the design solutions are appropriate for the market niches. Identifying niches, securing prelets or creating sufficient flexibility in the design of the development is important in this market position.[12]

In terms of cost criteria, spend will be closely related to budgets, again with fixed-price contracts being used. The construction may not be complex and even where it is, highly standardized techniques can be used. This helps to contain costs.

The sales effort will be stepped up, harnessing the personal commitment in a programme that may involve public relations, advertising and letting agents. This should be used to enhance and reinforce the promotion derived from local networks within which the executives and senior management operate.

At the **policy and project evaluation** stage, the project team management will carry out a cost–benefit analysis, which will relate both capital and revenue expenditure to the direct and indirect income generated by the flagship and by the surrounding area, together with the social benefits that have come about. The promotion will be evaluated in a 'broad brush' fashion, encompassing the political, social and economic outcomes. Statistical data will be used where available and the impact on organizations in the area and the physical appearance of the area and its surrounds will all be taken into account.

E-type project

The **E-type** project, encompassing the **service–national** dimension, shares some features with the locally orientated project, as Figure 5.7 shows.

Looking at the **policy formulation** stage, the idea for the project may be more original for this market position. The initial stimulation could come from elsewhere, or the idea could be entirely new. In either case the executive and senior management will work the idea up into a policy and project content that is unique to the circumstances and environmental context. In terms of the aims and objectives, the overall goals will be well defined, but the criteria for achieving these will be less clearly defined and subject to change. The sub-goals will tend to emanate from the various organizations involved. These will be imprecise for a number of reasons. Firstly, it will not usually be possible to go to that level of detail at this stage of the project. Secondly, each of the organizations – or different groups or departments – involved will have their own agenda associated with the flagship development. In many cases, their goals will be competing and therefore in conflict. They may even be contradictory. One common way of managing these competing goals has been to keep them implicit, negotiating each goal only under pressure.

Decision making will be taken at executive levels based upon plans drawn up by teams or departments. Cost implications will be similar to those for the locally-orientated project, although there may be differences in the average size of development.

Promotion may involve an intraorganizational executive, the public relations and sales efforts being planned for every level of the development strategy, into which the flagship is placed. The first task in any strategy for the market position will be to determine the image to be portrayed. This will not simply be a question of the 'style' of the subsequent development or indeed the 'lifestyle' that it is hoped to promote. Is any proposed image going to 'stand alone' for the development area, does it fit alongside other images for the city or city areas, or is there an overall image for the city that reflects its market position? These questions will be determined partly by the diversity of market positions that areas of the city implicitly or explicitly have, and partly by the segments being targeted within any one market position.

This type of issue has to be addressed for any of the market positions, but it is worth dwelling upon here because it is with the E-type project that the options begin to multiply. Image making for an area or city has to be carefully handled, for any image is saying something about the people who live and work in any area. The image is speaking for them. Of course, this is not a new phenomenon – it is consciously used by public and private organizations in their corporate identity and culture all the time, with employees being chosen because they can fit the culture and being asked to

Policy formulation	Project implementation	Policy/project evaluation
People: 1. Whose idea? – stimulated by external model or idea – new idea – executive and senior management 2. Formulating policy/ criteria – executive and senior management – well-defined goals – outline criteria, subject to change – imprecise, competing sub-goals – executive decision making and policy formulation derived from departmental plans	People: 1. Internal – executive control of project management team – analytical, problem-solving approach – managing for change 2. External – high level use of external contractors and services	People: – executive and senior management involved in project teams – may be contracted out – media
Cost: – important criterion – profit maxi-mization, cost control –defined budget	Cost: – close monitoring of spend to budget – flexible pricing according to changing require-ments – letting of packages on fixed price	Cost: – detailed cost–benefit analysis
Marketing and sales: – intraorganizational executive – levels within development strategy – use of external agents in public and private sectors	Marketing and sales: – intraorganization executive levels – external agents in public and private sector	Marketing and sales: – evaluation using well-defined goals and outline criteria • as a project • as part of a wider development strategy • raising profile of organization/area • attracting addition-al rent/asset value or investment in area

Figure 5.7 *E-type* market position

reflect it in their behaviour or role playing. For some people this raises ethical concerns about personality and individuality. It is not intended to discuss this issue, except to say that an employee enters into a contract with an employer under which a wage or salary is received in exchange for the conditions of employment and undertaking the work. In an urban context it is a rather different ethical issue because no economic exchange is taking place. The result can be patronizing, and is perhaps a further example of what Harvey has claimed to be the penetration of the 'market' in to every aspect of everyday life in an urban environment (Harvey, 1989a).

Imaging an area or city can also be seen to dovetail with postmodernism where people 'buy into' surface meanings of 'style' and fashion, ephemeral experience and hedonism (Harvey, 1989a). Ethical views about this will depend upon the support for postmodernism as a way of life or being. Problems are posed for postmodernism or indeed for the relative values of the humanistic tradition, which rest more easily with the middle class and elites of society. For the disadvantaged and labouring classes this may be an unnecessary luxury. To take bricklaying, how can a brick be laid in a postmodern fashion? If the bricklayers did it 'their way' it could offend the designs of the postmodern architect. Who has the choice and what relative values are being posed in an absolute way? One general qualifying observation is that the built environment, although becoming more flexible in use with shorter life cycles, is far from temporary or ephemeral. Even where buildings are demolished, development costs have a long life cycle. There is a conflict between the durability and cost of the built environment and postmodernism as culture. The modern culture analysed by Berman (1983) shows continuity and continuous development of the built form and social encounters within it.

The preoccupation in advertising during the 1980s was 'lifestyles'. This is instructive. Lifestyle analysis and market research focused upon segments within market positions. That preoccupation with distinctive compartmentalization, niche markets, is 'postmodern' in a sense, yet had little substance. It was essentially based on capturing additional income in a growing market among the increasingly affluent according to career and age profile. 'Lifestyles' did not address the complexity of people's lives, the different roles played in different situations, or conflicting aspirations, and certainly avoided the stresses derived from the importance given to seeking approval from others, and keeping up appearances in different roles that people fitted into, as opposed to fitting them. Using the marketing matrix in a 'modern' way places greater emphasis upon the process, albeit that the goals shift by design and by default as the built environment and the activities within it tend to move from **innovative-local** to **routinized-national** over a long period of time – a point which will be taken up again (see figure 8.1).

Labouring this analysis is important because it helps us to understand what could be appropriate for area or city imaging. The image should surely fit the people and place, and not be imposed upon the place and people. The image needs to embrace the local population, its history and dynamics, both physically and culturally. This requires effort and expenditure, but is likely to lead to a sustainable image for the area and in the market-place – an image of integrity. Achieving integrity avoids the 'short cuts' of patronizing people with pseudo-history and instant culture, and fossilizing a place through conservation that denies that people live in societies of change.

When the images of the 1980s are considered, few stand up overall and most of those tried in an urban context have indeed proved ephemeral, whether it is those provided through advertising and letting campaigns or those provided through the postmodern architecture of 'signs' that simply creates a pastiche of history and style in design.

Adopting bottom-up measures for image making is important. It may well be that in some cases this will demand a complete change in direction. Where dereliction is extensive and the local population overall want something entirely different, then a change may result. Change is therefore inevitable, for urban regeneration would not be necessary if it were otherwise. Therefore the return to the status quo is not being advocated, as was promoted by some pressure groups, for example in London Docklands in the 1980s, but it is the extent of change that is being raised. Burns (1991, p.64) comments:

> For a while, . . . Sheffield was 'The Cleanest Industrial City in Europe'. . . . we became 'Sheffield – City on the Move', by the 1970s. . . . The slogan changed again: unofficially, but with a certain pride, we were the 'Socialist Republic of South Yorkshire'; by the 1980s – socialist republics having lost their clout – we became the self-styled 'Sporting Capital of Europe', our most expensive reincarnation.

The extent to which this image was 'self-styled' may be debatable. By whom is more the issue. The long-term international stature of the sports developments may also be questioned, but clearly here is a city in search of a new role or roles. The image is important in the marketing package, but it cannot be the package. Expensive or not, the resources and skills have to be present for promotion and development.

External consultants can be the driving force, handling the public relations and advertising programmes to create the image and support the letting campaigns of agents. Newcastle City Council, in whose authority are a number of flagship projects as well as the Tyne and Wear Development Corporation, commissioned J Walter Thompson to undertake an audit of current perception and develop a campaign (see Robins and Wilkinson, 1990; Wilkinson, 1992). In this case, and on a limited budget, the campaign concentrated upon existing positive features in the city, which were not reflected in the audit. Subsequent city campaigns and those of the Development Corporation did tend towards the 'lifestyle' approach. This early experiment has demonstrated some of the scope as well as the shortcomings of campaigns.

Networks can be used effectively in parallel with external agencies. Glasgow Action is a 15-year programme to attract investment, and the private sector has utilized the contacts of directors plus the promotion of 'project champions' to gain support (Fox and Healey, 1991).

The main features of the **implementation** stage are that the executive will control the project management team, an analytical approach being required throughout because managing change is likely to be a key element, especially where the flagship and surrounding areas are large. There will be a tendency to let out as much of the work as possible. This is usual practice for developers and will be advisable for other initiating parties. Spend will be closely monitored and reassessed with each change of requirements. Changes will come about because of the nature of the project and the external economic environment.

The **policy and project evaluation** makes the same shift in level and detail as the shift between national and international orientations for routinized projects. In the service culture this shift occurs between the local and national scales of outlook. It is possible that the evaluation of promotion will result in a broadening of campaigns. For example, the Mersey Development Corporation took a promotion campaign to eleven cities in the United States. Potential investors were targeted through mailshots, the Royal Liverpool Philharmonic Orchestra toured the cities to promote Liverpool, and interested investors attended meetings that were held in parallel. This action was taken because Liverpool's image was closely associated in Britain with the Toxteth riots and the militant city council, whereas the American perceptions were of Paul McCartney and the Beatles or neutrality (*Financial Times*, 1992a).

F-type project

The **F-type** market position focuses on the **service–international** dimension. In the **policy formulation** stage, the executive level is instrumental in formulating the aims and objectives. Because of this and the international orientation there will be an absence of sub-goals. These will emerge in the next stage of the policy process, and will become part of the conflict because of the intraorganizational nature of this type of project. A steering group will represent the organizations and become the principal decision making body. Whether individual organizations will have to refer back to their own constituency for each decision will depend upon the nature of the policies and how accountable the executives wish, or are allowed, to be.

For public sector organizations this concerns the issue of **governance** that was raised earlier. The process will be predominantly top-down, although the supporting views of the local population may help to establish need, and hence finance (Figure 5.8).

Cost can only be established in outline, derived from the aims and objectives. Translating these into design concepts give some cost guidance, but the project will be value-driven at this stage and therefore in marked contrast to the routinized flagship developments.

Promotion will need to be carefully prepared at this formulation stage for subsequent implementation. Decisions will focus on the intraorganizational and executive levels. External promotional agents are almost certain to be appointed. Central government will need to be involved, and therefore securing its support will be necessary. Other governments and multinational companies may also be able to support the subsequent promotion.

Marketing may be two-edged at this stage. Formulating the policy may require active promotion to both the financial sector and government funding sources in order to ensure the project goes ahead. Therefore, marketing will involve demonstrating need and the commercial viability, or 'pulling power', of the proposed flagship, if not in the form of tangible demand at least as confidence among both key supporters and the initiators. Selling the scheme to the backers will be the first task.

In the **implementation** phase, external structures will probably be more dominant than the organizational ones. Thus, the intraorganizational steering group and those to whom work has been contracted out will be the prime movers of implementation. Those to whom key packages of work have been contracted out may well join the steering group. Each steering group executive will rely on their own organization to provide the management support and to resolve problems as they arise. There are bound to be numerous issues to be solved and the project will tend towards crisis management, especially at critical stages.

Part of the crisis management will be the control of costs. Outline budgets will be revised and detailed budgeting for packages should ideally be addressed as the project proceeds. This will not always be the case. For example, with fast track construction methods the detailed design of the project will be carried out during construction. The design should be one or two stages ahead of work on site, although in practice slippage can result in packages of construction work being let without full information about design and specification. Ironically, this can lead to design matters being determined in parallel and in liaison with the contracting team, which is similar to the craft-based process.

At this stage, the sales effort will be brought to bear, the same people and organizations being involved with the overseeing of the campaigns.

Project evaluation, and hence policy evaluation, will be multifaceted and fragmented because of the diversity of organizations involved and

Flagship type: *Service–International*

Policy formulation	Project implementation	Policy/project evaluation

People:
1. Whose idea?
  – stimulated by external model or idea
  – new idea
  – executive
 	
2. Formulating policy/ criteria
  – executive and intraorganizational with senior management support
  – well-defined overall goals
  – outline criteria, subject to change
  – absence of sub-goals
  – intraorganizational steering group and decision making
 	
Cost:
  – outline budget
  – value driven *vis-à-vis* promotion
 	
Marketing and sales:
  – intraorganizational and executive levels
  – use of external agents
  – use of central government, other governments, mediating institutions and multinationals
	People:
	1. External
	  – steering group
	  – contracted out services
	
	2. Internal
	  – steering group executives draw upon organizational management input
	  – contracted out services
	
	3. Process
	  – analytical, problem-solving approach
	  – tending towards crisis management
	
	Cost:
	  – revision of outline budgets
	  – detailed budgeting for packages
	
	Marketing and sales:
	  – intraorganizational and executive levels
	  – use of external agents
	  – central government, other governments, mediating institutions and multinationals
		People:
		  – steering groups
		  – government
		  – organizational
		  – external consultants
		  – commentators, media
		
		Cost:
		  – accountancy and cost–benefit analysis at a general level and at organizational level
		  – financial and cost–benefit analysis of packages or final elements
		
		Marketing and sales:
		  – 'broad brush' evaluation of political benefits
		  – evaluation of economic promotion value for money type criteria
		  – 'broad brush' social impact analysis
		  – detailed evaluation of packages and elements:
		    • as projects
		    • as part of the whole flagship
		    • raising profile of organization/area
		    • attracting additional rent/asset value or investment in area
		    • impact on population
		  – evaluation of above at level of each organization in terms of overall goals relating to organization

Figure 5.8 *F-type* market position

interests being served. It will be hard to determine the level of success or failure of the original aims and objectives categorically. The aims and policy criteria will probably have changed because of the diversity of involvement and the period of time taken for implementation, particularly for a large flagship development. Ideally, the original steering group should evaluate the regeneration, but upon project completion, the group is likely to be disbanded and resources extracted.

Evaluation will most likely be undertaken by each separate organization that was involved. While they may pay attention to the original aims, objectives and the policy criteria for achieving those aims, their preoccupation will be with their own agenda. These are the project and policy sub-goals articulated both at the policy formulation stage and during implementation. These goals would have been part of the process of change, part of the resultant crisis management, being negotiated according to the balance of interests and power wielded at any one time. It is also possible that some goals would have been present but not articulated at any stage, and would emerge only during the evaluation.

Organizations undertaking their own evaluation would be the initiators, local and central government, and public commentators, including the media and academia. Their roles in evaluation may be inversely related to the extent of their involvement; however, this may be positive, in that such organizations are more likely to look at the flagship and resultant regeneration as a whole. Accountancy and cost–benefit analysis for the whole scheme and for each organization will be used for evaluation. The necessary data will generally be published in the public domain. Analyses of the key elements and packages will also be undertaken, but these may be kept private by the organizations undertaking them.

The promotion will be evaluated according to the political benefits for interested parties. Economic activity will be evaluated in terms of the ability to secure value for money and profit levels through promotion and via effective market demand, and the social contribution of the scheme. More detailed evaluation of organizations' own involvement and the spin-offs for them will be undertaken by the organizations themselves.

5.4.3 Innovative culture

It is difficult to predetermine a management approach to innovation, except that flexibility will be important, allowing room for experimentation, adaptation and growth for successful projects or elements. Diversity will be one of the key components, to minimize risk and maximize opportunity. However, some principles have to be established, especially if buildings are to be provided as part of the flagship development, although this may not always be absolutely necessary. For example, the first Garden Festival in Liverpool had temporary structures and the Theatre Village in

Newcastle, which is one of the case studies, commenced on an area basis rather than with a building.

In theory, there should be a great deal of interest in the surrounding areas and what will become of the former flagship, if it is not of a durable nature as a project. The flagship as an entity will still receive attention, but the longer term objective is vital, for in many cases the flagship cannot be sustained as an entity in itself without the attraction of further investment and consumption. It may not be possible to determine what will come in the wake of the flagship development, so it may also be advisable to undertake schemes that help to shape the innovative culture. Under these circumstances the flagship concept becomes less of a defined project on a site and more of a concept being implemented through schemes across an area.

G-type project

The **G-type** flagship project occupies the **innovative–local** market position. The idea for the project will tend to come from an individual, perhaps an elected member, entrepreneur, dignitary or someone from a voluntary organization or a hybrid group. The idea will be visionary and will there-fore be developed with few goals, in outline form only. The criteria for achieving the aims or vision will be simple and open-ended or may even be absent at this stage. Decision making will be autocratic or through building a constituency of people who come to embrace and 'own' the vision too. The **policy formulation** stage will be dominated by this visionary approach (see Figure 5.9).

Cost will be a secondary issue, being addressed in some kind of plan or feasibility study that serves to show that the project is practical. Promotion will be intrinsically wrapped up in the policy development. The initiator will have to demonstrate the vision by comparisons with other schemes elsewhere, the sheer weight of need or the feasibility study and business plan. Personal commitment and disseminating the vision through the network of 'who you know' will be a vital prerequisite for the scheme to progress.

Implementation is organizationally simple. The initiator will be involved and will need active financial and political support. Other management will need to share the vision and thus have the enthusiasm to see it come about. Cost implications will continue to unfold. The project will tend to be led more by the finance that has been raised than by the cost. Herein lies the prospect for the flagship to be compromised. Those involved in the im-plementation may become more preoccupied with raising money during implementation than realizing the aims and objectives. The flagship can also be compromised by a lack of finance or because the finance is given conditionally. In all situations the 'vision' must lead, and it will be the

Flagship type: *Innovative–Local*

Policy formulation	Project implementation	Policy/project evaluation

People:
1. Whose idea?
  – elected member, dignitary, entrepreneur, community/voluntary organization or hybrid group
	People:
	  – initiator
	  – political/economic supporter
	  – management by shared vision, enthusiasm and experimentation within concise guidelines
		People:
		  – initiator
		  – political/economic supporter
		  – local commentators, general media

2. Formulating policy
  – visionary objective
  – a few, simple goals in outline form
  – open-ended criteria or absence of criteria
  – autocratic decision making or legitimization by demonstration		

Cost:
  – uncertain or unconsidered
  – vision/business plan in outline form only
	Cost:
	  – evolving, unfolding
	  – led by ability to raise funds (more than the budgeting of requirements)
		Cost:
		  – cost–benefit analysis
		  – revenue costs and returns
		  – capital costs will be discounted

Marketing and sales:
  – personal commitment
  – demonstration effect
  – grapevine/network and through association/social interaction, e.g. 'who you know'
	Marketing and sales:
	  – reactive rather than planned
	  – network-based
	  – personal commitment
		Marketing and sales:
		  – demonstration
		  – commentators, media
		  – reactive
		  – adoption by others as role model

Figure 5.9 *G-type* market position

ability to build support for the vision which will determine finance and remove the potential for compromise.

Having sold the vision to the appropriate people, the promotion of the flagship will tend to be mainly reactive. This reactive approach is necessary to build and maintain support for the idea. Promotion will be carried out through a combination of personal commitment and networking.

The **evaluation** of the project will be straightforward, with the initiators undertaking their own assessment, and local politicians and other interested parties, including the media, giving most weight to any perceptions of success. Cost will be important, but will only be focused upon in the event of the scheme being unsuccessful, when financial criticism will be extensive. Evaluating the marketing effort will be self-evident to those involved. It will include demonstrating the potential through the completion of the project and through the media, which will be picking up the innovative nature of the regeneration and reacting opportunistically to results and outcomes. Others seeking to adopt the same type of project elsewhere may undertake more thorough analyses of the project and related policy in order to establish methods and learn from mistakes.

H-type project

The **H-type** market position is concerned with **innovative–national** projects and is therefore theoretically aimed at drawing inward investment and consumption into an area that is innovative or pioneering in one way or another. The National Garden Festivals were of this type, although the subsequent investment was certainly not of an innovative nature. Innovative projects have been limited in number, although there is scope by attracting corporate R&D functions, linking with university and higher education research, generating commercial spin-offs, and developing centres for telecommuting and subcontracting.

The principles for supporting such activities may not always require an innovative style for project management. While the risk factor may be quite high, the nature of the buildings may not be demanding. Pharmaceutical research laboratories require a strong service rather than a strong idea to supply the accommodation. Figure 5.10 sketches out the basic parameters, and only a few cursory remarks need be made to supplement this.

The **policy formulation** will be carried out by a steering group that would be developing its own idea or that of an individual. The management style will tend to be autocratic and the costs, in theory, will be uncertain. Successful innovation must look as if it is here to stay and appear confident if it is to gain credence. In order to attract some innovative functions, a large development budget would be required in relation to the project size; for example, many of those involved in corporate or institutional inno-

Flagship type: *Innovative–National*

Policy formulation	Project implementation	Policy/project evaluation
People: 1. Whose idea? – elected member, dignitary, entrepreneur, corporation, hybrid group or consortium 2. Formulating policy – visionary objective – a few, simple, detailed goals – outline criteria, subject to change – creative steering group with 'autocratic' approach	People: – steering group – management by shared vision, enthusiasm and experimentation at controlling level – management by analysis, problem solving and cost crisis monitoring – contracting out of construction services	People: – self-evaluation by initiator of role – steering group – external consultants – media
Cost: – considered, yet uncertain – vision/business plan in outline form – some detailed projections of quantifiable elements	Cost: – rapidly changing, difficult to monitor, inability to control cost – led by perceived necessity to reduce cost escalation through project growth and cost overruns on agreed packages or elements – fund raising	Cost: – retrospective assessment – value for money
Marketing and sales: – personal commitment – organizational symbolic support – networking, especially 'political'	Marketing and sales: – steering group – executive, senior management in organizations – external agents for public relations and lettings – lobbying interest groups and government	Marketing and sales: – 'broad brush' evaluation of vision and extent realized – cost–benefit analysis of detailed goals – observation of criteria that emerged as important

Figure 5.10 *H-type* market position

vation expect very high quality surroundings and communications. Those involved in sectors that are developing products and services in start-up organizations may require grants and so a regeneration project will have to link its development to the programmes of other government departments. English Estates has played this type of role in the past, and although their efforts have tended to emphasize small business rather than the nature of the business, the principles hold.

The cost will be uncertain and, although a business or operational plan will be necessary, options or scenarios will tend to provide the basis for possible and outline costings. Promotion will be the most important in gaining financial support. The most successful way will be obtaining support from one influential figure or organization, especially if they are in a position to contribute finance. This will create the 'comfort' necessary for others to follow in their footsteps with finance and support. The approach will be personal, using networks, but there is likely to be a significant political role in order to obtain the initial support.

A national project requires a steering group for the **implementation** stage, management being carried out by shared vision and enthusiasm for the project. The more detailed components of the project will need to become clear in the early part of the implementation stage. This will be achieved by a combination of experimentation, trial and error and reacting to others who respond positively to the project and who may become operationally involved as tenants or in activities in the flagship or surrounding area.

The detailed management of each stage of the innovative project involves analytical and problem solving skills.[13] The selection of a developer at the implementation stage can be quite complex. If the buildings have to be designed specifically for single-purpose functions then the risk for the developer will be too high unless a subsidy or guarantee is provided from another source, such as the local authority, or where a public service tradition exists as in the case of English Estates. Failure to secure support will require either owner occupancy or an authority to take the risk by acting as the developer.

The buildings may be very simple in specification, yet for many start-up organizations and small pioneering sectors of the economy the type of development will not fit most property investment portfolios. The first difficulty is that developers would not wish to have a large number of small premises. The second reason is that most tenants would need a large service input in terms of reception, conference and meeting room facilities, and sometimes shared administrative and secretarial support. In both these cases the requirement is for a large management input from the developer. Developers have tried to minimize the management input since the reconstruction period, with Land Securities pioneering the full repairing lease and reducing both management and overhead costs (Smyth, 1985, p.133).

The main exception to this is the shopping centre development, where developers set up centre management teams. There are signs that the management trend is on the increase. Local authorities have begun to appoint high street managers to look after town high streets along similar lines to the shopping centre. Corporate business has seen rapid growth of facility management, following the example set by the United States. Some niche developers of the 1980s property boom began to look at management. Local London, prior to being absorbed through takeover, pioneered the concept of space retailing for offices, whereby serviced suites were offered to small companies or to large organizations that needed a base in a town or city away from their headquarters. All basic office services were provided as part of the 'rental'.

It is this approach that many innovative–national projects will demand and, indeed, will be a necessary prerequisite for creating further opportunities for flexible working practices and flexible profit making in the economy. Where the developer is innovative the risk will be minimized. The authorities will be unable to bargain about content because the visionary will not be prepared to amend the ideas. From a different angle, developers who have used their creative abilities and those of their consultants to produce a viable scheme that would otherwise be marginal cannot accept Section 106 agreements or negotiate content, because the scheme will again be marginal.

All developers with a social orientation will be constrained because profit margins are lower. For the corporate developer potential returns could be high, but so are the risks. Some kind of top slice of rental income could be negotiated, payable after initial development costs have been defrayed, where there is a public authority or charity partnership with the developer.

The cost of a project will vary according to type and the extent to which the content is known at the beginning of this stage. However, the costs will continue to unfold during the project. Where uncertainty exists, establishing budgets, monitoring spend and therefore controlling cost will prove very difficult.

Marketing will be undertaken by the steering group, involving the executive and senior management levels. They will be working alongside and under the direction of public relations and letting agencies, particularly for the lobbying of government and interest groups.

The **evaluation** will involve the initiator, the steering group, external consultants and the media. The actors will be different compared to locally orientated projects, but the purposes and functions will be very similar. Cost will almost certainly have to be evaluated retrospectively, concentrating upon value for money. This raises an interesting issue, which tends to dominate British policy thinking in both public and private organizations. When a budget is unclear or impossible to establish at the outset, then the evaluation has to be upon the outputs. The outputs are the cost and what has been received in the exchange process. This is what 'value for money' is supposed to be about, yet frequently the focus in public and private organizations is on inputs, in other words, just the money. In many of the policy analysis studies and assessments of value for money during the 1980s the emphasis has been on the inputs. It is quite right to focus on the cost, yet if all initiatives, investment decisions, policies and flagships become entirely cost-driven, then other important factors are being ignored. These factors include buying market share during a recession, increasing productivity through tooling up, compressing time and space through infrastructure investment and reducing flexibility to keep long-term costs down or profits up for public and private organizations, respectively. For innovative projects, this raises the financial issue of the loss of long-term competitive advantage in a way that cannot be quantified through accountancy practices (cf. Drucker, 1986).

This criticism begs two important questions. Where does this approach come from? Although this problem is not unique to the British case, it is prevalent in Britain and is driven by the stock market demanding short-term returns because that is the way it is structured. The problem also emanates from accountancy practices. In many cases accountancy 'procedures' and 'taken-for-granted' thinking are absorbed by executives, even though their accountant advisers may not always have a deep understanding of the operations of the organization, especially in research, production, marketing and personnel. This leads to accounts and accountancy thinking dominating decision making. Accounts, financial control and related practices are there to **serve** the operations rather than to **control** them. Service implies the provision of advice that is essential for decision making. Decision making should involve those with accounting and financial skills along with other key areas of operation. Such decision making does require sufficient resources, and where these are available the emphasis should be more heavily weighted to outputs rather than inputs.

The second point is that financial data is frequently more readily available. The input is known, the final cost should be close to the budget, but the value that is to be achieved may be unknown and qualitative. Fear that the desired value will not be realized in practice creates considerable tensions. Would a shortfall in value threaten financial standing, affect image, or affect career prospects for the decision makers, or is it simply easier to err on the side of caution when presented with budget data *vis-à-vis* qualitative output material? In the latter case, the input data – the financial information – is usually no more certain than the output material. It simply looks more authoritative because it is statistical and has professional backup.

This excursion into the realms of general finance and management perceptions is important because such behaviour is underpinned by attitudes to innovation and to risk taking. The attitudes pose a problem to the very existence of the innovative–national flagship development. For most proposals caution may well be advisable. Innovative project management must be structured around facilitating ideas, yet requiring each to be thoroughly developed for implementation. The outcomes for some less risky projects have not been all the initiators wished for, and some have yielded unexpected outcomes (Harvey, 1991; see case studies in particular). However, innovative projects can induce economic diversity, thus lowering the risk for the project, and can generate growth industries and services for the economy. Using the appropriate criteria for assessment is therefore important.

The debate set out above has focused on investment and consumption issues in a way that excludes housing. Some of the same issues arise for housing. New forms of housing in terms of design, the functions they serve and possibly the experimental lifestyles could all affect the perceived security of the properties, whether held as investment by developers for rental income and asset growth or for mortgagers for lending money against. In conclusion, cost evaluation has to be undertaken on an appropriate basis, treating the original affordability as separate from the value for money.

Marketing and sales will be rather different in approach compared to the local market position. The national orientation requires that a 'broad brush' evaluation of the original vision and the extent to which it has been achieved is undertaken. A more detailed cost–benefit analysis will be needed for the detailed goals. The goals and the criteria against which these were set will probably have emerged during the implementation stage, so the promotion strategy will have been reactive, evolving throughout. It may be difficult to untangle the marketing for the flagship as an entity and the extent to which it has generated further investment where an area-based approach is taken. The Theatre Village in Newcastle is a case in point.

I-type project

The concluding market position is the **I-type**. The **innovative–international** project is largely theoretical for there have yet to be any in Britain. Globally, it would be hard to point to any that have been totally innovative, although elements have appeared in some schemes, for example the leisure facilities in Baltimore (Harvey, 1991). Even these had precedents, for large-scale leisure is not unique. Had the first Disney theme park been an urban regeneration flagship project, it would certainly qualify. Perhaps the most likely flagships for the future would be communications- or environmentally-based. Communication-led developments would use shared computer technologies and practices (Edgington, 1990; Gann,

1991) and multimedia, such as telecommuting, teleconferencing and exploring the interface between real time and virtual reality in global communications. Environmental projects would be linking the principles of being good stewards of the environment with cost in use, planned maintenance and minimal energy costs.

Therefore, this concluding market position will have to be more of a marker or indication of the potential, rather than based on flagship project examples. Marketing practice will be drawn upon as the main means of describing the resources and skills needed (Figure 5.11).

The origin of the idea will probably be similar to the national case. The **policy formulation** would be handled at a larger scale, an intraorganizational steering group being the likely vehicle. In order to keep the vision intact, this group would be autocratic in both its organization and its leadership of others. It is not that an innovative idea can only be driven in an autocratic way *per se*, but in a market it is necessary to be harnessed to the political and economic structures that have power. The power of money and politics that can compromise the scheme towards other ends is more easily controlled in an autocratic fashion, assuming there is an absence of corruptive and fraudulent tendencies. The autocracy may emanate from a core group or from a person, the former providing a higher degree of protection from corruption, although it does not exclude conspiracy. Such autocracy can emanate from a popular and community-based organization in a bottom-up fashion.

The costs would be unknown and the business plan would not contain a cost plan, but perhaps a 'ball park' figure. Promotion would require a heavy input at this stage. Again, this would be as much to do with encouraging others to become identified with the project as with trying to attract further investment into the area. In some cases the one will be the same as the other.

The **project implementation** stage would be similar in terms of the people and organizations involved. The cost aspects would also be similar, except for fund raising, which would need to be more creative and might be phased, the first development phase of the project lending the confidence for investment in subsequent stages.

Promotion would almost certainly involve central government, particularly if the project is large in scale. It may well involve a number of governments, mediating institutions and multinational companies.

Following completion and a period of operation, an **evaluation** would be undertaken. Government would be involved, which would make the process more political. In essence, that would be the main differentiating factor in the evaluation process. In practice, any project would surely be of high risk. Success is therefore likely to be absolute or negligible. The economic and political stakes are high. Success would have a major impact. While this might adversely affect some, the overall economic outcome

Policy formulation	Project implementation	Policy/project evaluation

People:
1. Whose idea?
  – elected member,
  dignitary, entrepre-
  neur, corporation,
  consortium
 	
2. Formulating policy
  – visionary objective
  – a few, simple goals
  – fluid criteria
  – intraorganizational
  steering group, led
  by 'autocratic'
  individual or core
	People:
	  – steering group
	  – management by
	  shared vision,
	  enthusiasm and
	  experimentation at
	  controlling level
	  – management by
	  analysis, problem
	  solving and cost
	  crisis monitoring
	  – contracting out of
	  construction
	  services
		People:
		  – government
		  – steering group
		  – organizational
		  – external consul-
		  tants
		  – commentators and
		  media

Cost:
  – uncertain or
  unknown
  – vision/business
  plan without cost
  plan
 	
Marketing and sales:
  – steering group
  commitment
  – networking,
  lobbying
  – external advertis-
  ing/public relations
	Cost:
	  – rapidly changing,
	  monitoring at
	  package level with
	  crisis management
	  of cost control
	  – led by perceived
	  necessity to reduce
	  cost escalation
	  through project
	  growth and cost
	  overruns on agreed
	  packages or
	  elements
	  – creative fund
	  raising
		Cost:
		  – retrospective
		  assessment
		  – value for money
		
		Marketing and sales:
		  – 'broad brush'
		  evaluation of vision
		  and extent realized
		  – cost–benefit
		  analysis of goals
		  – observation of
		  criteria that emerged
		  as important

	Marketing and sales:
	  – central govern-
	  ment
	  – steering group
	  – executives, senior
	  management in
	  organizations
	  – external agents for
	  public relations and
	  lettings
	  – other govern-
	  ments, mediating
	  institutions, multi-
	  nationals	

Figure 5.11 *I-type* market position

would induce high positive social benefits for the locale.

It is perhaps understandable that there have been few – if any – examples of innovative–international projects, given the intense level of risks. The benefits are potentially extensive – economic, political and social – wherein rests the dilemma. Because the risks would be intensive, the blame for failure would fall on the few, from which scapegoats would be identified. The successes would be extensive, and while the initiators would be bound to pick up large shares of applause and praise, many others would seek to bask in the glory created by others.

This highlights a problem that exists to some extent for many flagship developments, particularly those with public sector involvement, that are large-scale and national or international in orientation: hijacking the credit. The innovative type of projects are the most prone to the hijacking of political credit. Political credit tends to be greater where the social benefits are greatest, especially where the social benefits arise from economic success. Appropriate management of a project will maximize the economic success and therefore have an impact upon the area, the people and those involved with the project. Thus, the nature of the impact will be dependent upon three factors:

- market position
- project management
- economic conditions.

The extent to which the process is top-down, bottom-up or a combination may affect who stands to gain and lose from any flagship development. Similarly, the extent to which the development team has a social or corporate orientation will affect who stands to gain or lose. The evaluation process, as used by the practitioners, can also be used for policy evaluation through research. Research usually covers a broader range of issues, and in this research, where the objective is to help to establish good practice, it is necessary to raise some of the important issues that can be looked for in the case study material. It is therefore to the subject of project impact that the analysis now turns.

Project impact

6.1 INTRODUCTION

The precise impact of a project upon an area cannot be determined in advance. Implicit are the realities that every location and cultural circumstance is different. In addition, every flagship development project is different, both as an entity in itself and in the immediate context for regeneration. Acknowledging the specifics is important; however, there are some commonalities and threads running through many, if not all, projects. The purpose of this chapter is to draw out some features common to a number of projects. Some relate to specific market positions and segments, others will be cross-cutting. From this, threads can be drawn out about what interests are being served, who is most likely to benefit from flagships, and the extent to which people and interests are being disadvantaged by the impact of a development and subsequent investment.

6.2 SHIFTING AIMS FOR URBAN REGENERATION

These fundamental issues raise the question 'why should there be urban regeneration?' While the question has a certain superficiality, underlying it are some conceptual shifts in thinking that have gone on in the minds of policy makers, which were detailed in Chapter 2. In summary, the initial concern was for the indigenous population, if the rhetoric is taken at face value. Perhaps the real concern was as much, if not more, to do with the image of an area, because the area-based policies and actions have tended to concentrate on regeneration that is most easily solicited from government spending programmes and the market. This seldom seemed to take much account of the indigenous population, and even where the rhetoric tried to build the bridges, the counselling, training and employment measures were absent or tended to fail.

Property-led regeneration, which was emphasized during the 1980s, depends upon unblocking the supply side. However, to what extent does the unblocked supply release the pent-up demand for employment and improvements in living standards among those who were abandoned by the previous economic activities of the area? The short answer has to be 'hardly at all'. Flagship developments are a part of this picture and it is therefore to be expected that the benefits for the indigenous population will also be negligible.

A large measure of caution is required at this stage of the analysis. A considerable proportion of the urban literature adopts a distinctly 'left wing' political stance. Many of these contributions contain a large number of penetrating insights, but the literature also tends, like the policies, to undergo shifts in thinking. The literature is particularly strong in analysing some of the intended benefactors of regeneration, namely 'big business'. The real outcomes for business are not always closely considered. These analyses frequently conclude or imply that if there are certain groups who stand to gain, then there must be those who stand to lose from urban regeneration (for example, Robinson and Shaw, 1991). Saunders (1990, pp.29–41 and pp.120–203) has made an excellent critique of this kind of 'leftist' literature in relation to home ownership, many of the same points being relevant here. The analysis of Saunders shows that almost every household has gained from home ownership. The data was collected during the boom, therefore some of the gains will have since been lost or eroded. There will have been a growing number of losers through repossessions, equity values falling and in some cases mortgages exceeding equity, but still the vast majority stood to gain from home ownership and not at the expense of others.

Is it, therefore, possible to say that all successful flagship developments are bound to have a positive impact on the social well-being of an area? In answering this question, it is useful to use home ownership in a 'compare and contrast' exercise. The first comparison concerns whether those not directly in the 'market' are losers. In the case of urban regeneration the answer is clear. The indigenous population or business does not stand to lose anything through urban regeneration, except where housing is demo-lished or activities closed to ensure that a flagship or projects are devel-oped. In this latter case, those that could lose will be in the minority because the very reason for developing is the degeneration of the area. The opportunities were therefore continually diminishing or absent. Social well-being would continue to spiral in a downward fashion unless regener-ation took place.

This analysis assumes that opportunities only arise from the existing political and market context. Many of the interest groups formed to lobby politically on behalf of the local population inevitably have lost their immediate case to protect existing employment or to attract similar employment opportunities, because the competitive advantage for these activities has been lost. The reasons for this loss may be related to the location, to historic investment or to the age and form of the built environment and infrastructure. These interest groups have also clearly failed in their second case, which was to mount widespread opposition to challenge the political and market context.

The next argument is that the local population become losers because of the opportunity cost. This is an internal critique, in other words, one that challenges decisions in terms of the political and market context. Essentially, the argument states that if money were not put into a flagship development or another urban regeneration project, it could be spent upon the needs of the local population. What are these needs? There are two. Firstly, they need another system in which to live, which immediately raises the external criticism that a challenge to the system should be funded. Any political system will not fund such a mission consciously, and in any case the local interest to support such a mission has not been present to date, as has already been noted. Or, secondly, the needs are for employment and better living conditions. Undoubtedly there is a strong case for funding housing and environmental improvements because these improve self-worth and respect for others. Counselling and training can help to relieve problems and provide new skills. However, the benefits of these are only sustainable if new employment opportunities are attracted into the area or if employers outside the area can be persuaded to employ those from a deprived area. In the latter case, this does produce redistributional benefits, but others will implicitly lose opportunities, so the overall problem is simply displaced. To obtain benefits from any investment for the local population requires longer term employment opportunities in the area. This brings the analysis back to the need for sustained urban regeneration.

6.3 REACHING THE DISADVANTAGED

In both the United States and Britain the private sector has been looked to as the means to induce sustained urban regeneration (Barnekov and Rich, 1989; Hambleton, 1990). This 'privatism' has been followed by academics, criticizing the claims of 'what's good for business will automatically be good for the city and its communities' (Boyle and Meyer, 1990, p.273; see also Barnekov, Boyle and Rich, 1988; Squires, 1991) and that the benefits will 'trickle down' to those in need. This has been countered in the United States by claims that regeneration has created a broader spectrum of jobs by income and skill, of which more reach the disadvantaged than is supposed (Frieden, 1990; Frieden and Sagalyn, 1989). Frieden and Sagalyn (1989) also say that constraints on local public sector finance have driven local authorities towards private sector, property-led solutions and that the failure of developments to reach local people has been the result of

economic trends beyond the city boundaries and shortcomings in education
and training, as well as the operation of free labour market policies. The
absence of links to the labour market and the attitude of employers
prejudices opportunities in most local labour markets.

The issue of local labour markets is fundamental to any trickle-down
approach and Frieden and Sagalyn (1989) are correct to emphasize it.
However, responses may differ between different administrations and
different developers. The extent of the project impact will be highly
dependent upon the degree to which this issue is addressed. However, the
other notion – that the control of the economy lies outside the locale –
should be challenged as a valid reason. It is true, but not the whole truth
because one function of marketing the city is influencing the distribution of
opportunities by creating new markets through innovation and developing
market strategies that take account of conditions in the economy.

It is an unsustainable argument to assert that 'privatism' and development, hand-in-hand with marketing the city, can be used to create and
keep competitive advantage in a regional, national or global sense, but that
the impact on development and labour market economics is somehow
'external'.

6.4 MARKET SHARE AND THE DISADVANTAGED

Perhaps Barnekov, Boyle and Rich (1988) exaggerate the coherence of city
marketing to date, yet their point is a fair one:

> Municipal marketing and civic entrepreneurship were responsibilities
> lodged firmly in the public domain. Cities that succeeded in
> their programs of economic development would create a favourable
> climate for private investment and this, in turn, would place these
> cities in a preferred position to win the urban sweepstakes. Cities that
> neglected economic development or failed to provide effective pro-
> grams would experience continued economic decline.

The authors view this as a retrograde step because of the absence of
public sector finance. However, there is nothing intrinsically 'good' or
'bad' about public or private sector money and, as the case studies will
show, the source of funding has little to do with successful implementation,
including any positive impact upon local labour markets.

Two points of qualification can be added. The argument that the local
population may not stand to gain from a flagship development is prompting
an area-based question and therefore simply mirrors the direction policy
has taken. However, it would be more compassionate to attract inward
investment to a locale where people are rooted and feel some sense of

'community', even if there is no agreement as to what this means precisely, than to favour moving people out or neglecting them.

Taking responsibility for this requires a policy that is not area-based. The marketing matrix accommodates this. The local orientation is geared to organic growth from within the city if the area itself has degenerated too far. The national and international orientations can encourage investment from geographically spread sales targets in order to provide employment within the locale. The culture being promoted would link in with the overall, but not specific, skill types that predominate in the area. Training programmes will enable the transition. There are other labour market barriers, which can be difficult to overcome; however, that takes the analysis closer to the policy futures discussion after the case studies. The main point here is that the arguments about there automatically being losers can be discarded.

Those who do receive employment are comparable with those who buy a house. They are participators in the regeneration process. It is sometimes claimed that these people are also losers. This argument is unsustainable. Purporters of this argument for regeneration make a fallacious comparison between wage and salary levels in former employment and the levels in new employment. The former employment is no longer an option, therefore the true comparison is between welfare assistance and the new earning levels. The commonly made criticism is that wages derived from newly created employment are frequently lower than those from previous employment. However, as the left wing economist Robinson (1964) said about developing countries, 'the misery of being exploited by capitalists is nothing compared with the misery of not being exploited at all'. This is not to suggest that achieving higher paid work or higher wages is undesirable; indeed, it is to be encouraged. Nevertheless, it has to be acknowledged that one of the main reasons for attracting investment may be the achievement of lower wages in order to generate a competitive advantage.

The work of Harvey (1989a,b,c, 1991) is of a far more sophisticated nature. His analysis not only acknowledges the progressive nature of a capitalist economy, but stresses the need for it to do so for its survival. The presence of low paid employment has frequently gone hand-in-hand with the creation of flagship projects that promote affluent, pastiche 'lifestyles' framed in postmodern architecture (Harvey, 1989a). The low paid serve the more affluent in their consumption and leisure pursuits and provide support services for offices. This type of social polarization is criticized with justification on ethical grounds and holds within it the seeds for social tensions, as well as being part of the dynamic that creates competitive advantage and hence the investment in the first place.

In a postmodern economic and physical environment, the experience tends to be different for each group. For the low paid and those excluded from employment, the affluence is a stark contrast. The benefits of new employment can seem ephemeral, while the low pay seems enduring. The polarization can be reinforced through the design of the flagship. While the architecture may embrace history as pastiche, the signs that are evoked are geared to increasing the rate of consumption and efficiency. The local population will not read the architectural signs as part of their history and will tend to feel that the culture is imported in many cases. This is socially patronizing and may render the economic foundation of the scheme ephemeral.

Clark (1985) shows that the culture need not be reflected in the planning and architecture. Indeed, a flagship could be designed fundamentally to reflect the history of the place, the population and the direction in which it is generating new activities. This echoes modernism, where the function and the integrity of the form are closely integrated. If this is treated in a contextual and non-deterministic way, rather than imposing an architectural approach or economic formula, then a continuity and sense of place can be sustained. In its turn, this can be an attraction to inward investors as well as respecting the local people and their culture. This point can be illustrated through Harvey's reference to elite avant-garde artists searching for locations that have a sense of place:

> Modernism look[s] quite different depending on where one locates oneself and when. . . . The particularities of place – and here I think not only of the village-like communities in which artists typically moved but also of the quite different social, economic, political and environmental conditions that prevailed in, say, Chicago, New York, Paris, Vienna, Copenhagen, or Berlin – therefore put a distinct stamp on the diversity of the modernist effort. (Harvey, 1989a, p.25)

The art world may have its own locational requirement, but so does any activity. In a postmodern culture, the tendency is for individuals to seek out different environments as part of the search for new experience, and for organizations to seek short-run competitive advantages. Consumption and investment in both cases are footloose. The agenda is not for the mass market nor for achieving economies of scale, respectively. Modern society is highly sensitive to location because it is seeking to establish longer term consumption and investment patterns.

The example from the art world is, in fact, extremely relevant when considering the project impact of flagship developments during the 1980s and early 1990s. There has been a massive growth in the arts in relation to urban development and flagship projects in particular. Fisher (1991, p.10), as Shadow Minister for the Arts and Media, wrote:

> Projects like these enrich cities. They add to enjoyment, they give cause for people to be proud of their neighbourhood. These are some of the things we look for in city life: variety, quality, surprise. . . .

They should offer public places, squares and parks and waterfronts, in which it is a pleasure to be. There should be choices of theatres and cinemas, of book and record shops, of bars and restaurants. Most of all there should be other people to meet, with whom to share amenities.

Whether people actually do meet in this way does raise questions about how the dynamics of such developments work in practice. The view may be somewhat idealized, but the concept has weight and it is to the arts that many local authorities have turned, albeit in a rather haphazard way (Fisher, 1991). The arts sector is not only the provider of a service and consumption, it is a major employer and contributor to the economy. The claim is that a redistribution of arts away from London into the regions, providing greater scope for local expression and identity, has begun (Fisher, 1991), although this remains an assertion rather than fact. The North American experience has been the opposite, whereby a more commercial approach has narrowed choice (Edgar, 1991).

What we are in essence dealing with here is the **perception** of different interest groups. Do the local population and business interests support the flagship development in principle? For those in business it is likely that support will be forthcoming where business is either positively affected or the affect is neutral. For the local population it may be more complicated. There may be resentment that a culture is being imposed upon them, but a feeling that it is 'better than nothing'. Alternatively, there may be total opposition. What can be made of these perceptions?

There are some material indicators that can be used. Shopping facilities that are pleasant and safe (Poole, 1991), housing that is private and safe (see Coleman, 1990; Stollard, 1991) and creates security, permanence (cf. Altman and Chemers, 1984) and diversity (Jacobs, 1965, 1972) may all be good indicators. However, what people feel is important. Returning to the work of Harvey, he invokes Simmil's essay of 1911 concerning 'The metropolis and mental life', which addressed the difficulty of assimilating the complexity and diversity of urban life. The problem is that we tend to treat each other as objects, not as feeling people, subjecting others and therefore being subject to the economic demands of managing our time in an urban environment, leaving us with the danger of reducing ourselves to some sort of mask of individualism. Perhaps there are different masks for different roles (Harvey, 1989a). The intensity of life in a postmodern culture, it is said, draws us towards emphasizing the superficiality of experience as each mask is worn, 'leaving behind' the subjective self beneath the mask. The flagship development can provide an opportunity for the population to reconstitute its masks as the environment is regenerated. This may or may not be a positive force and it may often be impossible to tell in advance. A flagship development may render the urban environment less diverse and perhaps more easily assimilated. That too can create a problem, for those who do not like the narrower moulds may resist or rebel.

The analysis therefore returns to regeneration as a tool of image making and social control in the city. People can be 'made' in the image of the environment, but not in any automatic way. The response to change can be qualitatively different. People may use the environment and the possibilities that the new activities create to induce a condition that is different from that originally expected. This type of action, currently labelled 'empowerment', comes from below, or is bottom-up in policy parlance. How this works its way out in practice cannot be predicted. It may be economically positive for the initiators, in the way that street theatre around the Pompidou Centre in Paris has been, helping to make it one of the most favoured tourist destinations and providing a model for others to copy, for example, Covent Garden, London. The response may be empowerment in a way that challenges authority, and possibly the economic viability of the area (Clark, 1985; Harvey, 1991).

Under such circumstances those interests that are generally assumed to have gained from the flagship, the developers, may well lose, as may certain segments of the population, as the recent riots in Los Angeles clearly demonstrated. Whether empowerment leads to social gains, however, is a moot point and is dependent upon political outlook. A social challenge to a flagship will certainly mean that the initiator will lose. For a developer that may mean lost profit, a loss or bankruptcy, whereby the loss is passed on to the financial backers. A private initiator, therefore, can experience a notional or real loss. A notional loss is anticipated profit which is not received, whereas a real loss is where the costs exceed revenues. For a local authority, the loss may be experienced as a loss of political power, and any costs are likely to return to the public purse, either at local or central government level. The extent of the social unrest will determine the scale and area over which the impact is felt.

The empowerment of the local population can be described as an 'externality' in a top-down approach. However, the local population, and hence any marketing strategy, need to be internal to the market, in order to have any opportunity to consistently bridge the national and international economic processes and area-based issues. Yet here is the dilemma. Capturing market share and successfully delivering benefits from that process to the disadvantaged brings the affected population, including the disadvantaged, into the realms of a 'product' for sale for investment purposes.

6.5 THE IMPACT OF RECESSION

Recessive conditions can also threaten the gains to be made by the project initiators. The political costs can be high, especially for large-scale schemes or sensitive ones, but the main gains are financial. A recession can threaten the notional and real gains for a developer. Similarly, a local authority can bear economic costs, which are passed on to the local population.

The recessive conditions have helped to expose the financial weaknesses of some developers and their flagships. The developments of Olympia and York, formerly the largest developers in the world, have been affected by bankruptcy. The management of their financial crisis is a problem for the banks that have lent money for a number of flagship developments in North America as well as for Canary Wharf, London Docklands, which proved to be one development too many. There are, of course, political consequences for these projects. In the case of Canary Wharf, the politics concern the relevance of a property-led policy, the contribution that the developer was to make to infrastructure costs, and, finally, the impact of the demise of Canary Wharf on the property market in general and Docklands in particular.

The impact of a project can be weakened during recession and potentially thwarted by the economic demise of a developer. The larger the scheme, the greater the pressure on banks and government to ensure its longer term success for reasons of economic and political confidence, respectively. That will surely be the unfolding destiny for Canary Wharf. What this demonstrates is that 'big business' is not always the beneficiary. It can be a loser, as can those closely associated with schemes at a political level.

6.6 PROJECT INITIATORS, IMPACT AND GOVERNANCE

At this point we return to a theme raised in the previous chapter – the extent to which private initiators underpin government policy and the extent to which the public sector underpins private profitability. The balance of investment has been addressed as an issue. Clearly, a relationship of co-dependence will help the security of a scheme, therefore maximizing the impact of the project in whatever form that takes. That type of **governance** may give security for the scheme, but for the impact to benefit the local population and business most, the governance needs to be very carefully and sensitively handled. Leadership should not be confused with management, which is all too easy with an intraorganizational structure. Leadership requires not only the ability to look ahead but a serving rather than a controlling approach where power compromises and potentially corrupts, in the sense that the population is not being served (Marshall, 1991).

Governance can also be important for large-scale schemes, and especially for predominantly single-use schemes where diversity is not being sought. Lead-in times and the construction programme create two problems when they span the 'trade cycle'. Gaining support can take time, and schemes may have to be redesigned and renegotiated with authorities over this period. The implementation phase can also be lengthy, during which the initial estimates of market demand can change dramatically. Governance here can benefit the developer where partnership with a local authority or government body provides political strength and economic covenant over the turbulence of the trade cycle. It is only government agencies and powers that can provide such an insurance policy for very large-scale schemes.

Such partnerships will involve some loss of power and therefore control over the content, yet yield greater stability. Political support and covenant is one option, direct subsidy being the other form of support that the developer will receive in exchange for some loss of control. The developer minimizes the risks in this way and is more likely to enhance the profitability of the scheme. In most cases the developer will not be located in the area so the rental stream accrues elsewhere; however, it is the activities within the flagship development that will contribute to the scheme impacting upon the area. This impact will be twofold – the scheme itself and the subsequent investment that is drawn in. Those who say that developers have simply been subsidized by the public purse (Harvey, 1989b) paint too crude a picture in analytical terms, regardless of what happens on the ground, although even here the case studies do not support this crude subsidization argument.

6.7 INTEGRATION AND SEGREGATION

The purpose of this chapter has been to look at the impact of projects upon an area. It has been shown that many of the analyses claiming that there are many 'losers' are fallacious. It has also been shown that while profitability and the impact on business locally and those investing in the area can be beneficial, the way in which a development can be experienced is both very subtle and highly unpredictable. Such impact can be far from positive in many instances, and the seeds of discontent have been sown in some locations. Eruption into broader social unease is difficult to prove, although Davis' book, *The City of Quartz* (1990), provided the analogy of new walls going up in cities, segregating people and groups through development, as the Berlin wall came down. One concern about those walls of development was that they turned their back on some of the poorest groups in the city – it simply took one small incidence too many to release pent-up anger, followed by open season for looters, in the Los Angeles riots of 1992. The 'City of Quartz' to which Davis refers was Los Angeles. It has also been shown that developers and business will not necessarily stand to 'gain', even where public subsidy is available. Furthermore, partnerships between private and public organizations provide greater stability, and hence, greater likelihood of a positive impact for the locale if the aims and objectives embrace the local population, but there are costs for accountability from the resultant governance unless genuine service rather than power is the motivator.

The impact of a flagship project is important for any local authority. The policy issues discussed can be addressed under the following summary questions:

- What are the income generating effects?
- What are the distributive effects?
- In what ways will the urban environment be experienced in relation to these effects?
- Is there a positive trade-off between governance and accountability?

This completes the analysis, and the case studies can now be reviewed in this light.

7.1 INTRODUCTION

This chapter introduces the case work, by addressing the selection of the flagship developments and their categorization. Firstly, a reminder of the purposes of a flagship development will provide a basis. Such a project is:

- a development in its own right, which may or may not be self-sustaining;
- a marshalling point for further investment;
- a marketing tool for an area or city.

These are the main criteria for a flagship development, and a flagship has to be seen in the broader policy context of endeavouring to regenerate urban areas. Defining what a flagship actually is, however, is not quite the same as seeing whether an actual project **is** a flagship development.

There are two problems. The first is that a flagship development may be labelled as one after its conception. The initiators may find it politically expedient to harness their development to a policy initiative. This may be to attract resources or simply to give greater prominence to a scheme that happens to be in an area of urban regeneration. This does not present a particular problem because there would seem to be a need for confidence building. Whether such an approach undermines other preconceived flagship developments in the area is a moot point, but again one that should not raise too much concern. The policy thrust is market-led and so such moves are simply using the marketing and sales techniques within that market to make the scheme successful. The initiators and their agents also pick up the parlance of the day, copy writers cash in on the imagery of the day and convert it into sales jargon. While this may devalue concepts over a period, it is of minimal concern. There have been phases in the property market when the cachet of a label has been tremendous for short periods. 'Science park', 'hi-tech' and more recently 'business park' are obvious examples of labels that have been worked nearly to extinction. This is simply a process of exploiting the label for a product to its maximum advantage and is part of the sales process.

The second problem is where the idea of a flagship development is used outside areas for regeneration. This is, of course, also part of the sales kitbag and in this sense there is no issue. The flagship label, when used in a different context to urban regeneration, loses or alters its meaning. The purpose of a flagship development is to unblock supply-side constraints, while meeting needs, in order to make the market work again. In other contexts, the market is presumably already 'working'. This means that it is the market that creates the further investment, not just the primary development. Indeed, the very same processes that attracted the first development into the area also brought subsequent investment to the location. In the case of the flagship, it is **because** of that first development that other development followed. It is not always possible to see 'on the ground' the balance between these fine points and, indeed, the initiators themselves may all hold slightly different perceptions where the margin is not clear cut.

7.2 CASE STUDY SELECTION

In selecting the case studies, the aim has been to try to avoid the problems of the labelling of projects, choosing those that were seen as flagships from their early days. Every effort has been made to eliminate any projects that had no special or perceived potential ability to attract further investment. The perception of the aims and objectives are crucial here, as each project is being evaluated on its own terms. Therefore, it was not a criterion for selection that further investment must have been attracted into an area. The reverse is true for some of the case studies.

Seven projects have been selected, covering a broad range of situations by location, character and circumstances, as well as by scale and involved parties. The selection has been governed in part by what has been practical under the constraints of the research.[14] It has not been possible to be comprehensive on any set of criteria. Although seven projects do not cover all the market positions, it has been stated that it is difficult to chose examples that do comprehensively cover every market position. The marketing matrix outlines the possibilities and potential as much as the actuality. Following on from this, flagship developments will not necessarily correspond to the matrix because the aims and objectives have been ill-conceived and perhaps poorly implemented. This is one of the aspects of evaluation, even that carried out on the terms of the initiators. Choosing projects by matrix position would be in danger of leading towards selecting the 'best fit' cases, and would therefore provide a bias in the results.

There are other methods of classifying projects, to which the discussion will return below, yet it would be impossible to satisfy every method of categorization. The projects selected have been chosen on a basis of geographical spread and concentration, and upon size and who initiated them. The case study projects are:

- The Watershed Complex, the Floating Harbour, Bristol
- International Convention Centre, Birmingham
- Hyatt Regency Hotel, Birmingham
- National Indoor Arena, Birmingham
- Brindley Place, Birmingham
- Theatre Village and Chinatown, Newcastle upon Tyne
- Byker Wall, Newcastle upon Tyne.

Three major geographical centres are covered in the selection, each with different characteristics. Bristol was among the first cities to restructure its economic base during the 1970s. At that time most inward investment was in the financial services, especially insurance, locating in the central business district. By the 1980s this was being superseded by business parks outside the city centre areas, driven as much by planning policies as by the market demand. The Floating Harbour, the docks in Bristol, was already being developed with the Arnolfini Gallery, and the Lifeboat and Industrial Museums. The Watershed Complex in Bristol is part of the regeneration of Bristol Docks and is perceived as successful. The Watershed has a public sector image, although it is in fact a private development, containing retail operations as well as having a strong voluntary sector involvement and user input, although funded by both the public and private sectors.

The industrial base of the West Midlands had suffered in the recession of the late 1970s and early 1980s. Light engineering, especially that associated with the car industry, had dominated. However, the entire car industry was undergoing massive global restructuring and a redefinition of market locations for production, linked to changes in manufacturing organization and automation. There was a need to find new forms of economic activity.

The International Convention Centre in Birmingham is located close to the city centre on land previously used by metal working industries. It is a public sector development run by the National Exhibition Centre management, NEC Ltd. It is the largest case example and has been targeted towards rejuvenating the area and economy through business tourism, plus the attraction of inward investment. The Hyatt Hotel was conceptually and is physically linked to the International Convention Centre. Its development was undertaken with a mixture of private and public sector funding as a joint venture partnership.

The Brindley Place scheme is located adjacent to the International Convention Centre. It has been developer-led, with the sale of public land funding the National Indoor Arena. The Arena also involved some public funding and is owned and operated through the NEC management on behalf of the local authority. The Arena is mainly used as an indoor sports venue, although its multiple uses also include concerts, exhibitions and conventions, which are facilitated by its proximity to the International Convention Centre. The remainder of Brindley Place is a purely private development. It started as primarily a development for speciality shopping and leisure attractions. Having undergone a number of conceptual transformations, it has emerged as a more traditional retail and office scheme, although development has yet to get under way.

The reason for including a number of projects in Birmingham is to explore the relationship between them. How many flagships can be developed adjacent to each other and are interdependent? Does this create opportunities for a momentum to be built up that induces its own economy, or is it very fragile, or does it perhaps just create conditions that satisfy latent demand? There is an important matter concerning the relationship of marketing as a management tool and the economics of the city market-place.

In contrast, Newcastle has been undergoing long-term structural decline. Coal, port-related functions and manufacturing have been disinvesting. The 1980s witnessed a new confidence in the city, not seen since the ill-fated civic development programmes of the 1960s. The Metro Centre, the Garden Festival site at Gateshead and various other development programmes by the Tyne and Wear Development Corporation (TWDC) and other public and private organizations were having some affect – perhaps not replacing what had been eroded, but adding something new on the ground and in the minds of many.

The Theatre Village and Chinatown is an area located in the centre of Newcastle close to the central business and shopping areas. The economic history of the area was based upon retailing and warehousing. The aim has been to generate arts-based development, harnessing an existing core of arts activities as a base for further development. The Theatre Village concept largely failed during the 1980s, although some improvements in arts facilities were made as well as retail, restaurant and residential development. Yet these occurred despite the Theatre Village concept. The flagship was run through a trust under The Newcastle Initiative, which was set up by the CBI, the industry interest and lobby organization. This makes it an unusual scheme, both because of the area focus, and more because of the CBI involvement. However, The Newcastle Initiative, it was hoped, would act as a role model and a pioneer for engaging the private sector in new ways of approaching urban regeneration, so it had a poignancy.

The reasons for selecting Byker as a project are threefold. Firstly, there was a wish to include a major housing scheme because of the innovative architecture and social approach to development. Secondly, although it strictly predates 'flagships', it has been an important role model and certainly would have been labelled a flagship if it had commenced during the 1980s. Thirdly, many of the projects are still quite recent, rendering analysis dependent more upon recent perception than long-term data, and Byker provides a longer time horizon. As a public sector development it is important to analyse the issues faced when adopting innovative approaches. Innovation can be an important part for some marketing strategies and will undoubtedly feature in future policy initiatives.

The case studies therefore embrace the arts and leisure, business tourism, retail, office and residential development. The urban regeneration projects are located, with the exception of Byker Wall, in the inner city. The areas have had contrasting histories, ranging from an international port, through manufacturing, to retail and distribution. Each area reflects the heritage and strategic economic history of the city in which it is located, and the cities occupy important positions within contrasting regional economies. The North-East has experienced long-term regional decline, in contrast to Birmingham and the West Midlands, whose experience of decline is much more recent. Bristol, on the other hand, is located in the South and has a more prosperous recent history, showing a flexibility towards adapting quickly to changing economic circumstances. Each of these case studies is very different, covering a spectrum of activities and, as the relevant chapters will demonstrate, reflecting different explicit and implicit marketing positions.

Finding ways to classify developments while acknowledging the differences is not easy. Developments have been classified in many ways according to what authors believe to be important. It is worth recapping some of these classifications (see Section 3.3 for full details and references). There are over two hundred urban regeneration initiatives, which essentially have three classifications by **vehicle**:

- area initiatives
- project initiatives
- enabling initiatives.

Projects also can be classified by:

- geographical location
- building or development type
- initiator.

A categorization by **initiators** is as follows:

- private
- public
- voluntary
- popular
- hybrid forms.

This is particularly useful for this research because the initiator's aims

Table 7.1 Case study categorizations

Project	Location	Vehicle	Building type	Initiator	Function	Purposes	Market position	Market outcome
Watershed	Bristol	Project	Leisure, retail, exhibitions, arts	Developer	Consumption	Marketing, commercial	H-type	E-type
ICC	Birmingham	Project	Conventions	Council	Consumption	Marketing	F-type	E-type
Hyatt Hotel	Birmingham	Project	Hotel	Partnership	Consumption	Commercial	F-type	F-type
NIA	Birmingham	Project	Sports	Developer, Council	Consumption	Marketing	E-type	E-type
Brindley Place	Birmingham	Area, project	Retail, arts/leisure, offices	Developer	Consumption	Commercial	B- and E-types	
Theatre Village	Newcastle	Area	Arts (leader), leisure, residential	Private interest	Consumption, commercial, self-help	Marketing	G-type	
Byker	Newcastle	Project	Residential	Council	Consumption, role model	Marketing	G-type	G- and A-type

and objectives are being identified and evaluated, which embraces the project **function**:

- exploitation of international competitive advantage of resource base, location and investment for the production of goods and services;
- exploitation of competitive advantage as a location of consumption;
- acquisition and development of key control and command functions.

The more immediate **purposes** of flagships are:

- primarily a marketing tool
- primarily a commercial development
- self-help
- combinations.

Using these definitions, we can classify the case studies and place them alongside their market position (see Table 7.1).

It is the marketing matrix that gives rise to each of the nine market positions, which become the prime organizing concepts for the individual cases and for comparing and contrasting the findings. The evaluation will bring out the particular lessons for each project, the implications for policy and development practice for each market position and the general lessons for flagship developments. These are developed further in Chapters 14 and 15 for development projects and urban regeneration policies, with particular reference to the future directions for regeneration and our cities.

Our hypothesis concerns social well-being, the likelihood of maximizing social benefits, especially for the disadvantaged in and around the areas of regeneration. This means the policy process is important. A top-down approach is far more likely to concentrate benefits in the hands of those with advantages. This is because self-interest tends to dominate, yielding a further concentration of wealth and power. This can be avoided in a top-down approach and can go beyond patronage or even philanthropy by incorporating social needs into market positions. This means that the population becomes an integral and key part of what is being 'sold'. The alternative model is to either devolve power down the social structures or let those concerned begin to flex their social muscles – empowerment. Both options result in a bottom-up approach. Both are less certain in the sense of how the process starts and certainly the direction in which it develops. The case study material will help in evaluating these aspects and their relevance for envisioning and hence policy making. It is to the content of each case study that the analysis now turns.

The Watershed Complex | 8

8.1 INTRODUCTION

The Watershed Complex is the first case study flagship development. Completed prior to the others, it provides the longest time horizon for evaluating flagship operations and parallel promotion activity.[15] It was an innovative development and investment project because of its emphasis on the arts. As a pioneer, it was at the time of policy formulation an **H-type** project (see Figures 4.1 and 5.10), occupying an **innovative–national** position in the marketing matrix.

Situated in the historic core of the city of Bristol, the Watershed occupies a prominent location at the head of the Docks, which in Bristol is called the Floating Harbour. Bristol is located on the west coast of Britain on the river Avon, close to its mouth in the Severn estuary. In the Middle Ages, Bristol was the second most important port in Britain after London. The Floating Harbour is a seven-mile stretch of non-tidal dockland area. The branch of the Harbour on which the Watershed is located, called St Augustine's Reach, was excavated from the river Frome in the 13th century. It used to stretch right into the heart of Bristol, but the Victorians built an arch over a substantial section so the head of St Augustine's Reach is on the edge of the central core of the city, marked by Neptune's statue, with the Watershed adjacent. For most visitors to Bristol, this view would be their first of the dock areas.

8.2 ECONOMIC BACKGROUND

Bristol remains a major city in the British economy, having undergone many changes since the port dominated activity. Motor, aircraft and light engineering took the economy into the production of the means of communication and defence. Tobacco, board and paint industries developed the economy into consumption and predominantly market-led industries. To an extent, these remain. However, education, administrative and financial functions increased during the 1970s, forming Bristol's current service-dominated economy.

In the 1960s the Floating Harbour ceased operation as a port after the new port facilities at Avonmouth were opened. During the 1970s, the majority of development was in the city centre, although not on the former dockside area. Nor was it sufficient to retard or recapture activities for the dock areas. Development in the 1980s was concentrated around the periphery of the city in business park locations, such as Aztec West, until the moratorium on office development came to an end, and office and retail development began to accelerate in the latter half of the decade in the centre.

There was a need to regenerate the entire dock areas. The run-down and subsequent closure of the docks had led to the demise of other activities in the 1950s, for example the retailing and public houses along the quayside and the Royal Hotel located behind the Watershed. The principal closures over the period were the warehouses.

The southern side of St Augustine's Reach had been slowly regenerated during the 1960s and 1970s to include the Unicorn Hotel, offices such as the Standard Life development at the head of St Augustine's Reach and the Arnolfini Art Gallery. The northern side of St Augustine's Reach remained in disuse, as did the adjacent site, Canon's Marsh. This key site occupies the corner defined by the Reach, the main artery of the Floating Harbour, the Hotwells district of the city and the Council Offices and cathedral situated at the foot of Park Street, which leads down from Clifton. Apart from the bonded warehouses developed by Imperial Tobacco, Canon's Marsh had been largely unused for around 20 years, and these bonded warehouses were also closed in recent years. Canon's Marsh is the main area that any flagship project would seek to regenerate. Indeed, this was the policy of the District Council.

The waterfront has four warehouses, comprising the Exhibition site and the Watershed Complex. The Watershed Complex consists of two warehouses. Unlike many of the brick and stone warehouses in Bristol, these were the first transit sheds and are built mainly of timber and steel. The site was under the jurisdiction of the City Corporation and the Society of Merchant Venturers until the formation of the Dock Corporation in 1803, and it was under their control in 1894 that Bristol architect Edward Gabriel won the competition to design sheds E and W, with the brief that the eastern facade facing the city should be of high quality (JT Group Ltd, undated). It is this gable end that has ensured the 'presence' of these sheds. They are listed today and the area is designated as a conservation area under the planning policy.

8.3 CITY POLICY

The city authorities took an innovative and enlightened view of the Floating Harbour, seeing it as an opportunity for sensitive scaled regeneration prior to the larger scale initiatives adopted in other locations across the country. The planning policies were not always backed up by – and through – other policy areas. The absence of a leisure department resulted in a lack of focus and the perception that leisure would not create desirable employment opportunities did, as shall be shown in the subsequent analysis, retard opportunities. Planning policies that have prevented commercial development, and particularly office development, have ironically frustrated leisure development in this area.

However, the approach was positive and relevant in the late 1970s and early 1980s, arising from a study commissioned by the City from Casson Conder and Partners (1972). The Industrial and Lifeboat Museums were being housed in similar sheds opposite St Augustine's Reach, the SS *Great Britain* had been moored and was being renovated in its dry dock further down the harbour opposite Hotwells, and local design and build contractors, JT Group, had restored the former Bush Warehouse as their head office and Arnolfini Gallery. The gallery has its origins as a grand stone China tea warehouse, built by Acraman, Bush Castle & Co. and possibly designed by R.S. Pope. It was also used for grain and tobacco during its warehouse life (Arnolfini Gallery Ltd and Building Partnership (Bristol) Ltd, undated). Outline planning permission was obtained in 1972 for the conversion of Bush House into an art gallery, cinema and restaurant with offices on the second to fifth storeys (Arnolfini Gallery Ltd and Building Partnership (Bristol) Ltd, undated). It has been a highly successful refurbishment, in terms of both cost and use. It acted as a pilot for the area in general and, specifically, for the Watershed Complex.

8.4 THE CONDITIONS

The city owned the Watershed site and sheds. Shed E was structurally restored at a cost of £115 000 with grant aid from the Historic Buildings Council for England, and in 1979 the sheds were offered on a 99-year lease for 'an attractive combination of public and commercial use' under competitive tender (JT Group Ltd, undated, p.1). The pump-priming complete, the first condition was therefore set by the City. Any competitive bid was likely to be secured not only on price but upon content that embraced the local authority's policy for the area. This flagship development, or more accurately refurbishment and conversion, would have to embrace public or voluntary sector uses, as well as private uses, as one of its primary aims and objectives.

8.5 THE PARTIES

The public sector had therefore taken the lead, yet the flagship was required to be a predominantly private venture as long as the use included public interest facilities. JT Group came forward as one of the bidders. Formed in 1961 in Bristol, the company had become well known in the region for high quality design and construction projects, a combination that has seldom been matched by contractors using in-house resources in Britain. JT Group had, under the direction of John Pontin, undertaken a number of leisure projects, had become developers in their own right and had added a measure of philanthropy to the business strategy.

The conversion of the warehouse almost opposite the Watershed into the Arnolfini Gallery and their own headquarters had provided a precedent and model to follow. The 'commercial' viability of this scheme was less problematic as JT Group were to provide the secured occupancy. The risk was negligible compared to the sheds on the opposite side of the water.

It is known that a speciality retailer was another bidder for the Watershed Complex and that their competitive scheme was very heavily commercially biased. A mixed-use scheme would prove more attractive, and JT Group was aware of the need to carry other parties into the arena to achieve the public uses. The umbrella organization to which JT linked was the Bristol Arts Centre, a diffuse organization, spread across a number of locations and activities in Bristol. Their main premises in King Square was nearing the end of its lease. Out of this melting pot came the idea to bring the activities into a single location, which would not only provide an improved profile for the Centre but in addition the tenants under that umbrella would mutually benefit and be stimulated by each others presence.

This was the idea at the bid stage, although the aims and objectives were in their infancy at this time and had yet to be developed. JT Group had identified the Bristol Arts Centre, which was to become the Arts Trust, as the primary occupant. Reversing the Arnolfini concept, the arts uses were to be located on the upper of the two floors of sheds E and W. Speciality shopping was to occupy the ground floor and provide the commercial content.

The four sheds, including those on the Exhibition Centre site, were to be put to different uses. Sheds U and V were leased to exhibition organizers and held by the city for exhibition use. Essentially, these sheds remain unchanged and their fabric has not been redeveloped. They are used for the annual Wine Fair and for intermittent exhibitions. They will be excluded from the subsequent analysis because of an absence of investment and because they do not attract any additional inward investment. Such economic activity as they do support is largely the result of their dockland location and proximity to the Watershed Complex.

Sheds E and W were those bid for by JT Group. It was their assessment that the speciality retailing would not only complement the arts use, but that the arts use would actively draw in trade and therefore support the speciality shopping (JT Group Ltd and Bristol Arts Centre, undated). It was hoped to attract one of the first local radio stations to the complex as a tenant, and indeed, GWR was granted a licence and became a tenant. The success of the Arnolfini Gallery led the director in charge of the tender to comment, 'We had proved to ourselves that, taking a waterside building and making it a mixture of god and mammon, art and commerce could work'.[16] It was on this basis that the bid was submitted, but its significance extends well beyond the essential content.

At the time of the tender submission, there was an absence of a leisure and arts focus for the city. The Department of Arts was formed in 1985, and Leisure, which encompassed the arts, in 1991. The Bristol Marketing Board was the effective body and was headed by Tony Byrne.[17] He was to become a major figure in the policy formulation for the Watershed. JT Group had its own charitable trust, which funded Tony Byrne's salary for a year, and Dartington and Co., a small merchant bank, provided accommodation.

The Bristol Arts Centre was constituted as an independent Arts Trust, which paid a peppercorn rent and a commercial service charge to JT Group.

JT Group linked with Dartington and Co. to fund the development through the Dartington Trust. The City remained the freeholder and the lease was held in a joint venture by these organizations, JT being the dominant partner in a company vehicle named Tiltyard (see note 16). The lease for the retail was structured as a geared ground rent related to the success of the development, the lease for the arts tenants being set up independently to protect their position within the flagship development. The JT bid was successful, not on grounds of price so much as on the content of the scheme. The project was given the name 'Watershed' at the tender stage and the name was retained, along with the logo.

This description of the content already raises some of the key aims and objectives. Before looking at these in greater detall, it is worth stating in summary form the current situation, in order to signpost the analysis. The arts umbrella was given an independent status as the Arts Trust. Underfunded from the start, the arts facilities have operated on a hand-to-mouth basis. Cross-fertilization between the arts did not take place, and the centre emerged as a media complex dominated by the film sector. GWR, the local radio station, has worked largely independently. Any possibility of cross-fertilization was deemed to be impractical or without sufficient benefit. The retailing was not fed by those attending the arts centre and, rather than being speciality shopping, has become a mix of predominantly craft and novelty trading. The leases are short term and the current recession is hitting trade and rents severely. JT Group does not believe that it has made any profit out of the venture, and at best has broken even to date.

The complex has a very high regional profile and the City uses it extensively in its promotion of Bristol. It has not yielded further investment into the area on any great scale. Canon's Marsh remains largely undeveloped, the principal occupant arriving since the opening of the Watershed being Lloyds' administrative complex, which located there against the tide of planning policy and in spite of the Watershed. The cause of the lack of inward investment is located beyond the Watershed in local planning policies. It can only be surmised, yet it is likely that the Watershed could have indeed attracted or helped to draw in further investment, including arts facilities funded in conjunction with commercial development, albeit on a scale or density beyond the normative content of the local planning policy. JT Group did not – and do not – believe that the commercial dimension of the Watershed could become profitable until Canon's Marsh is developed, so generating pedestrian traffic along the quay which provides the primary access to Canon's Marsh on which the retail development is located and ultimately depends for viable long-term trading.

8.6 MARKET POSITION

Bristol as an economy is dominated by the service sector and serves a national and international market-place. The geographical orientation is predominantly national, although its international history has a legacy and inward investors have helped sustain that outlook. In 1989, 46 000 people were working in insurance, banking, finance and business services, and 42 000 in retailing (Economic Development Office, 1992), and both education and public administration are major service employers. The city is well connected by motorway and rail, and has an international airport, although its location and services are not of major significance despite the programme to upgrade facilities. The Floating Harbour can be reached within a few minutes from the foot of the M32 feeder from the M4.

The Watershed Complex was an innovative scheme and, along with other pioneers, helped to establish arts-based economic and property development as a major thrust during the 1980s:

> A number of urban regeneration schemes have demonstrated that the cultural industries and the performance arts are among the best activities and businesses for reviving a run-down area and making best use of empty industrial buildings, shopfronts and warehouses. (Worpole, 1991, p. 146)

The ramifications and the constraints of this type of employment have been detailed in two local reports (Centre for Leisure and Tourism, 1989a, b, quoted in Worpole, 1991, p.148). However, what was innovative about the Watershed was the bringing of a number of groups with the Bristol Arts Centre under the umbrella of the Arts Trust. This not only provided a potential focus for arts activities, so complementing the Arnolfini Gallery and the established theatre activities, but also lent a visibility to these activities. The development of the Complex on the quay provided a powerful symbol for regeneration and a strong image of a dynamic, innovative city for both its population and its visitors, and, through the arts network, brought conference trade and promotion of the city to inward investors:

> Moreover, image becomes all-important in competition, not only through name-brand competition but also because of various associations of 'respectability', 'quality', 'prestige', 'reliability', and 'innovation'. Competition in the image-building trade becomes a vital aspect of inter-firm competition. Success is so plainly profitable that investment in image-building (sponsoring the arts, exhibitions, television productions, new buildings, as well as direct marketing) becomes as important as investment in new plant and machinery. The image serves to establish an identity in the market place. (Harvey, 1989a, p.288)

In this case we are dealing more at the level of marketing the city than the firm, but this is the point. In this case it was the City that set the parameters, but it was the private sector that took the lead, especially in image creation through the parties it took on board. It is interesting to note that, although the JT Group was commercially shrewd enough to obtain the support of the voluntary sector who serve the public domain, the Watershed is perceived as being a public sector scheme. While this myth may help to market the city, the scheme is clearly more innovative than that, for at this time the private sector was sceptical that any arts-based initiative could be harnessed to produce private profit. Perhaps the analysis was flawed given the turn of events for this scheme; however, careful mixing of arts and commerce has proved to be successful elsewhere, and had Canon's Marsh been developed the commercial viability may have been improved.

The Complex had a number of components in order to accommodate the mix of uses and activities. The speciality retailing occupies the ground floors of sheds E and W. The local radio station, GWR, occupies the end of the furthest shed, W, a broadcasting studio being situated close to the entrance and visible from the promenade along the quay, which adds to the spectacle. The arts components, entered from shed E, were to have contained a major screen, two dance studios, a gallery and exhibition space, performance/conference facilities, a crèche and a café-bar (JT Group Ltd and Bristol Arts Centre, undated). The spaces were configured to be flexible and multipurpose in order to facilitate the cross-fertilization.

During the policy formulation and implementation stages the mix of uses began to change. In content this meant a greater concentration upon the film industry. Two screens, dark rooms, an exhibition and conference area plus the café-bar were incorporated. The other functions were lost, as was some of the flexibility. This came about as a result of the individuals involved, who were instrumental in the 'policy formulation'. Although the balance of uses changed, the overall function was retained. There was no compromise to the market position. The Watershed has become established as a major regional–national film venue. The dockside location provided the right ambience and setting, as well as being a good central location.[18] The prominence and eventual dominance of the film side of the flagship arose because Steve Pinhay, who was a key figure in the Bristol arts milieu, had good connections with the British Film Institute (BFI) and because Tony Byrne, who was given responsibility for funding the project, set up and promoted 'Wildscreen', a biannual nature film festival, which used both the screens and the conference facilities and drew upon the presence of the BBC Wildlife Unit and HTV in Bristol.

The market position has shifted over time. What started, then, as an **H-type** project concerned with an **innovative–national** market position (see Figure 5.10) evolved into its current position as a **service–national** facility in the market, an **E-type** project on the marketing matrix (see Figures 4.1 and 5.7). There are a number of reasons for this, which can be divided into reasons internal to the project and external ones.

Taking the internal ones first, several points can be made. The first is that the concentration upon the film and conference trade had a number of implications. Limiting the diversity of activity, while always raising questions as to whether cross-fertilization would take place, did restrict the opportunities for different activities to expand and contract according to demand and with each phase of growth maintaining the innovative input. Keeping a balanced programme and raising the income would not have been easy, yet it has not been easy under the existing mix. Secondly, the first screen was fitted out to the highest specification with state-of-the-art equipment for its day – 1982. The second screen was not, and was too small to achieve cost effective use. The exhibition and conference facilities were fitted out to a minimum budget, so their useful life span as a unique and attractive location was soon eroded.

The current management has recognized these shortcomings and has planned to raise £450 000 for a refit in order to reposition the development as a media centre concentrating on film and photography in three areas (*Financial Times*, 1991a). These are (i) film-related events, such as showing those films not shown on the main circuit, and film industry events such as

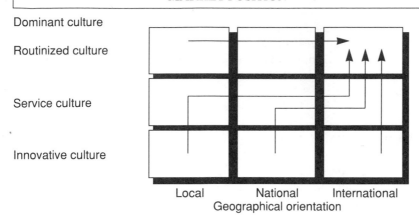

Dominant culture

Routinized culture

Service culture

Innovative culture

Local   National   International
Geographical orientation

Figure 8.1 Process of temporal market position shift

'Wildscreen' and 'Input', the international film-makers' programme festival; (ii) photographic exhibitions and an education programme related to these activities; and (iii) catering. This market strategy reinforces the service–national market position of the Watershed Media Centre.

The conference market is still sought; however, the sales edge has not only been lost as a result of the low budget fit-out, but also because of the development of hotels in Bristol during the 1980s. It is small and 'bottom-end of the market' events that tend to be attracted to the Centre, particularly from within the Bristol region. This brings the analysis on to the external factors. The first of these is that Bristol did not promote itself as a leisure or tourist centre, despite the reputation of the Theatre Royal, the Arnolfini, the Zoo, the SS *Great Britain*, Clifton 'Village' and the Clifton Suspension Bridge. Tony Byrne had wanted to do this, but this idea did not receive City support; indeed the local authority was hostile to the quality of employment that this type of activity might generate (see note 17). Had the City given more active support to the arts and leisure markets generally and the Media Centre in particular, direct finance or indirect income may have created the ability to invest to maintain the innovative nature of the scheme.

The last and overriding reason why this innovative project can be seen as service provision today is because of its success. It became a role model and an inspiration for other arts-based initiatives around the country. One of the characteristics of a successful innovation is for those with generic skills to take a concept and develop and refine it for other circumstances, taking it into a larger market. The long-term trend of success is for projects to become routinized in operation, the service provision that responds to particular needs being further packaged into a set of procedures and 'taken for granted' norms. The overall tendencies can be seen in Figure 8.1.

Even without any of the other factors, this innovative project would have

become a project based on the strong delivery of a service rather than a
strong idea. The market demanded it and the capacity for evolution, as has
been described, was already embodied in the project from the way in which
the 'policy' was formulated. It is now appropriate to concentrate on the
policy process.

8.7 POLICY FORMULATION

Looking first at the individual people and organizations involved, we can
examine the extent, coherence and content of the policies. There were
three main parties:

- The City Council *Provide context*
- JT Group *Developers*
- The Watershed Arts Trust (arising from the Bristol Arts Trust).
  Voluntary sector policy makers

The City provided the context through the tender process and thus laid
down the cornerstone policy. JT, as developers played the leading role,
drawing in the Bristol Arts Trust as voluntary sector policy makers.

The policy of JT can be boiled down to three main aims and objectives.
Firstly, they had an ambition to 'do an Arnolfini' (see note 16), so
enhancing their track record in the leisure field and maintaining a high
profile in Bristol. Secondly, the project would create design and build work
for the contracting side of the organization. Thirdly – and most importantly
– the scheme was a foothold into the Canon's Marsh area. JT had already
submitted one scheme for the main site, which could not be reconciled with
local planning requirements. However, the company saw it as a major
development and construction opportunity which was likely to be developed within the next ten years. The scheme would be the main gateway to
the site from the city centre and their land holding would give some
leverage for the development. Furthermore, the development of Canon's
Marsh would ensure the long-term commercial success of the Watershed.
'We thought and still feel the Watershed will come into its own when
Canon's Marsh gets going', according to the former director of JT, Roger
Mortimer. The development of Canon's Marsh has not proceeded as JT
had expected: 'Watershed is a key part of the major redevelopment of the
Canon's Marsh area which has been initiated by Bristol City Council' (see
note 16).

This was a reasonable expectation for a flagship development given the
policy assumptions. The assertion could have been tempered by the lack of
activity over the previous years. However, the tender could equally be seen
as a shift in policy stance and was supported by the Council Leader, who
stated, 'It is part of the overall package of schemes which the Council has
been keen to see developed to bring fresh life to the heart of the city'

Figure 1. The Watershed Complex, St Augustine's Reach, Bristol Docks. Reproduced by courtesy of the City of Bristol.

Figure 2. The gable end of 'E' shed before refurbishment. Reproduced by courtesy of the City of Bristol.

Figure 3. The entrance and gable end facade of 'E' shed after refurbishment. Reproduced by courtesy of the City of Bristol.

Figure 4. View across St Augustine's Reach, The Watershed Complex, to the City of Bristol. Reproduced by courtesy of the City of Bristol.

Figure 5. Hall 1, International Convention Centre, Birmingham. Reproduced by courtesy of the City of Birmingham.

Figure 6. Symphony Hall, International Convention Centre, Birmingham. Reproduced by courtesy of the City of Birmingham.

Figure 7. View of the Hyatt Hotel across Centenary Square, Birmingham. Reproduced by courtesy of the City of Birmingham.

Figure 8. Perspective of Brindley Place, Birmingham. Reproduced by courtesy of Brindleyplace plc.

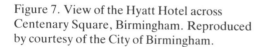

Figure 9. Masterplan of proposed Brindley Place development, Birmingham. Reproduced by courtesy of Brindleyplace plc.

Figure 10. Aerial view across Centenary Square to the Hyatt, International Convention Centre, National Indoor Arena and Brindley Place in Birmingham. Reproduced by courtesy of the City of Birmingham.

Figure 11. Chinese New Year Celebrations in Theatre Village, Newcastle. Reproduced by courtesy of Cityrepro, City of Newcastle upon Tyne.

Figure 12. The 'Chinatown' area in Theatre Village, Newcastle. Reproduced by courtesy of Cityrepro, City of Newcastle upon Tyne.

Figure 13. The refurbished interior of the Tyne Theatre and Opera House, Newcastle. Reproduced by courtesy of Cityrepro, City of Newcastle upon Tyne.

Figure 14. View of the Wall from 'inside' the Byker development, Newcastle. Reproduced by courtesy of Cityrepro, City of Newcastle upon Tyne.

Figure 15. View of Byker, Newcastle. Reproduced by courtesy of Cityrepro, City of Newcastle upon Tyne.

Figure 16. Aerial view of Byker. Reproduced by courtesy of Cityrepro, City of Newcastle upon Tyne.

(Watershed Arts Trust Bristol, 1981, p.2). The presence, profile and contact network of JT in Bristol put them in as good a position as any developer to assess this situation. With this working assumption, JT set about building a prominent team, and hence profile, for the project. Their view of the policy for the public content was as follows:

> Watershed will house Britain's first media and communications centre devoted to the ways in which people receive their information and entertainment, enabling public participation and enjoyment of television, film, radio, video, photography, printing and telecommunications. In addition to looking at new means of communication and the relationship between Art and Technology, Watershed will also examine the ways in which the traditional art forms have been treated by the mass media.' (Watershed Arts Trust Bristol, 1981, p.2)

This would create a destination in its own right, drawing people along the promenade and into the shops. Eventually it would become the primary access to the new Canon's Marsh development and in the interim to the 'Lochiel', a pub in a ship moored at the far end of St Augustine's Reach (JT Group Ltd and Bristol Arts Centre, undated). The arts facilities would be integral to the success of the speciality shopping, as well as creating a positive profile:

> The proposed scheme will create an almost continual 'shop window' for the community along this stretch of water. This will be enhanced by the presence of the Exhibition Centres, the Lochiel and the Arnolfini. Although the latter currently runs a joint film programme with the Bristol Arts Centre, which is extremely successful, the roles of the two centres are essentially different and complementary, and joint discussions on this scheme have taken place with Arnolfini. Arnolfini's policy is to 'look at' the arts, while people are encouraged to 'join in' at the Arts Centre, which is deliberately geared towards community involvement at 'grass roots' level'. (JT Group Ltd and Bristol Arts Centre, undated, p.9)

This would render the Watershed Complex the first of its type in the country, according to the Arts Trust. The Artistic Director, Steve Pinhay said, 'It is quite remarkable when you consider how all pervasive the media are, how little is known about them and how much they are taken for granted by the general public' (Watershed Arts Trust Bristol, 1981, p.3). This marked the beginning of a re-awakening of interest in and knowledge of the arts and media industries during the 1980s. It was not simply because the Watershed project and others in a similar vein, such as the Tate in the Albert Dock, Liverpool, the National Museum of Photography, Film and Television in Bradford (Bianchini, Dawson and Evans, 1990, 1992), or the cultural industries quarter in Sheffield (Fisher, 1991), created an interest *per se*, but that the drive to create and intensify the arts as a commodity was part of the economic drive in the 1980s (Harvey, 1989a).

The developers had set down a series of aims, responding to an idea from the City. The objective was clearly visionary and to this extent the position reflected those of the innovative–national marketing strategy, with a few simple and detailed goals, yet flexible enough to accommodate change. Change did occur. What was not in place was a creative steering group with 'autocratic' control. It was perhaps not obvious which party should initiate this. It appeared that JT, through supporting Tony Byrne to bring the arts side together, placed the responsibility in his hands along with Steve Pinhay, who also played a key role.

The overall vision was shared, but the policy for the arts side was devolved to these individuals. They proceeded to put the policy together in 'reverse' order. The first point was that there were no objectives and therefore no simple yet detailed goals written down for the centre. Tony Byrne appeared to wish to steer the centre more and more towards the film side with Steve Pinhay's support. The BFI wished to adopt the proposed centre as its 'own' regional film theatre (see note 18). This was a new approach and an attractive one, because the BFI won support from the Minister for the Arts to the tune of a £100 000 grant to equip what was to become a state-of-the-art screen (Watershed Arts Trust Bristol, 1981).

This meant that the film element drove the centre from this time. In order to get additional financial support, the film side needed further promotion. Hence, the evolving vision became driven by the need to sell the centre in order to raise finance to realize the vision. The vision did not drive the centre any more, and the absence of a steering group prevented it from being re-established. Its absence had two other affects. JT were reliant, at least until Canon's Marsh was built, on the arts side drawing in trade for the speciality shopping, yet their influence or monitoring of this evolving policy was less than that necessary for an innovative project. The second consequence was that the arts side, as it moved more and more towards a media centre, lost support from other vital interest groups.

The creation of the regional film centre was not supported by others in the local arts milieu. The Bristol Arts Centre and others that were to come from other groups under the new umbrella had varied interests. The emphasis on film drove out the dance studios and the crèche in favour of a second screen, which was not thought through carefully and could not have stood up to any cost–benefit analysis. The 'traditionalists' saw it as 'killing off the old arts centre', according to the City's Director of Leisure Services (see note 17), a view that has been echoed. The City supported the idea in principle, yet did not follow through: The City Council either wasn't told or didn't want to hear what the revenue implications were for the City' (see note 18).

In retrospect, it was probably the responsibility of JT to create a steering group on which both they and the City would be represented, not in order to control the arts policy, but to ensure that those responsible for the arts:

- set down a few detailed, simple goals;
- let the vision drive the costing;
- ensured that longer term revenue and capital costs were assured for the media centre;
- ensured greater spin off for retailing from the arts.

Other issues that will be raised ultimately come back to this policy shortcoming, which is firmly grounded in the need to **manage** a market position.

In the event, the financial side increasingly came to dominate, based on a tripartite interest configuration – BFI, JT and the City. The need for structured grant aid was not recognized at the outset. Voluntary sector support was relied upon. The BFI contribution was significant, but, despite Tony Byrne's success at raising money (see Table 8.1), it was insufficient.

Table 8.1 Watershed Media Centre capital and revenue funding

Organization	Funding (£)
BFI	100 000
London Life Assurance Co.	220 000
JT Group	60 000
Bristol Arts Centre	98 000
Historic Buildings Council and Bristol City Council	30 000
Other	16 000
Plus sponsorship in kind	

Sources: JT Group Ltd (undated), Watershed Arts Trust Bristol (1981).

The City was contributing indirectly by charging a peppercorn rent and JT Development made an £80 0000 allowance against the contract price for fitting out. The funding included some revenue grants over 6–10 year periods. The cost of redevelopment was estimated at £1.5m, of which the Watershed Arts Trust areas were estimated at £600 000 (JT Group Ltd, undated). Therefore, the arts side opened with a deficit of £350 000 and annual lease purchase costs of £28 000 (see note 18).

JT did not therefore have a large financial exposure to the project. The risk was minimal for an innovative project in terms of the size of the company. The returns, on the other hand, would also be minimal, with a risk of being negative, although the ground rent payable to the City for the retail uses was performance-related (JT Group Ltd, undated). The company was always going to receive more benefit from being associated with a prestigious project and for the competitive advantage created should Canon's Marsh be developed.

The marketing and selling of the development appears to have been addressed in a minimal fashion, the arts side being asked to lead the way. The potential for the regeneration strategy to be reinforced and given a higher profile was not realized at this stage. The City was encouraging development of Canon's Marsh, albeit on its own terms. However, a flagship project provides an opportunity to build a coherent economic development or tourist strategy (Bianchini, Dawson and Evans, 1990, 1992). This was not taken up, in part because of hostility to leisure-related employment and in part because the vision for Canon's Marsh could not be funded from the public purse and was not commercial for the private sector.

Promotion was driven by Tony Byrne, although the thrust of this was to raise finance rather than to spread the vision *per se*. In fact, it was difficult to determine what was being promoted, except to those directly concerned with the film industry. The absence of policy goals meant that the centre has been said to 'revolve around style' (see note 18) in the past. There was plenty of enthusiasm, energy and optimism for the project, but this is not a substitute for managing the marketing of a flagship. Once again, the absence of clearly defined aims and the support in funds and management that would be necessary for implementation signalled the way in which the project was to lose some of its marketing potential. The Watershed has a strong image and has served the city well from a marketing viewpoint. However, for many users and potential users the project lacked a focus or purpose in its first years. Its market was not clearly defined. The opportunity had been there to lend substance to the image:

> Each theatre company, artists studio, dance group is different. Arts projects can express the character of the community, indeed they literally give voice to it. In doing so, they are not merely decorative, they often capture the distinction between a community's identity and its image. It is true that some cities, such as Glasgow, have used their investment in the arts to promote or market an image, but the renewal of confidence, the pride and involvement of people in a city's cultural life goes deeper than mere image-making. (Fisher, 1991, p.3)

The image making has been extremely successful and has been derived from a combination of:

- dockside setting
- architecture
- content
- City marketing.

The sense of place has arisen through use rather than through active marketing and sales. Marketing could have enhanced the image of place and perhaps drawn out the organic potential, rather than the superimposed feel that hangs between the 'spectacle' and 'self-identity'. The issues addressed by Clark (1985) and Harvey (1991) and the potential for empowerment, in this case through active marketing, were diluted. Superficially, the causes for this can be attributed to the individuals responsible for putting together the finance and content. More fundamental was the absence of a steering group for the whole project.

In conclusion, the project stands up reasonably well to close scrutiny. The market position was defined overall, although there were gaps in the details of policy formation. Management processes were in place, articulated by individuals. What was absent was a structure to set the context within which people could operate and adequate finance could be sought.

8.8 PROJECT IMPLEMENTION

The speciality shopping was developed, but the tenants were of a rather different nature to those anticipated. JT had hoped to secure a chandler to service the leisure boating market and to have mooring facilities outside. This would have enhanced the visual attraction. The letting was not secured. Nor did negotiations with a specialist retailer materialize (JT Group Ltd and Bristol Arts Centre, undated). The Dartington Trust took the craft unit, as planned. However, the remaining units were let to craft, 'designer' and fashion goods retailers. It is debatable whether this really constitutes 'speciality' shopping, but it was not to prove special enough for people to make it a regular and specific destination, as similar goods are on sale elsewhere in the city. The Media Centre clientele were not regular buyers either.

Two of the consequences of driving the vision through the raising of finance were that the vision was not given time to 'grow' and be 'owned' by others. It had to be sold, rather than people buying into it. Had London Life not relocated to Bristol from London and made a loan of £220 000 as part of their public relations programme, the project would not have been implemented so quickly. This arose out of opportunism instead of commitment. Tony Byrne was well aware of the second issue; any innovative project that is finance-driven needs to be implemented rapidly, otherwise the momentum is lost, people lose heart and sponsorship is withdrawn, because sponsors wish to be present at the start in order to maximize the promotional value for them.

The only other reason to proceed quickly was that the main property lease for the Arts Centre was coming to an end. However, it has been outlined (see Chapter 5) that innovative projects need a sound financial footing, yet should be driven by the ideas and not by the finance *per se*.

The arts side of the Watershed faced problems in the implementation stage as a result of undefined policies. Policies remained vague and management weak. While the film-related activities performed strongly, the exhibition and catering functions were neglected. The shortfall in capital meant that, although the film fitout was to the highest standard, the exhibition and conference space was minimal at best and makeshift at worst. The café-bar was fitted out and proved a popular destination, despite being on the first floor and not 'on the way' to anywhere. People came to it as a destination, whether they were consuming the other facilities or not. It was a fashionable place to be and to meet people, especially among students and those interested in 'culture'. The café-bar was fitted out by JT in exchange for a lease purchase, a mortgage.

In the first years the City provided £4000 per annum towards funding. This could be seen as low and certainly was below revenue requirements *vis-à-vis* earned income. However, most other areas in the arts were cut during the period. The policy direction remained partially developed and the management was poor. The current Chief Executive of the Watershed Media Centre said, 'The organization opened in a wave of optimism, lots of hype; it worked during the eighties' (see note 18), reflecting the emphasis on style. However, the underlying financial issues began to show in spite of the large population throughput that was achieved. Apart from the funding shortfall, the management of the resources had been inadequate. The approach was described as a 'subsidized arts perspective' (see note 18), in other words, only seeking to break even and anticipating public sector support should the deficit grow. Income from other activities, such as the initially successful conference trade and the very successful café were spent 'in advance' and the revenue did not always match expectations because of the lack of control.

The current Chief Executive took control of management of the Centre in April 1991. The first Artistic Director was in post for 5 years, and two subsequent managers succeeded him. Debts had been £350 000 from the outset. During the 9 years of operations, debts have risen. For obvious reasons, the nature of these is sensitive. It is estimated that they were in the region of £600 000 in April 1991 and that the Centre was running at a loss of £250 000. It is thought that there has been subsidy given by the City over the years, perhaps in excess of £150 000. It is known that the turnover was £1.2m (see note 18), which is very good for an organization of this type, although this includes subsidies.

Clearly, there is some justification for the initiators adopting the 'subsidized arts perspective'. The Watershed has been very successful in a number of ways, especially from the viewpoint of marketing the city. Its position may look serious, but it is no worse off than many private sector companies during the current recession. What can be seen as irresponsible is that the situation need not have been like this, if:

- more finance had been forthcoming at the beginning to 'pump-prime' the operation;
- operational management had been as concerned with costs and income generation as with the 'style' and the arts.

It should be noted that the financial pressure constrained the ability of the project to remain innovative and the debts are reinforcing the need for a service orientation.

In terms of marketing itself, and indeed the area, the project has performed a good flagship function by attracting some major events. Most noteworthy is the biannual 'Wildscreen' film festival, which brings together organizations such as the BBC, World Wide Fund for Nature, Anglia Television, Central Independent Television and the Bristol & West Building Society in its organization (Wildscreen, 1988). 'Input' is another event concerned with programming during 1993. One of the key factors in locating 'Input' at the Watershed was the wide choice of hotel and hostel accommodation, permitting delegates from the broadest range of countries to attend at affordable rates (see note 18). These events lift the profile of the Watershed and have the indirect effect of marketing the area and city for investors and visitors.

The current period sees the completion of the shift in market position away from an innovative–national to a service–national approach. The steering committee structure was not in place, but attendant enthusiasm, experimentation and the shared vision have dissipated in favour of executive control of the constituent parts, managing the facilities in a rapidly changing environment and the building of intraorganizational dependencies – Arts Trust, City, JT – on informal levels and formally through contract on financial matters. This takes the analysis on to the final stage in the policy process.

8.9 POLICY AND PROJECT EVALUATION

The development from the developer's viewpoint has been a low risk one with large potential opportunities. With the passage of time, the potential has not come to fruition. It is the developer's view that if they had known Canon's Marsh would not be developed within 10 years they would not have entered the tender process. This has been coupled with the recession, which has hit the retailing sector hard, especially the 'speciality' and luxury end of the trade, such as the shops along the covered quayside promenade. Former JT director, Roger Mortimer commented on the shopping, 'it's struggling so hard to keep going', and tenants are finding they cannot afford to pay rent (see note 16).

JT has also helped to support the Arts Trust, buying the lease from them and providing financial support for the Trust. The continued support by JT for the Trust must be seen as part of the project politics that is informally worked out between the City, the Trust and JT. On a practical level, JT is committed to the development. Despite the difficulties, the potential remains, not only for Canon's Marsh, but also for sheds V and W. JT holds the lease on these buildings and has tried to attract a college of music to the complex.

The Media Centre sales have always been high, but undercapitalization and poor management have been the continuing problems. Despite the difficulties, 80% of all the income has been self-generated. This has come from the main screen when events, such as 'Wildscreen', are hosted, from external lettings to the conference market and from the regular income generated by the café-bar. Despite the fact that the café-bar was a major provider of revenue, it was seen as an 'adjunct to the arts', income being spent in advance and staffing and resources poorly controlled (see note 18).

Conference trade was strong in the early 1980s and actually penalized the photographic side as funding was lost due to the low profile. The poor quality exhibition space did not help. However, the conference trade did subside in the mid-1980s as hotel investment multiplied in Bristol. The conference, gallery and exhibition spaces occupy about 45% of the floor area, but this space is needed for the new strategy, providing flexible options for the future. The current emphasis is upon resource management, particularly cash flow and 'tying down and getting consensus on where the root problems lie' (see note 18). This approach will complete the executive control necessary by bringing the staff to a position where they can identify an issue as a problem and then bring their analytical skills to bear in the problem-solving process demanded by a service approach.

The current management is addressing a range of issues, including relations with funding bodies and with staff, the lack of clear-cut core activities and the need for a refurbishment programme in order to generate more of its own income. Concerning funding, closer relations with the BFI, the Arts Council, South West Arts, and Bristol and Avon Councils have been established through regular meetings. Addressing staff issues has cut costs and raised income by 12%. The new service strategy is to focus on film, photographic exhibitions, education and the catering operations. Although photographic exhibitions are large-space consumers and are not income-generating, they will underpin the revenue-creating education and community programmes. Exhibitions improve café and retail spend.

A £450 000 refurbishment is needed in order to achieve two broad objectives:

- cultural vibrancy
- financial stability.

The image needs renewing and the screen technology updating. The imperative is to second-guess new technologies and estimate where contemporary culture will express itself. There is a wish to move consumption away from the 'passive' model to a more active one, especially through links with schools, and further and higher education. The foyer will be upgraded in order attract further custom, hence income, and to introduce higher quality conference and exhibition areas, with the introduction of retailing opportunities. Raising the additional finance will be necessary to ensure the medium-term viability of the Centre in the market through its own activities. The arts dilemma, from the Watershed viewpoint, is:

- if it is commercial, it needs no subsidy;
- if it is 'pure' art, it is too amateur and does not deserve subsidy.

The cinema has been seen as 'commercial' and the photography as 'popular' and, by implication, 'amateur'. This dilemma, based upon a historic view of the definition of art, will need to be resolved, yet the broader problem for a local authority public subsidy for this flagship lies outside the domain of the arts. The switch from a commercial property rate to a uniform business rate means that the former incentive for local authorities to invest in image making development and programmes that will attract inward investment and consumption is eroded, because there will be little or no corresponding benefit derived from an increased rate base relative to enhanced property values (see note 17).

The Media Centre has proved itself as a major tourist attraction, third in the ranking for Bristol. The Hippodrome attracts 500 000 visitors per year, Bristol Zoo 450 000 and the Watershed Complex 350 000. Therefore, the image, the precedent and the presence that the Watershed Complex has achieved have been considerable. Although there have been shortcomings in the management and particularly in the financial side of the Arts Trust, the overall evaluation of the project from the viewpoint of the initiators has been either of success or of potential still to be realized.

It is probably the City that has derived most success from the Complex. As the Director of Leisure Services commented, 'In terms of perception for the City it has been tremendous' (see note 17). Furthermore, although community involvement was absent as the policy evolved for the Media Centre, it has helped to provide one of a number of foci for the city population. The people of Bristol have not seen themselves as a 'regional city', but as a series of 'urban villages'. This perception is changing or is having a regional dimension grafted onto it: it has broadened people's view of Bristol – and this despite the absence of a tourist and leisure strategy.

However, that is changing, which brings the analysis on to the impact that the project has had.

8.10 PROJECT IMPACT

In terms of image and its contribution to city life for a user of arts facilities, as a venue, as a place of recreation and tourist destination, and as a place with which the people of Bristol can identify, the Watershed Complex is a resounding success. As we have seen in the previous section, this is not quite the same as achieving the aims and objectives of the initiators. On these terms it has been less successful, although much of the potential remains and could be unlocked over the next few years.

Subsequent development and investment within the locale was only addressed to the extent that it related to the aims and objectives of JT and the Bristol Arts Trust as the primary initiators. The broader development impact and what interests are being served need to be considered in greater detail. The analysis cannot rely on the aims and objectives as an approach at this stage because many of the issues only relate in part or are separate from these. However, this is all part of the policy picture and aids in synthesizing the results for the case studies.

It is the Watershed Media Centre that has created the focus, although ironically its own economic health has been below par from the outset. The detailed nature of its economic performance is not available for publication, which tends to suggest that the position is far worse than any of the interested parties would wish to be made known, that is the City, JT and Arts Trust. It is known that JT has a far greater interest in the performance of the Trust today, compared to at the outset, because the Trust sold its lease to JT in order to raise money. The Trust was in the process of raising a further £450 000 for the new strategy and related refurbishment at the time of research, which has rendered the financial details more sensitive. The policy conclusion has to be that the finance must be at least met, preferably exceeded, if the Watershed is to continue to meet the evolving aspirations of the initiators and maintain the image from which the City Council has extensively benefited. The development of Canon's Marsh along City policy lines would require the Watershed to maintain its present profile.

The Watershed Media Centre, along with the growing interest during the 1980s in the arts in general and as a means for regeneration in particular, has contributed to the City Council commissioning an arts and cultural strategy, which was in preparation during the research period (see note 17). How this will relate to the policy proposals for Canon's Marsh cannot be discussed here, but will be an important issue for the future. The Watershed is part of a leisure mix in the Floating Harbour, which includes the Arnolfini, the National Lifeboat Museum, the Industrial Museum, the Maritime Heritage Centre and the SS *Great Britain*. Located at the head of the harbour, it is in the key position, which will be further enhanced as development takes place along that quay and in Canon's Marsh.

What development has taken place in the area and how much of this can be attributed to the Watershed Complex? The most obvious investment has been in the refurbishment and extension of the former Royal Hotel. Swallow Hotels have undertaken the investment to create a 250-bed luxury hotel with conference facilities. The Royal Hotel was one of the prime city hotels until the 1950s, after which it declined and then closed. The investment is estimated to be in the region of £40m (*Financial Times*, 1991b) and was part of a national and city trend of hotel development. In Bristol, Stakis Hotels, Shire Inns and Queens Moat House all had parallel developments. These developments have helped to upgrade the infrastructure and to some extent have competed with the Watershed Media Centre in the conference market. The Swallow Royal Hotel, as it now is, provides the closest competition, and has contributed to forcing the Watershed to compete at the lower end of the market. The presence of the Watershed was a contributory factor in the upgrading and redevelopment of the adjacent site, although it was not, of course, decisive in itself. The flagship function was in operation.

Other developments have taken place in the area. There has been the rebuilding of offices, let to the Council behind the Council offices, and proposals for further commercial development between that area and towards Canon's Marsh, although these have not materialized in the recession. However, the main focus is Canon's Marsh. The history of this derelict site is somewhat tortuous, and it is neither possible nor necessary to trace every step. Essentially, the site was owned by the City, British Gas, British Rail and Imperial Tobacco, and JT has an interest on the edge through the Watershed. The bonded warehouses owned by Imperial Tobacco were sold by the parent, Hanson Trust, thus rationalizing the site and permitting the development of the headquarters for Lloyds Bank. However, prior to this recent development there were been many attempts to set down a policy and create economically viable developments. Every attempt to reconcile the two goals of having primarily leisure use, and commercial development that would pay for the former has failed. This is because the City had always wished to see a high content of leisure facilities and low density commercial development where the commercial element could not fund the former. In addition, the landowners have been unable to reach agreement on a realistic pricing structure for the whole site.

The most recent City policy arises out of plans by consultants LDR for the site. The proposals included a 2500-seat concert hall, museums, art galleries and theatres, speciality shopping market, hotel accommodation and some commercial development. This policy arose at the height of the property boom and there was little interest in responding. It could only be funded with a very large injection of cash from the public sector, which was not forthcoming at that time. The conclusion to be drawn from this is threefold. Firstly, the Watershed project is unable to perform as a flagship because it has been unable to unblock the supply side of the equation, which is the main purpose of property-led initiatives. This first conclusion is somewhat unfair in that the policy belief of central government was that the blockage was located within the market overall. In this case, the blockage is a policy one of setting unrealistic development control policies. Even if one was to conclude that the landowners are causing the blockage through land price, the City is the major landowner and could use its position of leverage, especially concerning the 'ransom strip' owned by British Rail, which is also a public sector organization. This leads to the second possible conclusion, which is that the flagship is performing a latent function because it is constrained by public sector policy and practice. The third possible conclusion is that the planning policies are reasonable and in the best interest of the population, but are only workable with additional public resources. This latter conclusion would defeat the aims and objectives of central government policy for urban regeneration and restraint on financial involvement of the state.

What has taken place on the most prominent location within the Canon's Marsh site is the development of a new headquarters for Lloyds Bank, the first phase of which employs around 700 people. The completed first phase is located on the corner site created by the junction of St Augustine's Reach and the rest of the Floating Harbour, opposite the Arnolfini. It does not conform to either the former or the current planning policies for the area, and the chair of the Planning Committee, Andrew May, took the decision to accept the relocation from London as an opportunity not to be missed. Whether there was political pressure from higher levels is a moot point, but in any case the presence of the Watershed Complex had little or no role in attracting this investment.

The way in which the scheme has been implemented has militated against the successful regeneration of the remaining site area, which is still vast. The first point is that the postmodern architecture of the Lloyds headquarters is not in keeping with the warehouse genre. In front of the building is a large piazza facing the Floating Harbour. This is a large open space adjacent to another large open space – the water. It is not a 'public' space, but is a statement of corporate power because it does not provide a destination, and does not, therefore, draw pedestrians past the Watershed and its retailing. There is an absence of sensitivity or a sense of a 'place to be' on arrival. It was described as an 'anodyne and fascist space and is in contrast to the appearance of the Watershed on a Saturday' (see note 16).

The virtual severance of any sensible pedestrian through route and making the most of the quay for a round-trip stroll for tourism has been lost. The impact upon the area is therefore detrimental and is against the spirit of Bristol's planning policy of encouraging pedestrianization. Providing footpaths without a destiny has no more merit than a road without a destiny. The Lloyds employees drive to work or are picked up by coach from Temple Meads railway station. They tend not to go into the centre at lunch times, and so the Watershed does not benefit from passing trade. The City has also upgraded some of the pedestrian paths for those who do walk to the centre. While this is a good idea in itself, it is detrimental to the Watershed. The upgraded areas are those at the back of the Watershed and have smooth paviers, whereas planning policy insisted upon granite sets outside the retail areas of the Watershed. It is now, therefore, easier for pedestrians to walk into the centre bypassing the Watershed (JT Group, 1991).

Furthermore, high parking charges are discouraging motorists who have used on-street parking and the temporary car park on Canon's Marsh, once again reducing passing trade. Pedestrianization cannot be effected when seen as an alternative to other transport modes, but needs to be integrated with them. The proposed metro in Bristol will facilitate the reliance on public and pedestrian modes of communication. However, what has been achieved in the interim has to be maintained.

The impact of the Watershed Complex on the area has been less than the impact of policy on the area. The City still remains the chief benefactor because of the image of the Watershed. However, its own policies could potentially threaten the Watershed's existence and are preventing it from playing the flagship role of regeneration.

In concluding this section on project impact, it is useful to place the findings alongside the comments made by others concerning urban regeneration. The first point is that there are no 'losers' in this flagship project. There are a number of missed opportunities arising from a series of matters:

- lack of finance
- conflicting planning policy
- urban design and policy.

The retailers are in jeopardy; however, they are also in a risk business that has to accept the contingencies of recession and policy constraint. The developers appear to be accepting the risks, although they do lobby for change (JT Group, 1991). They still stand to potentially gain the most in the long term, but have not yet received much – if any – reward apart from prestige. Those that have gained are the users and, in particular, the City.

The City has benefited the most through the Watershed's image and through the fact that it is predominantly perceived as a public sector flagship. While the City has undoubtedly contributed to the Bristol Arts

Trust, the development has been privately led in conjunction with the voluntary sector. The case study does not support Harvey's (1989b) contention that the public sector underpins the profit of the private sector in urban regeneration. Both the private and public sectors have underpinned the voluntary sector in the case of the Watershed.

8.11 SUMMARY

The Watershed Complex has had the greatest benefit for the City, the aims of which in putting the development out to tender have been achieved and exceeded, despite the costs the City has borne in the financing of the Watershed Arts Trust in its running of the Watershed Media Centre. However, the City was not involved in the development. It was the innovative approach of developer JT, by linking with the Bristol Arts Trust (formerly the Bristol Arts Centre), that made the project possible in the adoption of an innovative–national market position. The high risk involved with this type of project leads to the conclusion that the project has achieved an extremely successful result in terms of image and the marketing of the city.

It has faced serious shortcomings in two respects. Firstly, local planning policy has thwarted the catalytic role of this flagship development, particularly the development of Canon's Marsh with complementary and integrated uses. Secondly, the lack of funds and poor management of the Watershed Media Centre has led to the innovative position being compromised and a service approach being adopted. This has been contrasted with some other arts schemes, for example Glasgow was selected as the Cultural Capital of Europe for 1990 on the basis of its financial plan (Wishart, 1991).

The other cause of the switch to a service–national market position is that many other schemes have benefited from the pioneering work achieved in Bristol. Heritage-type projects became very popular during the 1980s and the Watershed has an element of this, especially in architectural terms and as part of dockside regeneration, which Bristol helped to pioneer (cf. Bianchini, Dawson and Evans, 1990, 1992). The arts angle was innovative too, and, combined with the latest media technology, had the effect of inducing a duality of 'hi-tech' and 'soft feel'.

Overall, the project has to be seen as a success, although strictly on its own terms it is a qualified success. In terms of maximizing the potential for marketing the city, it would have been necessary for all main parties – JT, the Bristol Arts Trust and the City – to have produced a strategy for the project. This could or should have fitted into a city strategy. A steering group would have been the vehicle for achieving this. It would have had the added potential benefit of formulating and implementing the aims and objectives for the flagship more coherently and successfully for all parties concerned. This would have yielded greater benefits for the initiators but also for the users, both visitors to the city and the local population.

<table>
<tr><td>

The International Convention Centre

</td><td>

9

</td></tr>
</table>

9.1 INTRODUCTION

The International Convention Centre (ICC) in Birmingham has two things in common with the Watershed Complex. Like Bristol, Birmingham is one of Britain's foremost cities. Those with allegiances to Birmingham say that it is the nation's second city, just as Bristol was once the second most important port after London. Birmingham retains an important industrial base. It was a communication node at the heart of the national canal network. The ICC site is located a stone's throw from the main canal interchange in England. Like Bristol Docks, this historic heart of Birmingham has undergone long-term decline as canal transportation was superseded and the traditional 'metal bashing' industries closed.

The second commonality is that the regeneration, through the ICC, has a strong arts and cultural component, namely the Symphony Hall. However, the similarities largely end there. The two most striking features of the ICC are:

- its scale
- it is the first in a series of neighbouring flagships.

The ICC is one of the largest flagship projects developed in the UK during the 1990s. Canary Wharf and Broadgate in London are both larger, but outside the capital this project is as large as any in cost and larger in vision.

This raises the second striking feature, and in some ways the more significant, certainly in terms of the impact of flagship developments on urban regeneration. The ICC was conceived as the first of 3–4 flagships located on adjacent sites, linked by bridges over Broad Street and the canal. The communication routes are the only physical barriers between sites. The ICC is located closest to the core of the city, but just outside the inner ring road.

Alongside the ICC, on the opposite side of Broad Street, is the Hyatt Regency Hotel. It is the second flagship and integrally linked to the ICC. Behind the ICC is the Brindley Place development area, which can be subdivided into two flagships. The National Indoor Arena (NIA) is the main public provision and has been developed as a separate package during the implementation phase; the majority of the rest of the site is for commercial development. This will be a mix of retail, leisure and office uses and has yet to get under way. These multiple flagships raise the question as to how many flagships can be developed on the back of each other. Subsidiary questions concern the extent to which they simply feed off each other, possibly at the expense of attracting additional development and consumption activity, or whether the critical mass has a multiplier effect on the local economy.

9.2 ECONOMIC BACKGROUND

The economic growth for the area was built up from the decision in January 1767 for James Brindley to investigate a canal link between Birmingham and Wolverhampton. Its construction led to other canals being linked to form a national network with Birmingham at the hub (Spectrum Communications, 1991). Birmingham became a major manufacturing centre and was particularly associated with light engineering, metal work and jewellery production. It did not develop prestige, or a high profile, among visitors and the local population:

'Its reputation as a sprawling, blighted, industrial zoo whose citizens sported a collective inferiority complex dates back more than three hundred years.' (Lister, 1991, p.53)

The interwar years brought growth through automobile production, but much of this was located on the urban fringe while the industry in the core of the city declined. The 1960s produced a fervour to improve both housing and communications. The City embraced this with ambition, creating a new inner ring road, which in turn created a two-tier property market – that within the ring road and that outside. The industrial area was outside the area and new developments tended to locate within the inner ring road or towards the suburban satellites, for example at Five Ways and Edgbaston.

The downturn in industrial production during the 1970s led to major restructuring at the end of the decade and throughout the 1980s. For the city as a whole, manufacturing employment declined between 1981 and 1987 by 48% from 304 000 to 159 000 jobs (Birmingham City Council, undated). This was catastrophic for the regional economy. However, in the vicinity of Broad Street, where the ICC was to be located, the process of decline had been very severe for many years, the Inner City Partnership Area losing 11 000 manufacturing and construction jobs between 1971 and 1981, the remainder of the city losing only 8000 over the same period (Franks, 1983).

9.3 CITY POLICY

In 1980 the City set up an Economic Development Committee (Loftman and Nevin, 1992). The priorities were to create new opportunities for the people of Birmingham, and it was the City Council that took the initiative and developed the ICC. This was in contrast to the private sector development approach of central government, which encouraged public involvement in either a facilitative or partnership role. The City developed this flagship. There is a certain irony that it was national decline in manufacturing and its effects upon employment levels in the Midlands, rather than the longer term decline within the inner city, that prompted the City to act.

The City already had experience with the creation of a major exhibition centre, the National Exhibition Centre (NEC), on the eastern fringes of the city adjacent to the international airport. Opening in 1976, it proved successful both in terms of making a profit and in job creation through construction and operation (Franks, 1983). However, it would not create large-scale employment for those in the centre of the town, nor was it encouraging visitors to spend or invest in Birmingham or contributing to any change in image of Birmingham for the people of the city or for visitors.

This early perception of the NEC's success was justified by a study undertaken at the turn of the decade by Peat Marwick McLintock for the City. It showed that over 100 exhibitions and 120 concert nights, plus other events, each year had created a throughput of four million visitors annually, generated £200m expenditure in the West Midlands, supported 11 000 full-time equivalent jobs, was producing an annual turnover of £54m, creating a surplus of £17.4m and had contributed £3.4m to the City's General Rate Fund (Franks, 1983). The NEC was attracting around 33% of the UK's exhibition spending (Economic Development Unit, undated) and, as a result, had given the City confidence and set a precedent. The issue was whether this could be repeated in another form.

9.4 THE PARTIES

The public sector had the will to take the lead in the early 1980s and according to the Conservative Councillor, Bernard Zissman, they were the only ones who could: 'In bad times the only people who can afford to look

forward are central government and local government'. His own perceptions had changed when he was among some young unemployed school
leavers who told him they would never be given the opportunity to work.
His response was: 'We've got to do something to give these people hope
. . . . We've got to create an industry that depends on people'.[19]

This perception was to be shared by a broad alliance of members and
officers and between Conservative and Labour members. This led to urban
governance that was remarkably different from the ascendant views of the
time. On the one hand, central government was reducing local government
expenditure and trying to reduce its long-term involvement in service
delivery and provisions. On the other hand, leftist local authorities were
trying to 'go it alone' through 'local socialism'. Although the nature of
politics has ensured that history is being rewritten in Birmingham and that
everyone remotely involved with the ICC is trying to claim credit over and
above their just deserts, the importance of the 'teamwork' cannot be
underestimated because the continuity in commitment to the project,
regardless of who was in local power or leading the officers, was essential
to the raising of the finance and implementation. This arose out of the
see-saw of political control during the 1970s, which eroded predetermined
ideological stances (Loftman and Nevin, 1992; Robson, 1988). It was
reinforced by a shared wish to avoid central government imposing urban
policy initiatives on the city, yet a willingness to take on board close
working relationships with the private sector, especially for development
initiatives (Birmingham City Council, 1991a; Carley, 1991; DiGaetano and
Klemanski, 1992; Jones, 1990).

This continuity ensured project success in the formulation and implementation, at least in terms of the aims and objectives of the initiator,
that is the City Council. The main purpose is to contrast what was happening within Birmingham with events elsewhere, which made this project
possible in a way that would not have been possible elsewhere. Indeed,
other authorities have endeavoured to commission conference and concert
facilities and most have failed to deliver to date, for example Manchester,
Bristol and Newcastle. The precise reasons vary in each location.
However, any project of this type and scale requires a shared commitment
and vision, which the City achieved.

As for success, many within the City believe that the project is already a
success. Others would wish to reserve judgement until the utilization and
cost implications can be judged over a longer time span. Most observers
have praised the initiative, although a number of people have been critical
of the architecture. One commentator has praised the City as follows:

> The transformation in barely a few years of Birmingham's image
> from cultural wasteland to England's most dynamic concentration of
> cultural activity outside London is a remarkable story of local-

authority commitment and imagination. The achievements have put the city on the international stage' (Lister, 1991, p.54)

It was the ICC that started the repositioning of the city, not only in the arts and convention markets, but as a destination and location in its own right. The cost of the ICC was always going to be substantial – the final costs exceeded £180m – and had to be sufficient to recreate hope, create enthusiasm and provide opportunities. Building upon the success on the NEC, by developing a convention centre in the centre of the town, Bernard Zissman summarized the approach as:

for centuries the sales men of Birmingham went to the four corners of the earth to sell their product; . . . now what we are doing is to bring people to Birmingham.' (see note 19)

The notion was to use industrial wasteland close to the city core to create a project that would change the economy and so regenerate the area in the process. John Vergette, chair of architects Percy Thomas Partnership (PTP), described the idea as 'taking the City from tin bashing to business tourism'.[20]

The significance of a project of this scale, initiated by a local authority, and implemented through urban governance, is that the traditional competitive politics of the locale and the frequent oppositional role to central government was shelved in favour of trying to be more competitive in relation to other locations. In other words, not only was the scale of the project large, but the vision for the city was international. This takes the analysis on to the next stage, which concerns market position.

9.5 MARKET POSITION

The market position for the ICC is that of an **F-type** project (see Figures 4.1 and 5.8), that is, delivering a strong service and being international in orientation. However, it is more than that, for the aim of a flagship development is to draw in additional consumption and investment. The type of consumption the ICC would directly draw would be through international delegates, and investment would be international too, if not in origin, then in outlook and markets. Luqman Khan, Property Information Officer in the City's Economic Development Unit commented, 'We are trying to promote ourselves as an international city'.[21]

The role of the ICC was to provide the best purpose-built convention centre in Europe and one of the best concert halls in the world (Franks, 1983). In so doing, it would not only attract business tourism to the city, but also act as the basis for changing the outlook of people concerning Birmingham. This image making would be addressed to both the local population and those across the country.

In achieving the service–international market position in broad terms, the following market segments for the ICC were identified:

- international association market
- national association market
- international corporate market
- national corporate market.

The market was seen as a volatile one, but one that would have an underlying growth rate of 2.5% per annum, allowing for recessive conditions. The main target growth areas were identified as industry, technology, medicine and natural sciences. Birmingham was perceived as a good location, for the UK share of the convention market had been growing, rising from 9% to 11% between 1980 and 1983. The main competition in the UK was the Barbican in London, Bournemouth, the Winter Gardens in Blackpool, the Brighton Centre, St David's Hall in Cardiff, Harrogate, the Royal Centre in Nottingham and the Wembley Conference Centre in London, but each had at least one major deficiency in the convention market. The NEC would not be competition, concentrating on large-scale exhibitions, shows and concerts (Franks, 1983; see also note 20).

The perception of demand for conventions was supported by two other factors. The first was that the City's experience of the recession gave rise to the perception that its economy needed to move away from a production base towards communications as society moved to become information-based. Secondly, the facilities would be far more flexible and user friendly than in any previous venue. A series of venues or halls would be incorporated within the ICC, including the Symphony Hall, which could have a dual purpose to meet a wide range of convention sizes and needs. This would help the marketing of the centre and provide the competitive edge to capture market share (Franks, 1983).

The international association market is small although the events are large, and significant in prestige, attracting the largest spend per delegate. Their size can be around 2000–3000 delegates for each event and they require substantial promotion. Favoured venues tend to be pleasant environments – what are known as 'incentive destinations' – a perception that Birmingham had not enjoyed. The UK had around 500 each year, most of which were London-based. It was found that half of all international conferences were held in Europe because most organizations have their headquarters in Europe. Although the USA was the most popular venue overall, France and Britain came next and the following seven most popular venues were also European (Franks, 1983).

The national association and corporate market had an estimated value of £600m, of which around 15% was from national associations' conventions seeking UK venues. The overseas delegate spend is estimated to have been

2.3 times larger that the British delegate spend and 2.5 times more than that of the international tourist (Franks, 1983). Therefore, the market would attract considerable consumption into Birmingham and the surrounding region.

The market was not growing overall at the beginning of the 1980s. Smaller conventions of around 500 delegates were growing quickly, and there was some blurring at the upper end with international conventions. London was again seen as the favoured venue (Franks, 1983).

In summarizing the demand side of the equation, it was clear to the initiators that there was scope to attract existing market share from both mainland Europe and from London.

The supply side was also analysed. The United States had around fifty convention centres, nearly all of which were funded by the city or state authorities. The main market was targeted towards exhibition purposes as well, so most centres had flat floors rather than raked theatre-style facilities. Almost every convention centre is situated in a city centre. The top international venues are set out in Table 9.1.

Table 9.1 International venues, 1982

Rank	Venue	Number of events
1	Paris	266
2	London	242
3	Geneva	147
4	Brussels	118
5	Vienna	90
6=	Copenhagen	70
6=	New York	70
8	Rome	69
9	Tokyo	55
10	Strasburg	52

Source: Franks (1983).

The function of the ICC, therefore, was to spearhead a tourism strategy. There are parallels with Glasgow and its efforts to establish the Scottish Exhibition and Conference Centre and with Bradford's National Museum of Photography (Bianchini, Dawson and Evans, 1990, 1992), although in the case of Birmingham the plans were based upon business tourism and have been far more ambitious. The international orientation, it was hoped, would filter into the local culture, and indeed, the language school is more popular than ever according to one of the key initiating individuals (see note 19).

The outworking of that international orientation continues. It is recognized that Birmingham is a city in transition and that perceptions are confused, sometimes inaccurate:

Therefore a Strategic Plan is being prepared to provide the direction for the effective positioning, marketing, and image building of the City towards the year 2000. (Birmingham City Council, undated)

Thus, the market position has been established and the subsequent evolution of related policy has been to refine and reinforce that overall market position for the city, which has taken its cue from the ICC.

9.6 POLICY FORMULATION

The analysis now turns to the policy for the ICC itself and the immediate surrounds. It has to be remembered that the policy process intricately involves the ICC, the Hyatt Regency Hotel and Brindley Place, which incorporates the NIA, and these comprise the other Birmingham case studies in Chapters 10 and 11. The analysis in part anticipates those chapters where analytical flesh is needed to be put on some of the bones of this chapter. This makes it possible to capture their significance as neighbouring flagships for reinforcing the process of urban regeneration of the area.

The overall goal has been summarized as being the creation of 'A city with the confidence and vision to re-invent itself and meet the future face-to-face' (Spectrum Communications, 1991). The same City source of publicity states:

> The impact of the ICC is much wider than this, for the conference delegate or tourist does not visit a city only to sit in a meeting. They need good transport, shops and places of entertainment, somewhere to eat and something to see. In fact they want what the people of Birmingham want as well! (p.115)

The vision for the ICC goes far beyond the boundaries of the Broad Street area of Birmingham's inner city, across the whole city, spilling into the regional tourist markets of Stratford-upon-Avon, Warwick Castle and other popular destinations. It covers more than business tourism, general leisure and entertainment to include corporate investment, local consumption and the perception of the city among the local population. The vision for the initiators focuses upon Birmingham as a dynamic city in the market position of service provision with an international orientation (see Figure 4.1).

The vision began when some members of the council visited Phoenix, Arizona in 1981 and wondered whether a convention centre could be a feasible proposition for Birmingham. Contact was made with convention consultants and organizers, Spectrum Communications (Franks, 1983).[22] Three people from the council were driving the idea, Councillor Bernard Zissman; Chief Executive, Tom Caulcott; and the Treasurer, Paul Sabin (see notes 19, 20 and 22), which conforms to the ideal guidelines that this should be at executive level based upon an external model or idea for the **F-type** service–international flagship project (see Figure 5.8).

The formulation of the policy would be expected to be carried out at the executive level, bringing in other interested parties with senior management backup. That is precisely what happened. For a project of this potential size and vision considerable drive would be needed. Paul Swan, Managing Director of Spectrum Communications said that Tom Caulcott is a 'completely brilliant man, and therefore immensely powerful at knocking down walls', although it was this strength that later led to his demise (see note 22).

The key, yet unusual, interorganizational aspect of the emergent policy was the support the project received across party lines. Spectrum Communications was receiving a number of enquiries at this stage from cities across Britain, but these had neither the drive nor the consensus to take the projects through this first stage and successfully into the implementation phase (see notes 19, 20 and 22). Birmingham City Council had established in April 1982, through its General Purposes Committee, a Working Party to investigate the idea of a convention centre. This was headed by a Project Controller (Franks, 1983). The Working Party, whose membership was to include Spectrum Communications, an NEC management representation and other consultants and organizations, was to remain an important feature throughout.

A number of outline criteria began to be established. It was clear from convention centres elsewhere that a prestige, five-star hotel would be needed alongside the ICC (Franks, 1983). The ICC would have to be located close to the city centre for ease of travel, because the most needed to be made of Birmingham's central position in and nodal point on the transport network of Britain. Another criterion was to encourage spend in the shops and leisure facilities. The City had also been promising the City of Birmingham Symphony Orchestra a new concert hall since 1920, and there appeared to be a possibility to include this (see note 19).

It was clear, even by this stage, that the flagship project was not property-led. Paul Swan of Spectrum Communications commented 'it was a socio-economic concept' and not confined to arts, culture or tourism, for the motto was 'let's look at the service industry' (see note 22).

The next step was to undertake in 1983 a feasibility study in order to establish whether such a centre was possible, and to develop the criteria in greater detail and define some of the sub-goals for the ICC (see Figure 5.8). The feasibility study would therefore perform two roles; it would clarify the policy direction and act as a bridge to the implementation stage of the policy process. There were five components to the study. There was the centre itself, and Spectrum Communications was commissioned to undertake that part of the work. There are three international hotel groups who have the perceived expertise for convention trade, Hyatt, Sheraton and Marriott. Hyatt was asked to contribute their expertise alongside specialist hotel consultants Pannell Kerr Forster. Bovis Construction offered expert advise on development phasing, costs, programme and management, and finally, the consultants, JURUE, were commissioned to undertake an economic impact study (Franks, 1983).

The findings supported the concept of a convention centre. The market was defined at the international end, where delegate numbers are largest, although the turnover would be 'lumpy'. The City later decided in favour of a smaller centre on a number of grounds, cost being the overriding one. There was a steadier market for smaller scale conventions. The implications for hotel provision would be expensive, especially as there would be a funding gap for the five-star proposal. The other issue would prove to be the constraints of the chosen site (Franks, 1983).

The city was able to attract Simon Rattle as conductor for the Symphony Orchestra, subject to the proposed symphony hall being of the highest quality. This hall – one of 11 – would be multipurpose. The standards would be driven by user needs. Therefore, ahead of the appointment of the design team, Spectrum Communications was retained to advise on user needs for the convention facilities, and acoustic consultants, Artec were appointed to advise on the needs of the symphony hall. This was one of the crucial policy decisions in preparation for the implementation stage. A few quotations from the promotion document to commemorate the opening of the ICC are instructive for this complex and fast track development project:

> the involvement of Spectrum Communications was a crucial factor. Spectrums expertise both as conference organizers and as experts in the design and marketing of convention centres was called upon at an early stage. As users, they knew what the conference delegate and its organizer needed for a smooth and successful ride.

> All buildings are unique, but some are more unique than others. Some involve a relatively simple arrangement between client designer and builder. Others invent new rules as they progress.

> It was to be a building that the people of Birmingham were proud of because they were involved in it. It would be a centre for the arts as well as for trade, a place to visit and stroll through, to hold a party or go for coffee: a People's Palace, as well as a Convention Centre. In short it was to be part of the City. (Spectrum Communications, 1991, pp.61, 63 and 66)

The last rather extravagant statement would certainly have been building images beyond the ability to delivery had it been written prior to the completion of the ICC, but it still uses hype for 'selling the city'. However, in order for the ICC to be part of the city, the inner ring road, which acted as a barrier between the city centre and the Broad Street Redevelopment Area, identified in the feasibility study, had to be crossed. Wide bridge links were needed and became part of proposed pedestrian routes across the city. A mass transit system would need to be considered along North American lines and access to shopping, restaurants and entertainments would be necessary. The initial proposal was to incorporate the shopping down a covered mall in the ICC, which would act as the circulation and link between convention halls. This was later scrapped in favour of retail and leisure at the Brindley Place development on the other side of the canal. The canal was to have been opened up as a feature, although site constraints have left it somewhat hidden at the rear of the ICC.

Offices were also considered as a development proposition in the area, so linking the commercial locations of the city centre and Five Ways: 'The convention centre may act as a 'magnet' for private sector development which will bridge this gap and ensure good rental rates; however, the centre may not of itself generate developments new to the City' (Franks, 1983, p.69).

Finally, it was recommended that 1% of the capital cost would be spent upon works of art with the aim of adding quality to the centre and area environment. This cost and the previous issue of rates raise the cost implications of the policy.

Therefore, the second aspect of the policy formulation stage is cost. This has to be seen against the projected spend the ICC would attract within the local economy. The feasibility study estimated a contribution in excess of £27m per annum from 250 000 visitors once operations were fully under way. The direct employment created was thought to be the equivalent of 1330 new full-time posts and 630 indirect posts. Most of this would be located within the area and thus the total additional income for the West Midlands was estimated at £38.6m at 1983 prices.

The essence of costing for a service–international flagship development is to budget in outline and adopt a 'value-driven' approach, whereby additional costs are estimated to yield more than comparable returns concerning the fulfilment of the aims and objectives. It was not envisaged that the ICC would ever be profit-making (see note 20), which contrasts with the NEC. The outline costs are scheduled in Table 9.2.

The land cost included recommendations to use compulsory purchase powers. The proposal was to set up a company to operate the ICC, as had been carried out for the NEC. The income and debt charges were estimated, as set out in Table 9.3.

This produced for the ICC a 49.1% debt charge cover, which compared favourably with convention centres in the USA, which fell in a broad range

Table 9.2 Estimated ICC capital expenditure at 1993 prices

Item	Private sector (£m)	UDG/EC grants (£m)	Total public sector (£m)
Convention centre		51.20	64.00
Car parking		3.08	3.85
Infrastructure			
On site		0.70	1.00
Off site		7.00	10.00
Five-star hotel	30.00	2.50	10.00
Land acquisition within area	3.50		
Non-ICC land		1.65	1.65
Commissioned arts		0.70	0.70
Total	33.50	66.83	91.20

Source: Franks (1983).

Table 9.3 Projected deficit at 1983 and 1992 prices

Year	Income (1983) (£m)	Expenditure 1983 (£m)	Operating deficit 1983 (£m)	Debt 1983 (£m)	Total deficit 1983 (£m)	Total deficit 1992 (£m)
1984–1985			<0.1	0.1	0.1	
1985–1986			<0.1	0.5	0.6	
1986–1987			<0.1	2.0	2.1	
1987–1988			<0.1	5.4	5.5	
1988–1989			<0.1	9.4	9.4	
1989–1990	1.1	3.1	2.0	11.3	13.4	
1990–1991	1.9	4.8	2.8	11.8	14.7	
1991–1992	2.4	5.0	2.5	11.9	14.5	21.2
1992–1993	2.2	4.9	2.7	11.9	14.7	23.3
1993–1994	3.4	5.3	1.9	11.9	13.8	23.0
1994–1995	1.9	4.8	2.8	11.9	14.7	23.3
1995–1996	2.9	5.2	2.2	11.8	14.1	21.9
1996–1997						23.4
1997–1998						22.3

Sources: Franks (1983), Birmingham City Council (1992a).

from 21.8% for Cobo Hall in Detroit to 95.7% in Georgia, with Dallas, Houston, Memphis and St Louis all in the 40%–60% narrower range. The cost projections, therefore, appeared reasonable by international standards. However, the feasibility study projected that the total income brought into the region would exceed £27m and therefore be twice the deficit, inducing a net gain.

The funding strategy for the project was as follows. Around 40% of the proposed budget covered tax deductible items. Some of the additional activities in the ICC were proposed as income generating, particularly retailing. It was also hoped to obtain a grant from the European Regional Development Fund. At the time, Birmingham was not within the geographical coverage, but central government put a submission to the EC recommending its inclusion under Assisted Area status because of the severe experience of recession in the West Midlands. There was some controversy over this initially because the Local Chamber of Commerce feared that a stigma would become attached to the area (see note 19).

The City had presentations from architects to undertake the work – Richard Rogers, a local firm, two firms in consortia and a joint venture between two large practices. The joint venture consisted of Renton Howard Wood Levin (RHWL), which has a track record in both theatres and hotels; and PTP, an international British practice with a local office. Together they formed the Convention Centre Partnership, which was the successful team. While prestige was important it was not to be gained 'at any expense'. Working together as a team and being able to control costs, yet having sufficient backup, were important (see note 19). Their design team had not designed a convention centre before (although it appears that no architects have ever had a repeat order in this market). Paul Swan of Spectrum Communications said, 'I am passionately angry with architects', the reason being that the same mistakes were repeated for every convention centre. Having user consultants working with the design team was instrumental in overcoming this problem, and it has been stated that the ICC has only 'new mistakes' (see note 22).

Marketing is the next aspect of the policy formulation stage and the architects played an important role in this. An initial design was finished by November 1984 in order to complete the package for the EC submission (see note 22). The design concepts for the ICC and the Hyatt gave visual form to the ideas and therefore helped others to catch hold of the idea the initiators had. The brief was given to the architects by David Franks, the Project Controller (see note 20), and was derived from the feasibility study. The image to be projected is summarized in that document:

> It is important – not least from a marketing view – that the convention centre has its own architectural character and identity. However, the scheme should impress not so much by its novelty or boldness but more so by sheer quality and sense of scale, internally as well as externally. (Franks, 1983, p.74)

This statement was an important marketing proposition for the ICC, and will be returned to for the evaluation. The design concept also had a sales role for fund raising. In the wider context of encouraging investment and consumption in the city, the approach to marketing was set out as follows:

> Given the objective of bringing new visitors to Birmingham this centre will be marketed in a way which maximises the economic benefits to the City. This market strategy means that the centre will not operate on a truly commercial basis, which would aim to break even. (Franks, 1983, p.80)

Therefore, the aim in formulating a marketing strategy for the ICC was to 'sell' the city by adding value through expenditure on the ICC. This was in recognition that the city had an image problem that needed to be addressed if the implementation stage was going to be successful:

> Birmingham must be promoted first and foremost as a destination. It is no good, as sometimes happens at the moment, that operators of conference facilities deliberately avoid the word 'Birmingham' in their publicity material. . . . The image problem of Birmingham is one which must be overcome if new investment in business tourism and industry and commerce is to be obtained. (Franks, 1983, p.111)

Marketing was therefore taken seriously as the major factor in creating the benefits that the initiator – the City – wanted for Birmingham. The marketing of the city was strengthened through the creation of the Development and Promotion Unit plus the Birmingham Convention and Visitor Bureau. Here, the City Council was drawing on the experience and expertise gained from operating the NEC. The appointment of a manager and putting in place of the marketing capability had to take place before the design was complete (Franks, 1983). A management structure was put forward and was soon placed under the NEC umbrella, although operating from the site. Spectrum Communications was to develop a marketing role for the centre, their early involvement helping in this. Hence, the beginnings of an intraorganizational promotion package was being developed by the City (cf. Figure 5.8).

In summarizing this section, in order to draw out the main policy features and the management resourcing mobilized by the City, the aims and objectives were clearly defined at all necessary levels – overall goals and outline criteria. The management structure and financial resources were put in place to the degree required for proceeding to the implementation stage. The City Council must be seen as very thorough in what they were doing in adhering to the needs of this demanding flagship project (cf. Figure 5.8). The critical mass for the project and the momentum for the subsequent urban regeneration were present. This was captured in a phrase of Bernard Zissman, a key figure at this stage: 'A lot of things have happened as a result of the **decision** to build it' (see note 19).

9.7 PROJECT IMPLEMENTATION

There was some overlap between the policy formulation and implementation stages; however, implementation did not start in earnest until the EC grant was secured over two years later in January 1986. £37.5m was allocated on an inflation linked clause, so the final amount received was £49.7m (Spectrum Communications, 1991).

The management structure was as follows:

- Client: Birmingham City Council Chief Executive and Leader, and later the NEC/ICC Committee
- End user consultants: Spectrum Communications
- Project control: David Bucknall
- Acoustic consultants: Artec
- Design team: architects – Convention Centre Partnership; engineers – Ove Arup & Partners; quantity surveyors – Silk & Frazier
- Management contractor: Douglas Turner
- Catering consultants: Tricon Food Service Consultants
- Signage consultants: RSCG Conran
- Public Art Commission Agency.

The NEC/ICC Committee, now chaired by a Labour councillor because the Conservative Party had lost local power, took over control of the project. However, continuity was retained in the aims and objectives.

The design of the ICC was to be the crucial aspect during the implementation stage. The aim was to make only 'new mistakes'. The design team had not designed a convention centre before and the construction programme was to be a fast track one. Therefore, the detailed design and the production information would be produced just ahead of need on site in theory – the equivalent of just-in-time production and delivery in manufacturing.

A number of issues arose that would amend the design brief. The pub on the corner of the site, it was decided, had to be retained. The underground railway line ran under the site, so the Symphony Hall had to be sited within the complex in a position that minimized vibration. The retail element, it was decided, should be removed from the centre and would form part of the Brindley Place development. It was also determined that the City should invest in a convention centre that did not tap the largest convention market, but more the middle to upper range. Flexibility would be created by use of some of the halls for smaller events when these were needed for break out groups from plenary sessions in the larger conventions. The changes are noted in Table 9.4.

The design team was led by the Convention Centre Partnership, a joint venture of RHWL and PTP. RHWL had a great deal of theatre and commercial experience, while PTP was both local and large, as well as

Table 9.4 ICC design changes during implementation

	Formulation stage	*Implementation stage*
Hall 1	2800 raked	1500 raked
Hall 2	2100 raked	2000 raked
Hall 3	5000 flat	2970 flat
Hall 4	1400 flat	825 flat
Hall 5	600 raked	300 raked
Hall 6	100 flat	135 flat
Hall 7	600 flat	160 flat
Hall 8	600 flat	300 flat
Hall 9	400 flat	285 flat
Hall 10	400 flat	245 flat
Hall 11	400 flat	345 flat
Total	14 410	9065

Sources: Franks (1983), Convention Centre Partnership (undated), Three's Company Communications (undated).

having considerable experience in the design of large-scale public sector buildings. Although RHWL took the initial lead, the Convention Centre Partnership came to be dominated by PTP with RHWL focusing on the design of the Hyatt Hotel. It was said that problems arising out of the joint venture were offset by 'gains' in cross-checking (see note 22). Certainly, the Convention Centre Partnership played a key role. In selling the scheme for funding purposes they put together the brochure pack for central government and for the EC. This was the basis for the City's bid and there was extensive lobbying to secure the funds, the role of Euro MP John Tomlinson also being very important (Spectrum Communications, 1991).

The designs were geared to user friendliness, made possible through close working with Spectrum Communications, by providing detailed design solutions to common technical problems. It is a highly serviced building. The level of provision is well above that for most convention purposes – necessary for the 'theatre' of product launches, high profile conventions and where extensive simultaneous translation and outside broadcasting are required, for example during the 1992 EC summit. These sorts of services also increase utilization rates because the setting up time is reduced by 20%.

The main 'street', a covered mall originally conceived as a retail mall, is a public thoroughfare. It includes café facilities, information and reception areas and some souvenir shopping. It is designed to be used by delegates, but convention areas are kept separate with linking bridges spanning the mall and connecting all halls. The halls are highly flexible. The Symphony Hall is raked and is also used for conventions. Halls 1 and 5 are also raked. The other halls are flat.

Outside the building, Centenary Square was being moulded and embellished through the per cent for art policy. A number of statues, sculptures and commissioned designs for the hard landscaping were to provide the focus. The most prominent sculpture, 'Forward', is a heroic piece celebrating the working history through the people and form, yet the figures are marching towards the future and symbolically towards the ICC. Sculptures are also included at the entrance to the ICC and inside the building. The policy has endeavoured to make attractive spaces for the business tourist and for the local population. The analysis will return to the architecture and urban design in evaluating the extent of success.

inside + outside

The implementation also included a 30% clause for local labour to be employed in the construction process. The publicity implies that this was targeted at the Ladywood district behind the development area and that the introduction of apprenticeship schemes was successful in delivering new skills and opportunities to that population (Spectrum Communications, 1991). The position is far from clear cut and a number of qualifying points need to be made. Firstly, the local labour content clause in the construction contract was typical of many policies at that time. However, in the Birmingham case this had not been one of the original aims and intentions. It was a device introduced at a later date. Secondly, its implementation was seriously compromised. The management contractors, Douglas Turner, complained during the construction that deadlines were being missed and that costs would rise because the local employment clause was difficult to fulfil (Loftman and Nevin, 1992). The policy was introduced in reaction to rising unemployment and the Handsworth riots of 1985. However, Birmingham had a multi-billion-pound construction programme in progress during the late 1980s, causing prices to rise as a result of the demands on materials and labour. This was in part an effect of the property boom and could in part be seen as an effect of the urban regeneration programme. Finally, the Local Government Act 1988 rendered local labour clauses illegal, so the results of this policy were in fact negligible. Despite these shortcomings, it is estimated that the ICC construction work created over 1000 'man' years of employment for Birmingham-based operatives and orders worth £45m were placed with West Midlands companies (Birmingham City Council, undated).

Central government attention had begun to focus upon the setting up of training and recruitment agencies for providing jobs for those in Birmingham once the ICC and the other flagship developments were open and operating (Department of Employment, 1986; Loftman and Nevin, 1992). There has been considerable criticism of the failure of employment opportunities to reach the most disadvantaged, particularly in the report by Loftman and Nevin (1992). An evaluation of this report will be provided when assessing the impact of the project; however, many of their criticisms are unjust on a number of grounds. While some of the initial aims were to create new employment, it was not an aim that these would necessarily be for the disadvantaged. While Loftman and Nevin do acknowledge this, they state that there was an implicit trickle-down policy in the feasibility study. If this is accepted as true, the policy was not claiming that the trickle would reach down to the most disadvantaged, either through direct employment – as Loftman and Nevin would clearly like to have seen – or through indirect employment, in other words spin off employment, which their report ignores. What the feasibility study did state (Franks, 1983) was that tourism tends to provide more employment for women and minorities and that the Inner City Partnership Area would provide a source of labour.

However, this is not to say that the absence of many local jobs during construction and for operational activities does not create a political problem, which is what Loftman and Nevin are building upon. The political problem is a sensitive one, especially during recession. Yet the main aims and objectives of the ICC were to successfully reposition Birmingham in the urban market-place as a 'world city', which would help to secure economic and employment activity for the future. This will be reconsidered during the policy evaluation.

There is an issue of **governance** as the means for policy implementation. While not every decision, even ones concerning large spend, is put to the electorate, the authority is accountable. In the case of the ICC the authority was broadly accountable, although some specific matters made this process more difficult. Loftman and Nevin (1992) draw attention to initiatives involving the private sector in Birmingham where information was kept private for reasons of confidentiality. This can create suspicion. Furthermore, they claim a number of key financial decisions were made by only a few people, citing a sub-committee of six elected members with delegated power to approve requests to raise and underwrite loan stock for NEC Ltd. Finally, there has been an absence of public involvement until the Highbury Initiatives of 1988 and 1989. This brought together public officials, key private sector parties and international figures, covering a broad range of interests. The first symposium decided upon a strategy to downgrade the inner ring road, develop pedestrianization, communicate the new city image and encourage a series of distinctive city quarters. This process had already started (Convention Centre Partnership, undated) with the building of the £3.5m bridge link across the inner ring road to Centenary Square (*Architects Journal*, 1992). The second symposium endeavoured to accelerate the improvement and sales effort. The criticism was that the participants were exclusive (Loftman and Nevin, 1992), yet this top-down tendency is a feature of projects with an international orientation, unless the population are packaged as a central part of the urban 'product', which in this case they were not.

If social well-being was not a central aim and objective for the project, cost was certainly a major consideration. A large portion of the finance came from the EC, and the financial projections are detailed in Tables 9.2 and 9.3. During implementation costs rose as a result of inflationary tendencies in the economy, fuelled by the property boom affecting construction prices. The City was insulated from the worst of this because the EC grant had been given on an inflation linked basis. The City was financing a proportion of the project. Economic development costs for the City grew from £12.5m in 1980/81 to £67.8m by 1990/91 (Birmingham City Council, 1991b; DiGaetano and Klemanski, 1992), the year the ICC was opened. The total cost had reached at least £171m by 1991/92, according to the City (Loftman and Nevin, 1992) or £180m, according to NEC Group (1992). Additional funding has been raised through NEC Finance Ltd in the form of loan stock (NEC Group, 1992). This did not satisfy the entire capital requirements, and therefore other city services were curtailed, particularly education. The City, it is claimed by the chair of the Education Committee, transferred £51m from education into other areas which would create opportunities for local people. This included capital for the ICC and extensions to the NEC (Leake, 1991). There is a trade-off being made, which is probably more to do with expedient imperatives due to escalating costs, than to calculated risk. The operating deficit for the ICC was £6.8m for 1991/92 (NEC Group, 1992) compared to the projection of £2.5m at 1983 prices (see Table 9.3). The ICC is trading reasonably well, but the costs have proved very difficult to control and the project has proved an expensive one. The research hypothesis challenges the cost side. However, the evaluation will determine whether this is perceived as justifiable for the City. Before this can be carried out, the marketing and sales effort has to be considered for the implementation stage.

The feasibility report envisaged that 212 000 visitors would come to Birmingham as a result of the ICC development. Their spend was estimated at £27m per annum, most of which would be in the local economy, creating 1330 full-time jobs. The total income for the West Midlands was estimated at £38.6m at 1983 prices. The construction phase, it was estimated, would contribute £72.6m and 1933 jobs in 'man' years to the region. In order to achieve these estimates it was proposed that the marketing of the ICC should start as soon as the design team was appointed, because the lead time for the international convention market is 5 years upwards. The Birmingham Convention and Visitor Bureau was seen as a key point of contact between the City and the market. A management function was to be established for the ICC, which would have clear lines of communication with all parties (Franks, 1983). In the event, the management and marketing was developed within the NEC operation, with the ICC becoming a division of NEC Ltd.

Spectrum Communications was appointed by the NEC to promote the Centre and organize the opening. The local population were given priority, guided tours being arranged prior to the official opening, which generated crocodile queues for viewing and created a great deal of positive public opinion for the ICC (see note 20).

The ICC appeared to be attracting inward investment during the construction phase. The Symphony Hall had been designed to a very high quality in order to secure Simon Rattle as conductor for the City of Birmingham Symphony Orchestra. The arts economy has developed in the wake of this. In 1990 Sadler's Wells Royal Ballet relocated from London to the Hippodrome Theatre and was renamed the Birmingham Royal Ballet (Birmingham City Council, undated). The City contributed £4m to provide purpose-built accommodation and £1m over subsequent years to be spent on artistic development. In addition, the D'Oyly Carte moved to the Alexandra. Birmingham has Britain's highest concentration of live theatre outside London's West End (Economic Development Unit, 1992). According to Anthony Sargent, Head of Arts, who moved from London's South Bank Centre, 'It is possible to do things in Birmingham that cannot be done elsewhere thanks to simple, steadfast dedication to make the city a better place' (*Intercity*, 1991, p.37).

These incentives to the arts and development of the arts economy were part of the overall city marketing strategy to encourage tourism and leisure. Councillor Bore stated that the arts is 'a key point in selling the city to potential investors' (*Intercity*, 1991, p.37). A great deal of investment has been attracted from overseas, including the offices of twenty-three banking operations, plus a considerable amount of relocation from British companies. TSB moved its headquarters to Victoria Square in Birmingham, creating 350 jobs in the local labour market and saving TSB £10 million a year. The chief executive of retail banking, Peter Ellwood, stated, 'There seemed little sense in keeping such a large presence in central London where rents are high and the living and working environment has deteriorated' (*Intercity*, 1991, p.38).

How instrumental the ICC was is a moot point. What is clear is that this flagship was the first in a series of projects and initiatives which together have changed the perceptions of investors, whether from the finance or arts sectors. TSB was driven by costs in deciding to relocate. However, the pull to Birmingham was more forceful because of the developments and changes taking place.

Confidence was created in the wake of the ICC. A private sector marketing forum, Birmingham 2000, was created, aimed at making the city a centre for large corporate business, especially in the fast growing financial sector, which was growing at a rate of 30% compared to the national figure of 20% in 1989 (Birmingham City 2000, 1991a). At the other end of the spectrum, small-scale leisure and restaurant businesses were springing up to service the growth in the ICC and related tourist trade. Ronnie Scott opened a new jazz club, choosing Birmingham in preference to Paris.

The international orientation to the marketing strategy was being pursued by the ICC. The city was gaining extensive national and international media coverage. The ICC's audio visual promotion was being shown in key locations around the world as part of a programme to reach business decision makers for incentive travel and conventions (Birmingham City 2000, 1991b). In parallel, the City was raising its profile through the now defunct Birmingham Super Prix motor racing event and the failed bid for the 1992 Olympic Games.

9.8 POLICY AND PROJECT EVALUATION

The ICC had been developed with clear overall aims in mind and the objectives were put into a more detailed form during the feasibility study. In contrast to the Watershed Complex, a small group of people from the City were involved at the policy formulation stage. In line with the requirements for the successful management of a **service–international** project there was an almost total absence of sub-goals (see Figure 5.8). The main aims were to create a new economic base to the other key industries in the region. This excluded the incorporation of the local population into the urban regeneration strategy in a central position. Any trickle-down effect was perceived as a benefit, yet was secondary. It is ironic, although not surprising, that it is on the basis of the 'sub-goals' that the City is facing criticism (see, for example, Loftman and Nevin, 1992) – employment issues are sensitive. There is an element of *déjà vu* in relation to the conditions that first gave rise to the vision for the ICC.

The City was also successful in the implementation stages as far as adopting the appropriate management practices, and developing a steering group structure for the design, construction and cost control of the project. It was on the grounds of cost that the project exhibited weaknesses; however, in other respects the implementation was managed in an admirable fashion for a large-scale fast track project, where the only really substantial delays were in the raising of finance from the EC. The continuity of commitment to the project from all the political parties was a necessary feature, and particularly unusual given the political climate of the time. This surely had a major impact upon the projects successful completion and limiting any further cost increases resulting from political delay.

In terms of the design, the original aim was to produce a building that impressed by its 'sheer quality and sense of scale' (Franks, 1983, p.74). The ICC has come in for a great deal of architectural criticism. It is a very large complex, which does not overwhelm the surrounding environment, yet does have a strong presence, whether the architecture is liked in a subjective sense or not. It is predominantly 'modern' in style with 'postmodern' overtones, following a tradition for public theatres and conference facilities into which it does fit neatly. In terms of quality, most of the criticism has focused upon the visual aspects. However, it is the user friendliness and the incorporation of the services to meet those needs that make it outstanding as a venue. This gives it a competitive edge over any other European venue.

The arts policy was a secondary issue in the early stages, but emerged to take a more prominent position. Indeed, this aspect has received most of the cultural plaudits from the arts community. The architecture and urban design will be returned to in greater detail when the project impact is assessed. However, two points need to be made regarding the aims and objectives. In comparison to some other cities, especially Glasgow, the arts were not acting in a leading role to attract inward investment (Lister, 1991), with the exception of the Symphony Hall. They acted in a support role and were therefore part of the drive to create the appropriate environmental image – they were part of the sales effort for the ICC and the City.

Loftman and Nevin (1992) criticize the estimates of employment creation and delegate numbers in relation to the actual figures, calling them 'wildly optimistic' (p.75). This has yet to be proved, because the ICC was opened in April 1991 and, as with any 'commercial' venture, it takes time to build up trade and keep satisfied clients. It is unjust to compare numbers with the 'average' projections in the start-up period. Only 34% of the average delegate numbers were achieved in 1991/92, but one should remember that this was the first year of operation. The authors also cite the employment creation figure of 319 full- and part-time posts, but this was made in 1990, prior to the opening. Of course, the marketing effort began with the appointment of the design team and the Centre has been successful in attracting a large range of conventions and product launches, many of which are booked a year or more in advance. If there is criticism, then cost is perhaps the soft target. This must be assessed because the contention of the research hypothesis is that flagship developments are an expensive way in which to achieve urban regeneration.

It is difficult to make an assessment of the value of the ICC to date, for it is still in its start-up period. This has not prevented critics airing their views. There has been local concern about the impact the ICC has had on the Community Charge and about the sheer cost of the project. It cost £180m in total, and some have claimed that the money would have been better spent elsewhere (see Loftman and Nevin, 1992), arguing their case on the grounds of:

- the local social needs of the disadvantaged;
- the impact on the local economy through expenditure on needs.

Their points about disadvantaged groups are important on two counts. Firstly, they research an issue concerning political legitimacy. The perception of many is that the ICC is an expensive luxury, which is immoral, especially considering its location close to the Ladywood district, which contains a large number of disadvantaged within its population. This is an issue the City is having to address, and is difficult to defend politically. However, it is necessary to address the substance. This raises the second point concerning the social needs of the disadvantaged. A large proportion of the finance for the project, just under £50m, was raised from the EC as a regional grant. Again, two issues arise from this. Firstly, this was finance that was brought into the area from outside and therefore did not come out of 'local pockets'. Secondly, the finance was allocated against this particular type of project and therefore there is little or no opportunity cost argument that can be supported. However, it has also been shown that some of the finance was raised by cutting or restricting other budgets, particularly education. It could be argued that this reduces the opportunities for the local population, whatever opportunities the ICC may bring to those in the current employment market. The only reason in defence of the action is that it was done out of expediency. The costs of the project grew because of:

- delays in securing EC finance;
- the distortion a project of this size has on regional construction markets;
- the boom in the economy and construction markets during the construction phase;
- shortcomings in project cost control.

The causes that demanded the expediency were largely outside the control of the parties involved, except for the project management. However, this is not an easy exercise, as the position for the service–international project shows (see Figure 5.8). Initial budgets can only be drawn up in outline for a project of this size, complexity and time-scale. Many of the costs can only be accurately established just before the packages are put out to tender.

The second main point raised by the work of Loftman and Nevin, cited above, concerns the impact of spend on areas of social need and the impact upon the economy. The spend would indeed increase the rate of consumption of other products and services and could have had a marked effect upon employment, which again increases spend in the local economy. The results have an immediate impact and could be continued given the deficit costs the ICC incurs. Although this is fair comment, it could only be sustained as long as the finance permitted, even large sums of capital finance having limited affects on annual revenue budgets. Such comment does not invalidate expenditure on a convention centre, because it would be unrealistic to expect that it will have its complete impact upon the local economy immediately. The full benefits, and indeed costs, of the ICC have yet to be assessed. That can only take place in a few years time, no matter what political judgements are reached.

What can be said is that the ICC already has been shown to be very expensive and that benefits have also begun to flow. The benefits are threefold:

• creation of a new economic sector for the city;
• inward investment;
• creation of new confidence and pride in the city among local people and business.

Let us first consider the cost aspects in more detail. The operating deficit projections have been revised to figures that range between increases of 66% and nearly 100% of the original expectations (see Table 9.3). This is a large rise, even allowing for inflation. However, NEC Ltd is a profitable private company. Although it is owned by the City, the costs are being defrayed by the profits made from the National Exhibition Centre (NEC Group, 1992), so there is no direct cost to the local population from these rises. The NEC has put forward the following statement for the ICC and NIA:

> The management target is to minimise operating deficits and plan activity levels within agreed levels of financial subvention from the City Council, while maximising the revenue generated for the local economy. (NEC Group, 1992)

However, the passage also makes clear that there is financial aid to the NEC from the City. The precise nature of this is difficult to establish, but it appears to consist entirely of loan stock (NEC Group, 1992), which is guaranteed by the City, although Loftman and Nevin have pointed out that the City discussions on the financial issues are not all in the public domain.

It would appear, though, that the operating costs are not posing a direct financial burden on the local population. The capital costs have been detrimental in terms of the curtailment of other budgets, such as education and £5 on the Community Charge for every individual.

In terms of the benefits, a new sector of business tourism has been developed. In the first year of operation, the ICC secured 160 contracts, of which 55% were for the corporate market, the remainder belonging to the association market. This produced over 96 000 delegate days and the average spend per delegate day was £139, including the hotel cost, and £31 in the rest of the regional economy. Therefore, in its first year of operation turnover exceeded £13.7m (ICC, 1992).

The ICC and other initiatives have helped to attract inward investment into the local economy in office- and arts-based activities. This chapter has already documented these, including some of the additional City expenditure associated with these. However, additional finance has also been attracted. The City of Birmingham Symphony Orchestra attracted £1.2m from the Arts Council; the BBC Symphony Orchestra, Bournemouth

Symphony Orchestra and Royal Liverpool Philharmonic attracted more funding (*Independent*, 1991).

The successes have begun to show, although it is impossible to state categorically whether the benefits will justify the high costs. Perhaps the only way to gauge this is from the marketing and sales efforts for the ICC and city. As was commented in the *Financial Times*:

> The ICC and the NIA have not been in operation long enough for there to have been any marked effect on the local economy. Efforts are being made to market the facilities both in continental Europe and in the US, but, for these to succeed, it seems likely that there will have to be an expansion of direct air links between Birmingham and other European centres and the start of transatlantic flights. (1992b)

This passage raises the need to sell the ICC and that, in order for this to be done effectively, other requirements have to be met, in this case British Airways taking up its option as the first carrier to fly to the US. The ICC is part of a broader strategy, albeit a pivotal part of marketing the city. Therefore, the successful selling of the city can also feed back to create the demand.

The project has been generally well managed, with the possible exception of the cost elements within the control of the parties involved. There were clear aims and objectives from the outset, which were given the necessary detail and resources throughout the policy stages. One of the key figures (see note 19) at the outset had been prompted to create new employment opportunities in the face of recession in the late 1970s and early 1980s – an issue of concern to many. In this case study the circumstances unfolded in a more clear cut way than those cited by Harvey for Baltimore:

> I want to stress that the spectacle was not consciously planned (although some elements within it were thought out in terms of strategies of social control, community reconstruction, and political legitimation in the face of social unrest), but chaotically arrived at in response to the powerful forces that have reshaped urbanization since around 1970. (1991, p.59)

It seems that Birmingham not only observed and learnt from the Baltimore experience, but carried the lessons through in a strategic way. Taking the case study from the specific to the city level, it appears that the facilities themselves have been marketed and sold well in terms of perception and use. The Symphony Hall has had a very high level of utilization. It has been used for recordings and has given the arts a major profile in Birmingham. Jan Smaczny, an art critic and lecturer, wrote:

> The first few months of the Symphony Halls existence as Birmingham's major concert venue have fulfilled all expectations and more.

As with all most worthwhile gifts, Symphony Hall continues to reveal new and surprising benefits not the least of which is the challenge of the three-way relationship between acoustic, performer and audience. The superb ambience of the hall, with all its exciting potential, both demands and rewards the highest standards from performers. (Symphony Hall, 1991, p.2)

Such acclaims become part of the sales efforts. However, the Hall has been widely praised, as have the other facilities. Paul Swan of Spectrum Communications said it was his 'favourite venue in Europe' (see note 22) and Volkswagen–Audi used Hall 3 for the launch of their new ranges, David Westbrooke, their group marketing services manager commenting:

What we have done at the ICC has changed our ideas of how future car launches should be staged. . . . The ICC is custom-made for this kind of event. We couldn't have put on this show anywhere else in this country and there is no other way we could have attracted so many people (*Communiqué*, 1991a, p.1)

This demonstrates that the ICC achieved its goal of being user friendly and that it is beginning to pick up business, and hence market share, as a result. The management are pleased with the level of business, stating that it is 'unprecedented' for a new large-scale centre (NEC Group, 1992). It also hosted the 1992 EC October summit, which involved the EC dele-gates, their support staff and 2000 media representatives (*Financial Times*, 1992c).

The feasibility study (Franks, 1983) anticipated 212 000 people per annum visiting the city as a result of the ICC. This estimate has been revised upwards to 500 000 (Birmingham City Council, undated) and the centre certainly had over 500 000 members of the public visiting in the first year (ICC, 1992), but many of these people were from the city. It has been estimated recently that the ICC will create 2000 jobs in the city (Birm-ingham City Council, undated), which is broadly in line with the feasibility study (Franks, 1983).

Birmingham is a major tourist destination. Over 550 000 overseas visit-ors come to the city and it is claimed to be second only to London as a destination for overseas visitors. Annual spend is around £300m, which produces an average spend of over £500 per head. Clearly the ICC has helped to lift the city and region as a tourist destination, while the Symphony Hall has raised the profile of the city as a centre for the arts. Indeed, Birmingham was chosen by the Arts Council as the location to launch their UK's 'Cities of Culture Programme' in 1992 (Birmingham City Council, undated) and the three large-scale festivals covering jazz, film and television, and literature have national standing (Lister, 1991).

The ICC has been generally very well received by the public. Despite complaints about the cost and the 'benefits' to the local residents, many have visited the centre and take their own visitors to see it as well. It is something that the population feel proud about. It has boosted civic pride. One anecdote illustrates the point. A Partner of ICC architects, PTP, came to Birmingham from the London office. On taking a taxi at the station, the driver insisted on driving him past the ICC and telling him all about it.

A massive hotel development programme arose in Birmingham during the 1980s. National hotel development was common during the decade, yet a great deal of local expansion was stimulated by the expectation of growth in business tourism. The Hyatt Hotel, adjacent to the ICC, is the subject of the next flagship case study and was conceived as part of the regeneration programme. The Swallow Hotel, Copthorne and Novotel all benefit from the ICC trade and are part of the inward investment resulting from this flagship development. A total of 35 000 hotel beds are provided in or within reach of the city centre (Three's Company Communications, undated).

It was not anticipated that the ICC would produce new retail develop-ments (Franks, 1983). However, there has been a perceived need among the City to cater more extensively for tourists through the provision of restaurants and leisure facilities, with improved retail environments to be achieved at a later date (see note 19). According to Bernard Zissman, one of the initiating individuals, 'a lot has been achieved [and] we have convinced our own people that Birmingham is an exciting place'. He is convinced that the ICC was influential in attracting major inward invest-ment in the arts and in hotels, in addition to TSB, Price Waterhouse, Peat Marwick and others. This is difficult to substantiate because it cannot be said whether they would have come without the ICC. What is known is how the Economic Development Unit tends to operate. Usually the first step in courting a potential inward investor is to provide the *City Profile*, the 'glossies' and supporting documents. The second stage will involve responding to specific questions and issues. The third stage usually con-cerns helping with location and property searches, especially for overseas relocators. This will involve client visits to potential locations. The final stage will involve a tour of the city. At this stage the decision to chose Birmingham will have been made in principle, probably with a specific site in mind. The tour of the city and surrounding environment will have more to do with selling the location to relocating staff (see note 21). At this point the ICC is certainly important. This would tend to suggest that the ICC is not very influential but has an important support role. However, this process omits the extent to which the ICC has lifted the profile of the city nationally and internationally, enabling it to get on the location agenda in the first place. This is significant, but impossible to quantify.

It has had a positive impact on property prices outside the inner ring road (Sparks, 1991; *Architects Journal*, 1992) and, together with the

Heartlands regeneration initiative, is stimulating demands for the upgrade of New Street Station and possibly new stations, including proposals for a station for the ICC and NIA (*Intercity*, 1991).

Overall, the marketing for the ICC and its role in marketing the city has been successful, particularly given recent recessive conditions. It would be incorrect to say that the City had had a single and coherent marketing strategy; however, as this and other projects were implemented the sales effort has unfolded in a way that has strategic coherence. Certainly, the City perceives it as a success and current strategy undoubtedly has its roots in the formulation of this flagship project:

> the City Council pursued a strategy for regenerating Birmingham which has involved attracting private investment into the City, which has led to a change into that of a major European City. It has resulted for example in the development of the International Convention Centre, the Hyatt Hotel and the Birmingham Indoor Arena as the focal points of inner city regeneration in the western part of the City Centre. (Birmingham City Council, 1991a)

> Entertainment, culture, leisure and recreation have an increasingly valuable role to play throughout the City Centre. . . . Indeed such uses represent the very essence of a large scale International Centre. (Birmingham City Council, 1992b, pp.6–7)

The City sees Birmingham as an international city, second only to London, because it is trying to secure its economic future with a global outlook and endeavouring to regenerate its urban areas through that process (Birmingham City Council, 1992b). That strategy is a long-term one, and one that is rendered longer by recessive economic conditions. However, the evidence suggests that the sales and marketing efforts have begun to have a positive effect. To date it appears that the exercise has been an expensive one. After the initial boost to civic pride and with the onset of harsh economic conditions, the main 'sales effort' is to address the disquiet over the cost of the facility. Justifying an apparently luxurious item in recession is not easy, especially given its scale and the longer term strategy it implies. It is made more difficult for local people to comprehend when critics focus on local issues, despite the orientation being inter-national. Parochialism can and does break out. Yet the evidence and analysis of this research must conclude that the ICC has indeed had some considerable successes in:

- regenerating the site;
- acting as a starting point for further regeneration via flagship developments;
- boosting civic pride;

- attracting inward investments, particularly in hotel, arts- and office-based activities;
- changing the market position of the city, via its own promotion, to a **service–international** location.

Thus, the city image has been changed and is underpinned by activities. The image is being delivered to its market-place. It may involve some spectacle (cf. Harvey, 1991) but the marketing of the city of Birmingham is not hype. It is too early to say whether the momentum can be sustained in harsh trading conditions, and a great deal will depend on the length and depth of the recession. It is also too early to say whether the project has been too expensive as a means of urban regeneration and city repositioning. It is clear that it has been expensive, but this must be weighed against the long-term benefits. Should the project fail in this respect, the marketing and management approach to the project has been successfully implemented and therefore few criticisms can be made about this. Cost is probably the only area of 'failure'; however, the circumstances were diverse and have been shown to be largely outside the control of the project initiators.

One of the other reasons that a service–international project is likely to invoke criticism is because of the top-down policy process. The local population tend to feel excluded and trickle-down benefits to the most disadvantaged, while being encouraged, were secondary considerations. The dilemma is that if local people are to receive the maximum benefit, then they become part of the 'selling' process, in other words, a commodity in their own living environment over which they are unlikely to have either choice or control.

Having evaluated the marketing efforts, its is now appropriate to look in greater detail at the impact the ICC has had upon the city.

9.9 PROJECT IMPACT

The analysis will begin with comment upon the urban design and the impact on the built form. It has been said that the arts should involve a relationship with the everyday lives of citizens living and working in the city. This is the test for a civilized society (Birmingham City Council, 1990a). What, then, should be made of the design of the ICC and of Centenary Square, the focus of the per cent arts policy? Art has been used as a means to create a 'sense of place', a 'sense of community', invoking some idealized notion of a 'golden era', which always just seems to have passed (Williams, 1975; Harvey, 1989a). This can be expressed through the pastiche architecture from previous eras of some postmodern architects. It can be invoked by the activities whereby the urban form becomes the stage set for experience and living, in which an ephemeral moment of community is created or a more prolonged impression which is just beyond reach. A pop concert in the open air or the cafés along the French boulevards are examples.

The ICC is predominantly a modern building, which has a strong presence in the urban setting, yet does not dominate Centenary Square in an overpowering way; indeed, from any angle its full mass appears less than it is. The main criticism of the massing is that, together with the Hyatt Hotel and the NIA, it lines up along the canal, creating a new segregating wall between the areas behind and the city centre. This is similar to the criticism Davis (1990) made of Los Angeles, and poses considerable problems. The 'wall' symbolically divides the Ladywood district of the city from the centre, which is itself a division between the advantaged and disadvantaged parts of the city. This is only punctuated by Broad Street, which is rather foreboding and windswept as the pedestrian passes under the link bridge between the Hyatt Hotel and the ICC into Centenary Square, and by the public footpath through the 'street' of the ICC. This covered way is more attractive, yet the entrances to the ICC neither invite nor advertise this public right of way. It will be improved once the new link bridge is built and Brindley Place is developed. However, this raises the second point. The 'wall' will tend to create a property market barrier. Although not as severe as the inner ring road, it is an unnecessary one for speeding up commercial development and maximizing rents. It is hardly the type of urban form advocated by Jacobs (1965) in her criticisms of modernism.

It is Centenary Square that has received greatest acclaim (see for example Fisher, 1991; Lister, 1991), and the ICC that has received greatest criticism. Apart from the points already raised about the ICC design and its setting, it seems that much of the praise and criticism is misplaced. The sculptures and hard landscape design have been given plaudits on two grounds: firstly, the fact that they are there at all, and secondly, for their quality, which could be interpreted as meaning that they are by artists whom the critics and other artists support and admire. The ICC was not designed by one of the guru practices, nor is it highly innovative in aesthetics. It is solid, both in style and in the sense of competence. What all the critics have ignored is the user friendliness of the building, yet this is its most valuable asset. What the commentators have ignored about Centenary Square is that, although the sculptures do break up the square, they fail to create any focus or unity. Indeed their individuality adds to the fragmentation of what still remains a rather bleak space. Sufficient has been achieved from the point of view of on onlooker, but for the user, especially for the pedestrian, it remains rather anodyne. This will improve. The City has begun to create pedestrianized routes across the city, linking all the key sites and landmarks. However, Centenary Square needs the development of Brindley Place to generate more traffic. Yet this will not solve the problem, which is the lack of life and 'sense of place'. This is caused by an absence of visual contact of people at street level around the periphery. The are no views into the office buildings, no cafés or sight of activities to give life to the square and security to people.

The positive aspect of the pedestrianization is that it has linked two distinct property markets (Sparks, 1991; *Architects Journal*, 1992). There are plans to reinforce these links with the Midland Metro line and the improvements have created a perception of proximity between the city centre office market and the Five Ways office area, which is located further down Broad Street. A number of office developments have been undertaken as a result of the initiatives; 33 000 square feet of offices at Five Ways and 100 000 square feet at Tindal Bridge close to the ICC (Quantrill, 1991). A massive impact upon the office and property markets has not been felt. The Brindley Place scheme has yet to get under way and the Birmingham Heartlands private and public sector regeneration initiative, which covers approximately 2500 acres, is in a similar position. Whether 'life' comes into the Square and along the routes remains to be seen. The Square's design has, in the event, turned out to be rather elitist, reinforcing the business tourism image, and not really for the people at all.

The project is having a positive effect upon arts, entertainment, restaurant, pubs and similar functions. The development of the Gas Street Basin into a canal-side pub/restaurant area behind the Hyatt Hotel will be returned to in Chapter 10. Ronnie Scott's jazz club and bar opened in 1991 and the Classic Diners of America chain has announced plans to open Fatboys Seagull (*Leisureweek*, 1992). Therefore, the impact on the culture spans the Symphony Hall and D'Oyly Carte to Ronnie Scott's and themed American diners. However, many of the employment opportunities created in the hotel, leisure arts and restaurant functions are low paid, part-time and predominantly allocated to women. This raises the questions about the impact upon the local population.

The feasibility study (Franks, 1983) recognized that of the estimated 778 full-time equivalent jobs that would be created through service provision to visitors, 66% would be taken by women and many of these would be part-time and self-employed. However, reference has already been made to new local employment created through relocation, for cxample TSB, and a number of highly skilled and well paid jobs in management, exhibition and convention organizing, design and interpreting have also been demanded as a result of the ICC and associated development. The higher paid local jobs increase local spend and therefore have a multiplier affect, the extent of which is not yet known and will not be for some years to come.

The City has been criticized by the Minister for Education on their redirection of resources to capital projects (Arts Business Ltd, 1991). It has also been criticized for the poor level of access local residences have achieved to city centre employment, including the Broad Street area (Loftman and Nevin, 1992). There has been criticism that the new jobs created by urban regeneration have bypassed ethnic minorities to a large extent. Those who received employment, 42% of the 275 jobs at the ICC in September 1991, were in cleaning, catering and security services (Loftman and Nevin, 1992). Indeed, the City has become more concerned about the polarization of incomes and lifestyles during the 1980s (Birmingham City Council, 1989, 1992c). It is clear that the renewed confidence in Birmingham and among decision makers has made the city a relocation destination. The ICC has played an important role in that, although its success in attracting the financial services is no greater than that of some other locations. Birmingham experienced an increase of 14 000 jobs in the sector between 1981 and 1987, which was second only to London, and the percentage growth exceeded that of London in subsequent years (Birmingham City 2000, 1991a). However, Edinburgh, Bristol, Bournemouth, Reading and Southampton were more successful in increasing market share in percentage terms (Champion and Townsend, 1990).

These new jobs would not have been allocated to those in disadvantaged areas, for example the Ladywood district behind the ICC. Between 1986 and 1990 Ladywood moved from being the ninth to the third worst ward in terms of male unemployment, despite the construction boom. In addition, in common with other disadvantaged areas, City investment in housing was among the lowest in British cities.

Although there was an implicit aim to create new employment through the development of the ICC and the belief that this could have a trickle-down effect (Franks, 1983), it was neither the primary aim, nor was it stated that the most disadvantaged would benefit. However, it is clear that any positive trickle-down effect during the 1980s cannot necessarily be ascribed to the ICC and related flagship developments, at least not in any quantifiable way. Lower quality employment in pay and skill has been achieved, but any contribution it has made in disadvantaged households has been limited and has not turned the tide of polarized living. The task of doing this would be massive and it is perhaps naive to expect a project, even one as large as this, to have such an affect. It is also naive to believe that local labour clauses in construction contracts or training packages are going to overcome the effects of being disadvantaged over a long period of time. However, little has been achieved to date and this is a major political issue. It is likely to become a major business issue as well, as relocation decisions will take into account the stability of the local populations if riots and civil disturbances continue.

Opposition did begin in 1988, when the local residents group 'Birmingham for People' was founded (Bianchini, Dawson and Evans, 1990, 1992). To date disaffection has not set in, or there has not been an event that has triggered civil disturbance. The local residences are largely shut away behind the regeneration schemes (cf. Davis, 1990).

The ICC was also envisaged to have a positive impact upon the local environment, such as building refurbishment and the upgrading of areas like the Gas Street Basin (Franks, 1983). Loftman and Nevin in their critique (1992, see pp.150–151) exclude the Broad Street area from their characterization of the inner city. While it is important to acknowledge that the employment opportunities may not have reached those in most need, it is also a sign of the success of the ICC that its immediate environment is no longer perceived as an inner city area in need of regeneration.

However, the environmental improvements have not penetrated into Ladywood. Like the economics of the ICC, there is an environment for the business tourist, which contrasts with the experience of the local population. This is summarized in the City's promotional document:

> Great buildings such as this spread their influence a long way. As you approach the Convention Centre, crossing Paradise Forum and the bridge over the Queensway, it feels as if you are entering a new city . . . . The business world now has a magnificent new conference venue, the first truly purpose built and most modern facilities in the whole of Europe. (Spectrum Communications, 1991, p.89)

The ICC and Centenary Square are not expressions of corporate power in the way that the Lloyds Building piazza in Bristol Docks is (see Chapter 8), nor is it classless space, albeit geared to consumption, as the Watershed is. It is for the 'business class' and the 'art establishment' rather than for the local population. The hard landscaping of Tess Jaray is attractive, the heroic sculptures of Raymond Mason and the others have the net affect of aestheticizing the space, even though this was not their individual intentions. Lister (1991) reports one local comment:

> Everyone is screaming about the quality of the international work, but a quarter of a mile from the convention centre are run-down areas like Ladywood Springhill, where there is really no provision. Here in Highgate a lot of people get mugged; the lifts don't work in the high rise flats, and when you talk to local people about the arts they don't want to know. They look at the millions spent on the convention centre and they say they would prefer to have the lifts working. (pp.57–58)

This is not just an issue of finance; it is an issue of management. The management of the market position and implementation of the ICC was nearly exemplary. It was a sort of corporate 'single mindedness' that brought it to fruition. The process had more in common with corporate management than democratic accountability, except in its most top-down form. The Birmingham approach verges upon **governance**, given the secrecy over some of the financial matters *vis-à-vis* loan stock and NEC Ltd set up as a private company. While there is nothing intrinsically wrong with this, it is only sustainable while governance is serving the population and other interests in a way that has political legitimacy. This is a difficult notion to pin down, but most people are aware when it is abused, usually in favour of power and wealth. Drucker (1986) makes an interesting point concerning the 'institutions of the new pluralism', which have no purpose except outside of themselves, in the context of corporate management. The purpose may be satisfying the customer or the constituency. He states:

> they need a considerable amount of power over people, and coercive power at that . . . to bestow or to withhold social recognition and economic rewards. . . . The individual is thus, of necessity, subjected to power grounded in the value system of whatever specific social purpose the institution has been created to satisfy.
>
> And the organ through which this power is exercised in the institution is the organ we call *management*.
>
> This is quite new and quite unprecedented. We have neither political nor social theory for it yet.
>
> This new pluralism immediately raises the question, Who takes care of the commonweal when society is organized in individual power centers, each concerned with a specific goal rather than with the common good? (pp.175–176)

In this case the goal was to resposition the city in the world market-place. This management question was resolved by directly excluding the population from the prime aims and objectives. The constituency for power becomes the customer – inward investor and consumer – rather than the local population. In turn, they begin to feel ignored and resent it. They experience **governance**, which may benefit them in the longer term, but does not seem to be serving them in the short term. The immediate lesson for the City is to address the local populations needs, especially those of the most disadvantaged. This is necessary to retain stability and therefore to sustain the momentum of the marketing effort for the city. It is also necessary on social grounds.

The second lesson is that the City, or any other administration for that matter, could have incorporated the local constituency into the aims and objectives. In other words, the marketing of the city is for the benefit of the population. The one serves the other. However, this is a two-edged sword, for incorporation means that the population become part of the 'product' of the city. As Drucker points out, the institution needs to use coercive powers to deliver the goods, so while the population are being served, they are simultaneously being coerced.

It is the **successes** of the ICC to date and the marketing of the city of Birmingham that raise these dilemmas. If cities are to be marketed, they must be managed. The logical long-term outcome, if the business analogy is used, is that just as an employee is subject to the employer's contract, so the resident is subject to the city management. On the other hand, if the population is excluded, management of flagships, other initiatives and marketing the city will be top-down and the benefits will rely on a trickle-down process which will be subject to a plethora of decisions outside the control of the authorities and the population.

9.10 SUMMARY

The marketing and management aims have clearly evolved throughout the project and policy process. The project has had a pivotal role in revitalizing:

- the area
- confidence among the majority of the population
- confidence amongst inward investors, especially arts- and office-based activities.

The city has been repositioned in the **service–international** market. The main criticisms that have been levelled against the project have been to do with the benefits to the most disadvantaged in the local population. However, it has been shown that this was not a primary aim. The other criticisms concerning the level of expenditure cannot be upheld at this stage. If there is any criticism of the project management it was the inability to restrain costs, although some of the factors were outside the project team's control. It is too early to say whether the project has been too expensive. However, the trading levels at the ICC and the early successes of the marketing for the city suggest it may well prove to have been justifiable, even in recessive conditions.

What has been less satisfactory is the low level of financial commitment to social programmes. These include earlier training and job placements for newly created employment and, more fundamentally, the absence of investment in housing and the transference of money from education budgets. Much of this is the result of cost overruns and the product of expediency. In order to redress the social balance, as well as for the image of the city, these areas should surely become a priority.

The success of the project in marketing, and therefore management, has raised fundamental issues about the role of local government, particularly the trend towards governance and the absence of accountability which comes in its wake. This in turn raised the issue as to whether the population can more effectively benefit by being incorporated into the sales process, hence becoming a 'product' themselves. This will be a fundamental issue in any consideration of the sort of cities we wish to see in the future.

The Hyatt Regency Hotel | 10

10.1 INTRODUCTION

The Hyatt Hotel is located in Birmingham across Broad Street from the International Convention Centre (ICC). The history of the area and a great deal of the background have already been covered in the first sections of the previous chapter. The origins of the Hyatt are very closely bound up with the ICC and in some senses the two should be seen as an integral package. An international convention centre needs a five-star hotel and this hotel, with Hyatt as operators, would not have been built without the ICC. The idea for a hotel was developed in the feasibility study for the ICC (Franks, 1983).

The Hyatt and the ICC share their origins and the hotel is dependent upon the ICC to a large extent. Yet there are conceptual differences, which do make the Hyatt a flagship development in its own right. The major difference is that the hotel has been developed as a partnership, each of the three parties retaining equity in the development. The partners are Birmingham City Council, Hyatt and Trafalgar House. The design and use are different too.

Hyatt is an international chain of luxury hotel operators based in the United States, which has a perceived reputation and expertise in running hotels associated with convention facilities. Trafalgar House has its origins in property development, but over the years through diversification and takeovers has become a conglomerate in property, construction, hotels, shipping, steel fabrication and process engineering.

The hotel, as developed, contains 319 rooms, including 12 suites, and has a club, restaurants, bars, ballroom, swimming pool, gym and health club. It is linked on the Broad Street side to the ICC by a covered bridge and behind it is the Gas Street Basin. This is a canal-side area that had become run down, and the Hyatt development has included the development of bars in the Basin, which has been separately branded as the 'Glassworks', so that it will appeal to a mainstream pub-going clientele.

10.2 MARKET POSITION

The Hyatt development is a consumption-based scheme, the primary function being to cater for the business tourist. It is therefore geared to providing a service and the operation is looking to the national and international markets to achieve the utilization and room rates. It is therefore an **F-type** project (see Figures 4.1 and 5.8). Its client base includes both delegates of the ICC and those who come to the city as part of the inward investment in business and arts. The Hyatt is predominantly occupying the **service–international** market position. The exception to this is the Glassworks, which has separate premises within the development as well as its own brand name. There is some spillover between the users of the ICC and Hyatt. It is certainly aimed at tourists in general as well as the local population who live and work in the city. In order to keep the tourist trade, its orientation needs to be national. Because of this outlook the management welcomes competition from other pubs and restaurants in the Basin,[23] as this will give the appearance of a lively place in which it is worth spending time, people first choosing the location, then the venue. However, the culture is a routinized one. The market position of the Glassworks is **routinized–national** (see Figures 4.1 and 5.4).

10.3 POLICY FORMULATION

The City came to an early conclusion that a successful convention centre would require a high quality hotel alongside (see note 19). This was borne out by the feasibility study, which advocated a 500-bed luxury hotel, costing in the region of £40m at 1983 prices. The conclusion was reached for the following reasons (Franks, 1983):

- British conference facilities that lacked adjacent or integrated prestige hotel facilities suffered as a result;
- European and North American convention facilities without a prestige hotel failed to reach their full potential.

It was realized that a hotel operator with convention centre experience could have an important input to the study (see note 19). Although the experience is clearly useful, there is nothing exceptionally difficult in servicing the convention market compared to any other five-star service for business and tourism. The other main motivation was that having an American operator would lend credibility to the ICC in the formulation stages, particularly for raising finance, and in the marketing of the ICC in the North American market. It would also help to reinforce the **service–international** market position for the ICC and for the marketing of the city of Birmingham.

Hyatt, Sheraton and Marriott were seen as the main contenders in the convention centre market, and Hyatt was asked to contribute to the feasibility study, receiving first option to become operator should the scheme proceed.

The original concept for the hotel was a glass pyramid (see note 20), and at that stage the parties involved were the City, Hyatt and Tarmac as developer–contractor. The design was created around the specification established by Hyatt in the feasibility study (Franks, 1983):

- 500 bedrooms
- two restaurants: one premier, one café-style
- quality nightclub
- ballroom with a capacity for 600 and banqueting style seating, and divisible into three units
- six small conference rooms
- business centre, comprising six offices with shared office service support
- fitness centre
- medical suite
- specialist shop units
- casino
- foyer, reception and bar areas
- back of house facilities.

Britain had a shortage of five-star hotels outside London and the hotel market offered traditional facilities under three- and four-star ratings. This project would be the first five-star hotel and would act as a flagship development, both to the immediate area of regeneration, and to the city hotel market.

The Birmingham hotel market was dominated by mid-week business-related demand, occupancy in the tourist market being very low. This was supplemented by peak demand arising from the NEC around ten weeks of the year, plus conference trade throughout the week, which tended to produce turnover and profit from the catering activities rather than from overnight stays. The occupancy rates were highest during January to May and September to November. The convention market however, was estimated to be strongest in May to June and in September, which would help to keep occupancy rates more consistent through the year. However, conventions tend to be held mid-week. Although incentive travel tends to have a larger spin off, which enhances tourism, the weekend trade would only be substantially increased if the ICC, the urban regeneration and the marketing of the city helped to create a greater long-term independent tourism demand.

It was hoped that the proposals for Brindley Place, the subject of Chapter 11, would generate tourism through the provision of speciality shopping and leisure facilities. There was also discussion about a

Birmingham Theme Park being developed at a later stage (Franks, 1983). This has been shelved as a concept. There was certainly opportunity to develop business tourism on the back of the ICC, especially for corporate conventions, where incentive travel is part of the perks. The Hyatt as the base, coupled with a social programme, can be an important incentive. The type of package can be derived from a number of options, thus making the city a regional tourism base:

- concert at the Symphony Hall
- attending the theatre, opera or other city arts venues
- Ronnie Scott's jazz club
- visit to Stratford-upon-Avon
- visit to Warwick Castle
- golf at the Belfry, a Ryder Cup venue.

Although the ICC was instrumental in creating this potential, it would be the Hyatt that would lend the credibility and necessary substance to the tourism concept. This would be the case, whether incentive travel and mainstream tourist users actually occupied the Hyatt in the main or not, for it would be the role of the Hyatt to act as a flagship in this way.

Hyatt acted as consultants in the feasibility report and were keen to investigate a hotel location in Birmingham for two reasons. Firstly, they wished to increase their presence in Europe, and second, although they have two London hotels they had only two second-city hotels, and this led to the company adding Cologne, Germany and Birmingham at the same time (see note 23).

10.4 PROJECT IMPLEMENTATION

The Hyatt specification was based upon a cost of £80 000 per room, compared to the average room cost of £60 000, which produced a construction and fitting out cost of £40m at 1983 prices for a 500-bed hotel. The final construction costs were just over £30m in a boom market, implying that changes took place between the feasibility study, during implementation and completion. There were two basic changes. The first related to confidence in the size and quality of the hotel market and the second concerned the ability to raise finance for the project. These factors were interrelated. It has been stated that Pannell Kerr Forster, hotel accountants and management consultants, did not believe that the ICC and other hotel demand could sustain a 500-bed hotel with the level of facilities envisaged by Hyatt. If this is the case, the subsequent development of a new Swallow Hotel at Five Ways with a five-star rating must put this into question. However, the feasibility report assumes occupancy rates at 1983 levels and the current recession is placing tremendous strain on occupancy and room rates, which could be used to support the consultants' contention, at least in the medium term.

In addition, cost questions were being raised. The original pyramid design by an architectural joint venture between Percy Thomas Partnership (PTP) and Renton Howard Wood Levin (RHWL), was estimated to be costing an additional £10m over and above the £40m using the Hyatt specification. There would have been advantages to constructing a hotel of striking appearance, lending credibility to the **service–international** market position for the hotel, the ICC and the city. However, public subsidy, the usual source for such an approach, was not forthcoming and indeed the ability to raise finance for the project was being brought into question, not just in terms of size, but at all.

Most hotel companies do not own the hotels, they are merely operators. It is the developer that takes the risk on the property investment. Tarmac was replaced as the private sector developer by Trafalgar House, the company taking 30% equity and securing the construction contract for its contracting subsidiary, Willetts. Hyatt also took 30% equity in the development, which was exceptional for the company, and provided the covenant necessary to raise the remaining finance, because for Hyatt to have a stake gave the perception that there was confidence in the hotel market generally and in the ICC particularly. The remaining finance had to come from the public sector. This was to prove to be the main compromise to the size and design of the scheme. What was originally conceived as a glass pyramid for 500 beds eventually was redesigned by RHWL as a vertical box of reflective glass containing 319 bedrooms at a cost of just over £30m. While a tall box acted like an advertising hoarding, a 'flagpole', across the city, the modern style contrasted with the more postmodern and vernacular approaches to hotel design being undertaken in most other locations.

The finance depended upon securing a central government Urban Development Grant. This proved difficult for government and the Minister for the Department of the Environment. Government felt that it should be letting the private sector take the lead in general and that, in particular, it was not government's role to subsidize luxury five-star hotels. What was not appreciated at this stage was that the operation of this business tourism market was dependent upon a public contribution and that the five-star status was necessary for the credibility and image of the proposals. This can be viewed at a number of levels:

- to ensure the development of the hotel took place;
- to lend credibility to the ICC as a flagship;
- to permit the Hyatt to act as a flagship in the hotel and tourism sectors;
- to help market the city.

In the end an Urban Development Grant was secured for £6m for the project, but the reasons for the grant were presented as being as much to do with job creation for local people as for sustaining a commercial proposition (Committee of Public Accounts, 1990; see also Loftman and Nevin, 1992). In this way an additional set of aims and objectives were imposed upon this flagship through the implementation process.

The City provided the site. It also raised £17m through a loan from the European Investment Bank (Loftman and Nevin, 1992). The exact structuring of the partnership becomes complex at this stage. It is assumed that the City retains just over 30% equity in the development, the balance being held by Trafalgar House and Hyatt. However, the £17m loan was lent to the partnership company, called Hyatt Regency Birmingham, with a second mortgage as security for the loan (Birmingham City Council, 1990b). This gives the impression that the City contributed over £6m in grant form plus £17m as a mortgage, or over 70% of the costs of project (Loftman and Nevin, 1992). This could simply provide the one-third portion of equity in the scheme, the remainder of the money being used to:

- **either** underwrite the hotel operations to eliminate loss or guarantee a certain profit for a period of time;
- **or** subsidize the rent so that the equity partners receive a guaranteed income flow according to the business plan;
- **or** the second mortgage buys outs a large proportion of Hyatt's equity as developer during the mortgage life.

In any case the result is the same from the City's viewpoint, that is to ensure commercial viability and provide more financial certainty for all those involved. This could be perceived as the public sector underwriting the public sector, yet this type of arrangement is quite common in a purely private sector scheme. It is usual that the hotel developer takes almost all the risk and the operator has minimum exposure, quite often being insulated from operating losses, especially in the start-up period. Although in essence no different from rent-free periods in the office market, the terms are usually more onerous and provide one of the reasons why financial institutions are more reserved about funding hotel development projects. In this case the financial institution will have been willing to make a development loan to a local authority because of its covenant.

What is not clear in this case is the share of risk Trafalgar House is taking. If operating losses are being underwritten, then their rental stream may be affected, but if rents are being subsidized, then the company has few risks. The same question also has to be raised concerning Hyatt in regard to its interests as developer rather than operator.

This also raises the question about the second mortgage. If the money has been used as a loan to Hyatt, this reduces their effective stake in the development for the life of the mortgage. If this is the case then it would imply that Hyatt's covenant for raising the finance and confidence in the project was politically charged. In reality it would be less than has been presented to other parties, for should Hyatt withdraw as operator at any time, depending on the legal conditions, the City could be very exposed in terms of risk. However, the act of providing the second mortgage, or indeed the money for the other purposes, removes a substantial amount of the risk and thus the City is increasing the security of the public grant contribution as well as retaining its operator.

The original feasibility study only considered rental guarantee and excluded underwriting operating costs and a second mortgage, although a second mortgage of some type would appear to exist. In concluding the discussion on financing, it would be incorrect to accuse the City of under-pinning the private sector in an exceptional way, because this is what often happens in a purely private sector development. However, it does beg the question as to whether it is appropriate for the public sector to act as the private sector does. At this point the analysis raises similar questions about the 'corporate management' of projects and the urban environment, and hence issues of **governance**, that were raised in the previous chapter concerning the ICC. The lack of financial details precludes some accountability.

Implementing the project had a marketing component. For the City this took two forms. The first was the presence of the hotel in support of the ICC. The Hyatt therefore had a passive role in the selling of the ICC and the marketing of the city which flowed directly from that project. However, the Hyatt had a second and more direct role in marketing the city. This has two elements:

- encouraging other hotel developments and operations in the city centre;
- promoting the city through confidence building for relocation and tourism.

Concerning the first of these, Luqman Khan of the Economic Development Unit commented, 'The City experience is that when large hotel operators are looking at Birmingham, they are looking at confidence among hotel operators' (see note 21).

The Hyatt contributed to confidence in the hotel market, both through the reputation of the operator and because it was the first among a wave of hotel developments in the city during the 1980s. The £11m five-star Swallow Hotel at the other end of Broad Street to the city centre, at Five Ways, has already been mentioned. The Copthorne Hotel, another glass design, is located close to Paradise Forum at the other end of Centenary Square, which is the main public space between the ICC and Hyatt and the city centre. The Wharf is a £2.5m budget hotel under the Beefeater & Travel Inn brand located in Bridge Street. A £9m Novotel, containing 148 bedrooms was built on Broad Street on a plot at the furthest corner from the Brindley Place development, which is the subject of Chapter 12, and thus added to the process of urban regeneration in the Broad Street area.

A number of other schemes were completed throughout the city, and an even larger number of planning applications, plus some schemes remaining in the development pipeline, indicated the extent of competition and growth in the hotel market during the 1980s.

The hotel investment was fuelled by general demand in the economy and the presence of the Hyatt as a flagship development, not just for the hotel market, but also for urban regeneration, as the Novotel demonstrates. This brings the analysis to the stage of project evaluation, both as part of the policy process and for the purposes of this research, to determine whether the project met its aims and objectives.

10.5 POLICY AND PROJECT EVALUATION

The Hyatt opened in July 1990, nine months prior to the opening of the ICC. Trade after one year of the ICC's operations was 80:20 in favour of the convention and exhibition market, which includes some contribution related to the NEC (see note 23). This means that the trade from other business travel and tourism has yet to be fully established because the target split is 65:35 in favour of convention trade. However, non-convention trade depends upon building up a reputation which goes beyond that of the Hyatt brand. Corporate functions and usage were slowly growing and the rates are competitive with those in London and other hotel conference facilities. The manager believes that once this corporate market is established, the tourist business will also grow. Tourism is dependent upon marketing the city and the regional attractions, and the manager believes that 'Birmingham is the best kept secret in the country' (see note 23). The main problem in the interim is the recession and the pressure from other hotels cutting their room rates. The Hyatt has been reluctant to cut its room rate because it is difficult to re-establish a reasonable rate, even after demand picks up. However, it did appear that there was scope to negotiate for each booking (see note 23).

In the first year occupancy was at 35%–40%, but it was claimed to have reached 65% in the second year, which compares well with the expectation of 70% set in the feasibility study for year five, albeit for a 500-bed hotel (Franks, 1983). Hyatt views the development as a success to date, but believes the full potential has yet to be realized:

> [In 1993] we will really start seeing more consistent occupancy, more consistent business levels. That's when we start getting a return on investment. . . . In five years time, when Brindley Place is up and running, everything will all come together. (see note 23)

The only other constraint on the development of trade is seen as the control British Airways have upon international flights to North America at Birmingham International Airport. They have the option over the first route, so while they operate no service, no other airline is able to fly those routes. This is a constraint not only on the Hyatt and the ICC but upon the whole international outlook that the city has adopted.

From the point of view of the operator, the project appears to be a success. Trafalgar House, as a development partner, has been facing a number of corporate problems arising from the recession, including over-exposure to both property development and to hotels as operators (Trafalgar House, 1992). While the exact risks the company faces in terms of the Hyatt are not clear, the involvement is probably one the company would rather not have at present, although its interest is minute compared to other property commitments and at least the building has an occupier.

The City's perception of the scheme is almost indivisible from the ICC. Therefore, as both the Hyatt and the ICC are trading well, the development is working on its own terms. In its flagship role, it has lent credibility to the ICC and the interdependent relationship in marketing the regeneration area has worked in part for inward investment in terms of restaurants and pubs, and other hotels have come into being. It has also contributed to the city strategy for its marketing by encouraging further hotel development and by beginning to serve the business tourism market beyond the needs of the ICC. Overall, it has added to the image of Birmingham as a vital city, second only to London. In other words, it has added to the efforts to reposition the area and city as having **service–international** orientation.

Although the Glassworks is more routinized and national in market position, it too has helped build confidence in the development and refurbishment of the Gas Street Basin and canal-side. The canal will be improved through the Brindley Place development, adding more competition, but generating more pedestrian traffic. The Glassworks therefore complements the **service–international** market position of the other schemes and the area in which it is located.

The one objective that was added during the implementation process was the need to create new local employment opportunities. This objective came with the Urban Development Grant. The project was not set up with this in mind and the absence of this objective initially is reflected in the implementation process. Loftman and Nevin (1992) criticize the hotel management for failing to monitor equal opportunities in their personnel policies. This seems to contradict a further accusation that applicants were asked to submit photos of themselves, which would seem to imply that the monitoring was all too close; as one Councillor said, this could have been used as a means to discriminate against ethnic minorities (see Loftman and Nevin, 1992, p. 109). While this practice does flout the Race Relations Code of Practice, no evidence is provided of the number of ethnic applicants compared with those actually employed in the Hyatt. It was found in

1987 that 17% of all employees in the Birmingham hotel industry were from the ethnic minorities (Commission for Racial Equality, 1991). This is a high proportion, which can be explained by the low pay and frequently poor terms of contract typical of the sector, plus the dominance of female labour. However, for some people, it represents an employment opportunity that they would not otherwise have had. This is not a justification of the terms and conditions, but it is an observation of new employment opportunities, especially as the hotel sector was an area of rapid expansion during the 1980s (see Table 10.1).

Table 10.1 Impact of hotel development within the Broad Street corridor, 1990

Development	Casual employment	Employment	Total employment
Hyatt		248	248
Swallow	36	109	145
Novotel		55	45
Copthorne	50	145	195
Wharf		45	45
Total			688

Source: Birmingham City Council (1990c).

The extent to which the project initiators took on board the objectives subsumed within the grant aid is minimal. The City could have used its financial leverage to renegotiate the terms of the partnership to ensure the implementation of the new goal of creating local employment. This brings the analysis on to the broader impact the development has had.

10.6 PROJECT IMPACT

The employment opportunities created by a successful flagship development in the hotel sector are not going to result in a large number of jobs in terms of skill, pay and conditions. Because of this, there is some evidence that these jobs do reach the most disadvantaged. While the benefits may not be that great, it is worth reiterating the point made by Joan Robinson (1964) that for the most disadvantaged it is better to be exploited than not exploited at all. However, with social investment, particularly training, it is possible to provide better opportunities for the most disadvantaged and this would put pressure on operators to improve working conditions.

The impact of the hotel on the ICC was to reinforce its credibility in the market, thus reinforcing its flagship function. It is an interdependent relationship because the Hyatt was conceived out of the need for the ICC.

The Hyatt has had a positive role as a flagship in attracting further investment in its wake in the Broad Street area and in the hotel sector.

The City at first sight looked as if it was underpinning the risks of the private sector, a criticism levelled at flagship developments and local authorities by others (see for example Barnekov, Boyle and Rich, 1988; Harvey, 1989b; Boyle and Meyer, 1990; Robinson and Shaw, 1991; Squires, 1991; Loftman and Nevin, 1992). Certainly Hyatt were having their operations underpinned by the local authority, yet this appears not to be any different to the way than the private developer does so on a purely private sector scheme. What the City was clearly underpinning was the credibility of the ICC through creating more economic certainty for the hotel. The original feasibility study for the ICC demonstrated that convention centres without a prestige hotel alongside consistently underperform (Franks, 1983). The City was successful in undertaking the project as a partnership development even though the private sector developer–contractor changed in the earlier stages. It is interesting to note that the assertions that the public sector takes the risk away from the private sector or that the public sector threatens the long-term viability of schemes by failing to invest, especially in infrastructure, are crude. In this case a partnership scheme was in support of and closely related to a public sector project. The City was the catalyst in policy terms, so – like the ICC – the Hyatt was not a private-sector-led flagship in the way envisaged within the thrust of central government policy.

10.7 SUMMARY

The success of the Hyatt Hotel development depends upon the trading success of the hotel. This is a commercial flagship, which is modified in three ways:

- the largest segment of the market is from the ICC and NEC, which are publicly owned;
- the funding came in part from central government;
- the funding came in part from private money borrowed by the local authority, which contributed towards the capital cost and adds security to the operation.

However, this last factor is common in commercial practice. All these factors have brought the flagship into being and have to date made it a successful one. Continuing success depends upon:

- the operational success of the ICC in generating business;
- the development of business and mainstream tourism;
- the length and depth of the recession.

The first two factors are dependent upon the effective functioning of both schemes as flagships for the area and marketing the city. Their presence becomes self-reinforcing for the trading success of the Hyatt – a case of success breeds success through the sales process of the city, in which the ICC and Hyatt have played and are playing an important role.

The one area of failure for the scheme is the inability of the initiators to absorb the objective of the Department of the Environment. This was to create employment opportunities, particularly for local disadvantaged people.

The Hyatt also raises two other questions. The first concerns how many flagships can be developed on the back of each other. Two certainly were attainable in this case. This could be put down to the interrelationship between the two projects, but it must also be attributed to a successful partnership and the project policy implementation, for which the City must take a great deal of the credit. The second issue arises from this. Partnership schemes tend to remove local government one step from their electorate because they come to serve two constituencies – their electorate and their partners. In a complex partnership agreement such as the development of the Hyatt, it is difficult to assess how accountable the City becomes to its electorate for the partnership, especially when two factors can promote a degree of secrecy:

- respect for their partners' need for confidentiality, especially on financial matters;
- the City's preparedness to act in a private sector management style, which is top-down and can be secretive.

It would seem that there is a lesson here for authorities. Just as authorities sometimes demand private partners to run an 'open book' where the private sector partner is taking the lead, so a local authority could always run an open book when it is taking the lead and could insist that all partners do in all cases. This would overcome the problems of governance, where direct accountability, for all its imperfections, is seriously diluted.

Brindley Place and the National Indoor Arena

11

11.1 INTRODUCTION

Brindley Place and the National Indoor Arena (NIA) are located in Birmingham on a 26-acre derelict site behind the International Convention Centre (ICC) in the Broad Street area of the city. The history of the area and a great deal of the background have already been covered in the first sections of Chapter 9.

As these two flagship developments follow on from the case studies of the ICC (Chapter 9) and the Hyatt Regency Hotel (Chapter 10), the question, again, is how many flagships is it possible to develop on the back of each other? It has already been shown that the ICC is achieving the aims and objectives of the City, which was the initiator. The Hyatt Hotel development has an interdependent relationship with the ICC and has satisfied most of the objectives to date, although the aim of creating local employment in return for receiving an Urban Development Grant has fallen short. Can further flagship developments be sustained on their terms through the economic momentum of the previous projects, or are there perhaps limits to the number of flagships that can be developed, the former ones rendering later ones less economic?

Addressing these questions requires an analysis of the extent to which flagship policies unblock 'supply side' constraints in the process of urban regeneration, and manage, through marketing strategies and the sales effort, to link with effective and latent demand. These are particularly interesting questions for Brindley Place and the NIA as flagship developments. They are two separate projects which share a common site, and the concept for the development was orchestrated by the City. However, the actual development activity is being led by the private sector – initially a consortium and currently a single company.

The NIA has already been developed, although development has yet to get under way on the remaining commercial part of the site, the design and content for which have gone through a number of changes, starting as a predominantly leisure and speciality shopping scheme with some traditional retail and office uses, before emerging as a concept largely for standard office and retail uses. The sales literature describes it as:

> Birmingham's premier new location for leisure, entertainment and business. Situated adjacent to the new International Convention Centre and the National Indoor Arena, Brindleyplace is just a couple of minute's walk from the new focus of Birmingham, Centenary Square. (Brindleyplace, undated, p.2)

11.2 CITY POLICY

When visiting convention centres, City representatives had become exposed to a number of concepts and processes for urban regeneration, including the Baltimore experience.[24] 'Festival markets' and 'speciality shopping' had become a means of urban regeneration, creating business opportunities for small retailers and providing shopping as a leisure activity for the consumer. Harbor Place in Baltimore was completed in 1980 by the Rouse Corporation, which first pioneered the festival market concept in 1975 at Faneuil Hall in Boston (Kester, 1990).

This became the concept for a large commercial development on the Brindley Place site, which would capture a market from the ICC, Hyatt and related regeneration and would reinforce those developments by becoming a national attraction. Design concepts and indicative masterplans were developed for the City, which included a festival market-place, an aquarium, an indoor arena, hotels, restaurants and canal-side features plus some office uses. Early interest was expressed by Novotel, although they developed a hotel on the top corner of the site facing Broad Street (see Chapter 10) ahead of the rest of the development. In other words, the site was earmarked for a combination of business tourism and mainstream tourism.

The City, as the site owner, planned to put the site up for sale to the bidder that kept within the concept brief and produced the greatest site value. The proceeds would be used for funding the non-profit elements, particularly the indoor arena.

11.3 MARKET POSITION

The original concept, therefore, had a very clear market position. The outlook was national in the business and leisure tourism markets. The niche and specialist markets envisaged for the retailing and leisure also emphasized the quality of service where an analytical approach is needed rather than standard products and services for a mass market. This produces a **service–national** market position according to the marketing matrix (see Figures 4.1 and 5.7). However, this position was to be compromised and split during the implementation stages, because the greater emphasis on multiple retailing and the command functions of routinized office functions introduced a parallel market position of **routinized–national** (see Figure 5.4), which could become the dominant element once the NIA part of the development is excluded. The NIA, which is built and operating, occupies a **service–national** position (see Figures 4.1 and 5.7), but the remainder of the scheme has yet to materialize.

11.4 POLICY FORMULATION

The management of policy formulation did not match the coherence of the policy formulated for the ICC and Hyatt. The ICC was a concept before the city centre location was found. It was inevitable that a project of the size of the ICC would involve urban regeneration on land owned or acquired by the City, but the convention concept drove the policy process. In the case of Brindley Place the policy was more diffuse.

The ICC was the catalyst for the development of business and leisure tourism on the site, thus trying to regenerate an area as a flagship on the back of another flagship. The NIA was originally conceived as part of the strategy to bid for the Olympics and would have been located on the periphery of the city, as is the NEC (see note 19). However, the City did not wish to lose the idea for a major sports facility that would be better than any other venue, including the Wembley Arena, London. To realize the project, private finance would be needed, which could come from land sale and planning gain on Brindley Place. The Arena would also be complementary to the ICC and could be used in conjunction with the ICC for conventions, rallies and exhibition purposes as well as for some concerts. The multistorey car parking facilities could be shared by both the ICC and the NIA. Inclusion of the NIA in Brindley Place was somewhat of an afterthought in terms of the strategic aims and objectives of the project, although chronologically it was part of the scheme from the very early stages.

The policy formulation was thus guided by the City briefing for the site, and the detailed work, which required developers to form their own policies, occurred during the first stages of the tender process, because these policies constituted the bid for the site.

The commercial tender for the site was put out by the City under the condition that the NIA would be provided, in terms of the majority of the finance, and that construction would proceed before other development work took place. The bidders included:

- Merlin International
- Shearwater Laing
- Ladbroke
- One other bidder who dropped out in the early stages.

Merlin International, which was pioneering speciality shopping in Britain, had links with the North American pioneers, the Rouse Corporation. Their architects were Percy Thomas Partnership (PTP), part of the Convention Centre Partnership that designed the ICC and Hyatt. Shearwater Laing was a joint venture between contractors, Laing, and Shearwater, the retail development arm of Rosehaugh. They were seeking to develop a mix of speciality and multiple retailing and leisure facilities. Their architects were Fitch Benoy, specialists in retailing. Ladbroke was contemplating a more traditional retail, hotel and leisure mix. Merlin Shearwater Laing emerged as a consortium bidder at the second stage of tender against Ladbroke, PTP being retained as masterplanners, and Fitch Benoy becoming the retail architects. HOK, the US practice specializing in stadia and arenas, joined the design team for the NIA (see note 20). This consortium was the winning bid.

11.5 NIA IMPLEMENTATION

The cost of the Arena was £51m, of which £23m came from the sale of the remaining 15 acres of the Brindley Place site to Merlin Shearwater Laing. The Sports Council contributed £3m (*Architecture Today*, 1992) and the remainder was financed by the City, through NEC loan stock issue (NEC Group, 1992).

At this stage Laing withdrew from the development consortium because their prime interest was the construction of the NIA. The maximum capacity of the NIA is 13 000 people and it has been designed by HOK Sports Facilities Group to be a flexible sporting facility. There are telescopic seats, temporary seating and mobile raked seating units in order to create all kinds of sporting 'stage'. It is equipped with a demountable six-lane 200-metre athletics track accommodating 8000 spectators. Emphasis has been put upon a quick change around in usage to maximize utilization rates. In fact, the whole emphasis of the design has been geared to turnover, a visit to the NIA being described by the architects as 'car–cola––seat–cola–car' (*Architecture Today*, 1992). There are twelve separate entrances from the concourse to the arena area, each of which has kiosks and toilets located strategically nearby. There are VIP boxes and a suite of function rooms, including a banqueting capacity for 380 people (Three's

Company Communications, undated). Catering will provide an important source of revenue for the NEC, which is managing the NIA on the same basis as the ICC. The NEC is a limited liability company owned by the City and the Birmingham Chamber of Industry and Commerce. There is also provision of a community sports hall for the public, when it is not being used as a warm-up facility by competitors. The construction of the arena incorporated a dedicated multistorey car park, providing 2600 spaces, for NIA and ICC users (NEC Group, 1992).

The quality of the facilities for the participants and for the spectators has not been a paramount concern, however, because the budget for the flagship was limited. The NIA has a great deal of flexibility and advice was provided on fitting out and provision for use as a large convention and exhibition space (see note 22), but the specification is far less demanding than that of the ICC. Herein lies its main weakness in the market place. It has a capacity of 1000 more people than the Sheffield arena (*Construction Weekly*, 1992), but its competitive advantage in the market may be short-lived, depending on the completion and specification of other arenas such as the one proposed for Manchester. However, as the greatest problem for building arenas is raising the finance, the competition may be staved off until another property boom, unless central government were to take a contrary view.

Maintaining the building and the service is contingent upon the operating costs. These are detailed in Table 11.1 which shows that the main financial burden is the servicing of the debt costs.

Table 11.1 Projected total and operating deficit for the NIA

Year	Total deficit (£m)	Operating deficit (£m)
1991–1992	9.8	2.2
1992–1993	11.9	
1993–1994	11.0	
1994–1995	11.0	
1995–1996	10.8	
1996–1997	11.1	
1997–1998	10.9	

Sources: Loftman and Nevin (1992); NEC Group (1992).

However, NEC Ltd has financed all costs out of its surpluses, there being in effect a cross-subsidization from the NEC, which produces an operating profit.

The marketing strategy for the NIA began with the financial support given by the Sports Council. The design was produced in consultation with the Council and with other governing bodies of sport. This gave credibility to the arena and its central location in Britain was easy to capitalize upon.

The City also developed a sports strategy (see note 21) to complement the one for arts in order to further emphasize Birmingham's claim to be the second city in England. The city was awarded the title of 'European City of Sport For All 1990–91' and the NIA opened in 1991 (Birmingham City Council, undated). This created a tripartite thrust – business tourism, arts and sports – in marketing the city.

The city has managed to attract the relocation of the Sports Association and is trying to encourage the financing and development of training and coaching facilities in order to replicate the same level of success as the arts sector has seen. There has been discussion of a national stadium to rival Wembley (see note 19). However, there is still some way to go to match the success in the arts, and the recession makes this more difficult. The NIA has acted in the same way as the ICC, that is to give credibility to the policy and therefore substance to the image.

11.6 NIA EVALUATION

The policy for the NIA was first formulated at the start of the Olympic bid. It could have developed along strategic lines. In the event, as the prospects of securing the Olympics became remote, the policy evolved in an *ad hoc* way. The emphasis moved towards the opportunistic mode of getting the project implemented where the property development market permitted. There were clear advantages to having the NIA located adjacent to the ICC for two main reasons:

- continuing the process of urban regeneration;
- mutual benefits from proximity, namely shared car parking, management and venue use.

The NIA has been successful in attracting a large number of events of varying types, which has demonstrated its flexibility. These include (Birmingham City Council, undated; *Communiqué*, 1991b; NEC Group, 1992):

- Sports events:
  - The Diet Pepsi Indoor Tennis Challenge, 1991
  - World Power Lifting Championships, 1991
  - World Championship Boxing, 1992
  - World Gymnastics Championships, 1993
  - World Netball Championships, 1995

- Other events:
  - Verdi's opera, *Aida*, 1991
  - Great Moscow Circus, 1991

- Walt Disney's World On Ice, 1991
- Eric Clapton in concert
- World Genetic Congress, 1993 plenary sessions, in conjunction with the ICC.

Confidence in the NIA and its reputation appear to be increasing, but this does not guarantee it long-term success. While the City may feel fortunate to have funded it at all, taking advantage of a buoyant property development market, the basic specification is in stark contrast to the ICC, even taking into account the differing functions and markets. This raises a question mark over its long-term viability. There are a number of reasons for this.

The internal specification caters mainly for the circulation of spectators, using this as a means to encourage expenditure on drink and snacks. The level of servicing necessary to maximize the flexibility of use and minimize the downtime has not been incorporated, leaving the area vulnerable to any successor that does consider the organizers, users and spectators in the way that the ICC has in its market.

Externally, the NIA is also very unsatisfactory. It is a bulky building that completes the 'wall' between the city centre and Ladywood – a physical barrier which symbolically and literally cuts off the affluent centre from disadvantaged neighbourhoods (cf. Davis, 1990). It can also be interpreted as the City turning its back upon the disadvantaged. This 'wall' has proved an expensive one to build and, it has been argued, has deprived citizens across the city of investment in housing and education (see Table 11.2).

Table 11.2 Capital spend, 1986–1987 to 1991–1992

Projects	Expenditure (£m)	Percentage of total
ICC, NIA, NEC and city centre projects	379.5	30
Public housing	335.7	26
Education	66.8	5.3

Source: Loftman and Nevin (1992).

The development also fails to integrate with the rest of the projects, apart from its 'function' as a wall. The massing of the ICC is discreet, given its size, yet the NIA turns its back on the canal at the historic junction of the British canal network. The canal is an important feature of industrial archaeology and tourism, which the sheer bulk and blandness of the NIA overpowers:

The forms that develop from this make an efficient piece of people-processing, but do they add anything to the urban grain that Birmingham is trying so hard to build?

The Arena . . . is an object standing in uncertain space, the quaint canals unable to bind the bulk of the Arena and the Convention Centre into the city fabric. (*Architecture Today*, 1992, p.34)

Although the canal area is used more than in the recent past, this is despite the NIA. The ICC may fail to make the most of its presence at its rear; however, the landscaping has won an award and neutralizes the effect. The proposed footbridge to link Brindley Place to the ICC will further enhance the environment and help to break down the wall of urban regeneration, and hence segregation, by encouraging pedestrian flows through the ICC main street. Whatever is being done to mitigate the effects of the ICC on the urban landscape has been outweighed by the imposing mass of the NIA on the canal and the skyline.

Evaluating the NIA on the terms of the initiators' aims and objectives, judgement has to be reserved. However, the medium to longer term does not look promising. On the positive side the City can justifiably claim:

- it was fortunate, as a result of City management skills, that the NIA was funded;
- the bookings are at reasonable level, given the recession;
- it complements the ICC for certain functions;
- it has been part of the urban regeneration process;
- it has lent credibility as a flagship to the city as a centre for sport;
- it has helped to attract some limited inward investment to the city.

However, there are also a number of negative and potentially negative features of the NIA:

- insufficient attention has been given to the requirements of the users – both spectators and competitors – which will affect its reputation;
- insufficient servicing has been provided to maximize current flexibility and adapt it to emerging demands in the future;
- it has proved costly to build and therefore adds to the NEC Ltd debt burden, which is guaranteed by the City;
- it is running at a deficit and has yet to prove it can draw in sufficient inward investment to justify anything but a break-even account;
- it has an obtrusive impact upon the local environment, discouraging further urban regeneration and undermining those positive features of regeneration;
- its completes a 'wall' of development between the city centre and local disadvantaged districts;
- it has no real competitive advantage over Sheffield apart from its central location;
- its long-term ability to maintain market share is very vulnerable to

future arenas which do take into account some of the omitted user requirements;

- the needs of the local population are excluded except for the tokenism of the community-cum-warm-up facility.

The needs of the local population take the analysis towards the broader impact of the scheme beyond the aims and objectives for the NIA as a flagship development and its contribution to the marketing of the city. Before considering that impact, the evaluation of the development as a flagship is summarized.

The project has had some economic benefits for the city in promoting the city generally and specifically selling the city as a sports venue. This has added to the overall marketing efforts described in Chapters 9 and 10. However, it is doubtful whether the project would have had these successes had it been a stand-alone flagship, rather than following in the wake of the ICC flagship. It has therefore benefited from its predecessors, particularly the ICC.

The benefits have been shown to be limited and certainly very vulnerable to change. The ability to sustain the momentum that has been built up over a long period of time is highly questionable. If it does not suffer because of recession, then it will suffer because of growth in the economy as more severe competition emerges from new arenas.

In the light of these limited benefits, the capital costs are high. Although it is perhaps too early to make a final judgement, all the indications are that the capital costs will far outweigh the benefits. This is compounded by the operating deficit, actual and forecast, which shows no indication of being eradicated in future years. These costs could have serious implications for the viability of the ICC and the NEC. It erodes the leeway that the NEC Ltd management have to maintain and sustain the operations of the ICC should trading conditions fail to improve in recession. It also places considerable pressure on the NEC to continue to generate profits to subsidize the other projects. This research has shown that the market for the ICC and marketing of the ICC in a city context is worth underwriting in this way (see Chapter 9). The same cannot be said for the NIA, and it could threaten the former.

The NEC has itself entered into an expansion programme of £45m (NEC Group, 1992). This risk may be well advised given the trading and profit level of the NEC. However, there is a saturation point for every market under each set of economic conditions. Therefore the NIA:

- exposes NEC Ltd to too many debt risks;
- is not justifiable in cost–benefit terms;
- fails in its role as a flagship.

It therefore has to be concluded that the NIA is a case of one flagship too many. While the **service–national** market position is not in conflict with the international one for the ICC and Hyatt – and, indeed, helps to underpin it in image terms – what the NIA delivers is insufficient to justify the costs. It will probably fail to further establish Birmingham as the second city in the national context. It will definitely fail in encouraging further urban regeneration in the Broad Street area, or indeed in Birmingham, except for some other sporting investment.

The reasons for this failure of the flagship function were not so much to do with the implementation stages, because these were controlled well by the City in the terms for bidding for the site, the private sector being largely responsible for the development. The shortcomings arose in the policy formulation stage. The Olympic bid may have helped to raise the profile of Birmingham on the international stage, but it also 'locked' the policy thinking into having to have an arena, when it would have been more appropriate to have looked at alternatives. For example, another capital project of smaller scale, using only the capital raised from the land sale, would have maintained the urban regeneration process, at no cost to the City and may have been more effective in encouraging further regeneration because of massing, design, different function and avoiding the continuation of the physical wall of segregation. Citing another example, and in view of the political problems caused by the ICC and Hyatt, the land sale proceeds and planning gain could have been introduced into housing and education. These are the policy areas that, respectively, were neglected and had funds transferred into urban regeneration projects (Loftman and Nevin, 1992). This would have ameliorated recent criticism of the ICC and Hyatt projects. If the investment had been concentrated in Ladywood, the result would have been substantial urban regeneration from the edge of the inner city areas towards the city centre, thus boosting the commercial viability of the intermediate areas, namely Brindley Place, as well as substantially improving the social conditions for the local population by improving their environment, self-worth, and education and employment opportunities.

It is at this point that the analysis can turn to other impacts the NIA has had, particularly in the local labour market.

11.7 NIA IMPACT

The primary impact to be considered is the effect of the project upon employment. It was estimated that the NIA would create 84 new posts (Birmingham City Council, 1990c). By September 1991, just prior to opening, 71 permanent jobs had been created, the majority of which were in cleaning, catering and security. While the employment levels are not

Table 11.3 Relationship between employment creation and capital cost

Project	Capital cost (£m)	Number of jobs	Cost per job (£000s)
NIA	51	71	718
Swallow Hotel	11	145	75
Novotel	9	55	163
The Wharf	2.5	45	55
Hyatt	31	248	127

Sources: Compiled from Birmingham City Council (undated; 1990c).

insignificant compared to hotel development, the capital cost per post is far greater for the NIA, as Table 11.3 indicates.

The capital cost is between four and five times greater than that of the nearest hotel. The comparison with a hotel is interesting because the employment opportunities are similar in skill, although the hotel image issue may open up the NIA jobs to a wider section of the labour market, and probably to more males than hotel work.

The capital cost per job may have been justifiable if the NIA was attracting inward investment and stimulating business confidence in the way that the ICC has done, which has a similar capital–job ratio, but this is not the case. Therefore the broader impacts, that is those that go beyond the original aims and objectives, further undermine the case for the NIA. Taking this into account, the conclusion is that the policy for the NIA has been top-down in approach with few real benefits filtering through to the local population. Failure to serve the local population through this top-down approach has left the City wide open to attack for its spend on flagship developments. While such attacks have focused upon the leading and most expensive project, this research has demonstrated that the ICC is the most viable of the projects considered and that criticism can more justifiably be levelled at the NIA. A top-down approach that really benefited the community (see Section 11.6 for alternative suggestions) could have avoided the City getting 'carried away' with its own enthusiasm for grand flagship developments and thus alleviated criticisms. In view of the poor impact of the scheme on the labour market *vis-à-vis* costs, pursuing those alternatives through a bottom-up approach would have earned more political plaudits and would have met more of the needs of the local population. An opportunity for empowerment would have been a welcome balance to the top-down approach of the previous projects. It would also have been complementary to the previous flagships, as one of the main marketing concerns for attracting inward investors in the future will be social stability (see Chapter 9).

11.8 BRINDLEY PLACE IMPLEMENTATION

The remainder of the Brindley Place site, assigned for commercial development, has proposals for a £250m scheme. The site is largely derelict, with the exception of an old school, a church and the new Novotel, which was developed separately. Surface car parking is the main temporary use.

Development upon the site will provide the missing link between the city centre and Five Ways and Edgbaston (Quantrill, 1991). For the developers it is more than this. The aim has been 'making this place a real destination' for eating and recreation.[25] However, the developer has gone through a number of transformations. Laing had already broken away to concentrateon the construction of the NIA. As the property market overheated, Merlin International ran into serious difficulties; they were not only over-committed but were unable to survive without massive support and restructuring. They too withdrew from the scheme. Throughout the early 1990s, the Shearwater parent company, Rosehaugh, found the development and investment conditions too harsh, for the following reasons (Goobey, 1992):

- off balance sheet and limited recourse finance did not ultimately insulate the company from being too debt laden because it affected financial confidence in the company;
- the company had not anticipated the possibility of high interest rates;
- management had lost control of the key decisions across its divergent companies and joint ventures.

Goobey writes:

> many of the Shearwater developments proved impossible to progress with and it became known that Rosehaugh was an aggressive seller of assets. The final confirmation that all was not well was the announcement on 5 February 1990 of a rights issue to raise £125m. . . . The issue was not underwritten by the institutions in the normal way.[26] (1992, p.60)

Shearwater was removed from its schemes in Sheffield and Camberley for failing to raise the finance and it withdrew from the joint venture for the Blue Water scheme with Blue Circle Industries. By April 1990 Shearwater had written off £12m and the company was being run down by Rosehaugh.

The Brindley Place site concepts had undergone a number of changes. An American firm of architects was introduced to evaluate the masterplan and produce another one that was considered more appropriate for the changing market (see note 20). This was given added weight because of the discussions with another developer, Capital and Counties, for developing the office accommodation, but this exploration had come to an end by 1990. As trading conditions deteriorated in the property market, the only option for the Brindley Place site could have been to sell it. The property market at that stage was entering a very depressed state and other companies would not have wished to invest.

Brindley Place became constituted under its own development company, Brindleyplace plc, once Shearwater ran into problems and Rosehaugh closed the division. Despite the problems Rosehaugh submitted a revised scheme in December 1991, claiming it would proceed with the scheme on condition that buildings were prelet or sold ahead of development (*Financial Times*, 1991c). Terry Farrell was the new masterplanner for this stage, the aim being to plan and develop the site as a series of stand-alone developments, giving maximum development flexibility.

However, conditions continued to worsen for Rosehaugh and in December 1992, the company went into administrative receivership.

Now that Rosehaugh is in administrative receivership, it has to be expected that the site will either be sold, this time at the bottom of the market to an investor that is prepared to take a long-term view, or that parts of Rosehaugh will be sold by the receivers, which could include Brindley Place. At the time of writing there is no certainty of this outcome, although it should be anticipated that a sale will happen before development land prices rise. Any purchaser would have to take one of two views: either develop the site out and look to the long-term rental and asset values to justify the expenditure, or hold the site. The latter is a low risk option, but may not be permissible without renegotiating planning permission and development terms with the City. The former option can proceed by seeking prelets or presales as Rosehaugh had envisaged; however, there would be heavy infrastructure costs to carry. In one sense the conditions are better for the site because receivership has involved writing off £35m of costs. However, development must start within a short period, otherwise the 150-year leasehold for the site will revert to the City under the terms of the original sale.

In looking at the changing nature of the parties involved during the implementation stage, it has already become clear that the scheme was not a self-supporting commercial flagship, at least in the short to medium term. Indeed, so great has been the uncertainty about the scheme that it has undergone a series of changes in design and content. Therefore, it is also necessary to look in more detail at the significance of the conceptual changes for the scheme.

In the feasibility study for the ICC (Franks, 1983), it had been envisaged that the take-up of existing offices in the area would have happened by 1989 and that the Brindley Place site would then come on stream for office development. However, the demands for new office development in Birmingham were not as great as the property boom of the late 1960s and early 1970s (Loftman and Nevin, 1992). Although office development was included in the first concepts, it was the festival market, with its speciality shopping and street theatre, which was the main use that the City had wished to see. The experience of Baltimore's Harbor Place was one they wished to replicate. Although festival markets were not particularly profitable, they created the ambience and environment in which office users wished to be, and so were seen as an attraction for the inward investment of command and administrative functions (see Ashworth and Voogd, 1990). They were said to have a social control dimension through the presentation of spectacle, the ephemeral experience of leisure shopping and passing the time (Harvey, 1989a, b). Kester puts it this way:

> The festival market became the narcotic of the 80s, providing a welcome escape for American cities faced with growing unemployment, declining tax bases, and deteriorating schools, hospitals, transportation systems and social services. The last time this particular set of elements came together, in the mid-1960s, the result was nationwide rioting, and hundreds of millions of dollars in property damage. The festival market promised a solution; a waterfront development that would simultaneously catalyse downtown investment, attract tourist and convention business, provide jobs for dangerously idle inner-city youth, skyrocket the tax base, and generally pave the streets with gold. (1990, p.20)

It is doubtful whether Birmingham Council representatives, developers and other interested parties saw it quite so starkly, and perhaps such comment has only become possible as city property indebtedness came to the fore and as recession closed many of the speciality operators. It is clear that Birmingham was seeking to use the canal location to greatest effect in order to reinforce business and leisure tourism. Fitch Benoy, the retail architects for the development consortium, designed a tent-like structure that would maximize the spectacle from the ICC along the canal. This 'tent' would house the various operators. However, the withdrawal of Merlin International and the downswing in the development cycle in Britain prompted the developers to think again. Their concern was that a tent provided no flexibility. Development could not proceed piecemeal in response to demand in a more constrained market, because the original Fitch Benoy concept had to be developed at one time. The extent of the demand and the supply for festival shopping was also being questioned. Brindleyplace plc wished to maintain some speciality shopping and leisure, as well as encourage smaller scale multiple outlets. The need for piecemeal development, which was demand-led, meant a switch towards a more traditional retail pattern, using narrow streets and squares (see note 24). This would produce a scheme more in the mould of the Shambles in York or the Lanes in Brighton. Terry Farrell's practice was commissioned to develop a new masterplan. The new plan endeavours to reinforce pedestrian routes, drawing people over the proposed footbridge from the ICC, up through Brindley Place, and from Broad Street into the site. The festival market would have stifled pedestrian flows. However, a consultancy study demonstrated the scope for attracting people into a pedestrianized scheme, which made the most of through routes (see notes 24 and 25). The main points emphasized by the developer are:

- Chamberlain Square in the city centre and Five Ways have the largest pedestrian flows;
- Brindley Place in located between the two;
- New Street Station in the city centre is a 12-minute walk away;
- the City pedestrian proposals will encourage walking, the Brindley Place development providing the missing link;
- 750 000 non-delegate visitors walked through the ICC in the first 18 months;
- 110 buses per hour pass along Broad Street at peak times;
- the proposed Metro 2 will link Five Ways to the international airport and have a station at the development;
- a new rail station connected with the Heartlands development link would be of additional benefit;
- street theatre in the proposed squares will be an added attraction.

The thinking behind the proposed scheme was a hybrid between traditional retail, leisure and office development and the festival market concept. The changes needed City approval because of the changes in planning permission and the sale agreement. A deed of variation was negotiated and permission granted in detailed form for the retail and in outline for the remainder (see note 24). A City planning officer commented:

> The developers have not taken on board everything we have asked them but we have a fair degree of progress arriving at a townscape for the site which meets the council's strategy. (*Building Design*, 1992)

There were a number of implicit matters behind this approach, which can be summarized as:

- the City was prepared to relinquish the festival market concept, presumably acknowledging the questions over its viability;
- the developers required all elements of the scheme to contribute to rental income and asset values;
- the City wanted to ensure a small-scale development in contrast to the NIA-ICC-Hyatt 'wall';
- the City wanted to encourage pedestrianization;
- the City, it is assumed, wanted to retain a high retail and leisure content, even if the office content grew.

The result meant that the scheme was now in direct competition with other canal-side proposals, especially the £8m Regency Wharf scheme and the existing Gas Street Basin (*Building Design*, 1992). Hyatt was expecting competition to the Gas Street Basin – and welcomes it, for it will help to draw in a larger clientele (see Chapter 10). A festival market would have operated in a different market niche to Regency Wharf, so the development of one will postpone, if not cancel, the development of the other.

The Brindley Place scheme is likely to take priority and the planning application was negotiated with an understanding that phase one of the development would commence early in 1992, with completion over a 5-year period. Assuming the scheme goes ahead in its present form, the content is shown in Table 11.4.

Table 11.4 Commercial content of Brindley Place

Content	Phase one	Subsequent phases	Total
Bars, restaurants, speciality retailing	60 000 sq.ft	90 000 sq.ft	150 000 sq.ft
Multiplex cinema	–	–	
Science of sport exhibition	–	–	–
Offices	75 000 sq.ft	775 000 sq.ft	850 000 sq.ft
Residential	–	120 units	120 units
Crescent Theatre	–	–	–
Hotel	–	–	–
Car parking	600 spaces	1900 spaces	2500 spaces

Sources: Brindleyplace (undated); *Brindleyplace News* (undated); see note 25.

The proposals include an interactive exhibition, Science of Sport (*Brindleyplace News*, undated), which will help to reinforce the role of the NIA. The NIA will have acted as a catalyst for this element, but it is not possible to state that this is a positive flagship feature of the NIA until the exhibition is built. The proposed offices will plug a gap in the market, as it is claimed that the available office stock is largely in the 25 000 square feet and less bracket. There is an absence of new space at 50 000 square feet and 100 000 square feet (see note 25).

11.9 BRINDLEY PLACE POLICY AND PROJECT EVALUATION

At the simplest level of analysis the scheme has failed as a flagship development because development has not taken place. It is possible to go further than this. For a flagship to justify its label, then the policy should be coherent enough and the implementation robust enough for it to go ahead. If the policy and process are in place, then the concept of a flagship surely embodies the strength to override circumstances. In other words, the strength of the concept links needs and also demands in such a way as to justify unblocking any constraints arising on the supply side from urban degeneration.

What if the demand is not present? The defensive reaction to this could be that the property market had fallen away and therefore the scheme was no longer commercially viable. From any developer's viewpoint this has some credibility, but in the case of Brindley Place, the analysis must consider two things:

- changes to the concepts
- changes in the development team.

Both of these are supply-side changes in response to changes in demand. The 'product' in design concept went through a number of transformations, demonstrating a lack of confidence in the market for this type of development as it evolved. The changes in the development team demonstrated the absence of demand in the property market generally and in the specific markets for this development. Perhaps this suggests that it is purely external factors that have compromised the flagship function. This is true, but it is not the whole truth, for a flagship should be able to override the market to a large degree, inducing demand in its wake. The severity of the recession makes the statement true, but the truth rests with the flagship use, that is, the festival market. The flagship function was really lost when the festival market was shelved or diluted in favour of more mainstream leisure and a mix of speciality and multiple retailing. From this point, the scheme was competing in the development market place for funds and tenants like any other scheme. While it may still complement the ICC, NIA and other canal-side developments, it will not perform a flagship role of:

- encouraging extensive canal development;
- becoming a national tourist attraction in itself;
- acting as a stimulus to revitalize other city retailing;
- reinforcing the arts, sports, leisure and tourist functions to any great degree;
- encouraging further office development in, and hence relocation to, Birmingham.

It is simply trying to attract a developer and sufficient tenants to start the development.

Why has the festival market been lost? As this is central to the loss of the flagship function, it is an important question. In one sense, it is merely a case of another flagship too many, adding to the problems that the NIA is likely to pose (see Chapter 10). In this case the problem was experienced sooner, in other words, prior to construction. However, this is too stark. Because it is a commercial scheme, the market is the ultimate judge. It has been noted that a flagship should be able to override the predominant market sentiment to a large degree. Why could a festival market not do so? It is easy in hindsight to say that many of the pioneering festival markets in the United States are experiencing difficulty, so there was an opportunity to reappraise the concept in a British context. Perhaps the City should not have become 'carried away' with the possibilities for successive urban regeneration schemes. Although they did not control the implementation, they set the original policy context. There was reason for being optimistic during the 1980s. Even though the economics were always marginal for a festival market, they permitted sufficient commercial use.

History shows that innovative concepts can evolve into something more sustainable. While the festival market was beyond its innovative phase, it had not reached the stage of a mature proposition. Just as the boutique shopping pioneered in Carnaby Street of the 1960s was imported into all high streets, culminating in the 'high style' of interior design developed by Next in Britain, perhaps there was scope for the festival market to follow a similar route. In addition, market segmentation and niche marketing were the 'buzz' concepts of the 1980s. Interior designers, Fitch, initially applied the concept spatially within a shop or department store until the notion was lost in overcomplexity of design and unsustainable budgets. Expensive, serial shopping centres were repeating the same story. So, the writing was on the wall before retail sales began to fall. There were economic limits to how far the current retail trends could be pushed.

However, the City has allowed the market to judge and has proved flexible in that way. It could be said that the current recession is merely a pause in the process of refining these concepts, including the festival market. Current business approaches of returning to core business would seem to suggest the opposite – the search for new cheap mass markets. This takes the analysis away from this project. However, it would seem that the festival market is lost for good for this development, and therefore, so is the flagship function. Any influence the future development may have on the rest of the city will be no more than the same impact any other commercial scheme will have *vis-à-vis* its competition and contribution to the built form.

11.10 BRINDLEY PLACE IMPACT

There has been no impact to date of any substance. The other flagships have not managed to set this flagship afloat, nor any other form of development. There are three reasons for this:

- the 'wall' or barrier created by the Hyatt, ICC and NIA (cf. Davis, 1990);
- the operations of the above are in their early days, and have not generated maximum custom to date;

- the state of the property development market.

Ironically, the 'wall' created by the other flagships would be alleviated to some degree through the development of Brindley Place, by creating new through pedestrian routes.

The other main impact the development claims will be the creation of 6000 new jobs. Even though many jobs may come with companies bringing their office staff, others will be for people living in the travel to work area. This development is likely to have a significant impact on the Ladywood and surrounding labour market. The fact that many of the jobs will be low paid, in catering, retailing and cleaning, would benefit many local people, and in addition new and better paid employment would also be available in administrative, office and management functions. Indeed, it is the intention that many local people would benefit from new employment opportunities:

> A practical programme of measures to give local people a real chance of benefiting from the 6000 new jobs created at Brindleyplace is being planned. Developers Brindleyplace plc are co-operating with the City Councils Economic Development Unit, Birmingham Training and Enterprise Council and local organization, Ladywood Community Business to work up plans. . . . The programme will include specially designed training packages to ensure that local residents wanting to work at Brindleyplace have the skills to do so. (*Brindleyplace News*, undated, p. 2)

This is a challenging objective if it is to be implemented purposefully and succeed; the potential for the local population is greater than for the other flagship projects (see Chapters 9 and 10).

11.11 SUMMARY

Both the flagships analysed in this chapter have shortcomings. The overall conclusion is that the City became carried away with its own enthusiasm for what was possible. In the case of the NIA, insufficient resources were put in to make it a project that was ensured long-term competitive advantage. A smaller scale project of a different nature could have been pursued. However, it was pointed out that there was a major opportunity to channel resources back into the local communities through the sale of Brindley Place.

Brindley Place has failed to date on commercial grounds and, it seems, failed completely as a flagship development when the festival market concept was removed. The future of the scheme remains uncertain, yet the potential for creating a large number of local jobs is high and this must surely be the primary objective for the City and developers when the project proceeds.

In conclusion, there do appear to be limits on the number of flagships that can be developed on the back of each other, or on the size of them, if Canary Wharf is considered, because the regeneration process rides over the economic and property cycles. While it is the case that flagships should be able to override market sentiment, they do not operate outside the economic context, even public sector ones. Thus, they are subject to the long-term disciplines of the market. Flagships can lead the market, but they are still part of the market. Any of the market positions that a flagship development occupies must recognize this. In these cases this aspect has tended to be overlooked. The NIA did not have a coherent strategy behind it and sufficient funding was not present. Brindley Place did not have a concept that was commercially viable and, although this is more clearly visible with hindsight, the number of changes to the concept and developer gave ample warning.

Theatre Village   12

12.1 INTRODUCTION

The Theatre Village is located in central Newcastle. Those living in the city may not even be aware of its existence. The Chinatown quarter is known, and forms part of the area. The Theatre Village takes its name from the Tyne Theatre and Opera House, as its focus; a hundred years ago there was a strong arts base in that part of the city. The area, situated immediately north-west of Central Station, is about 400 metres in width and 600 metres running north to south, covering about 60 acres in total.

The Theatre Village flagship is an area concept (see Table 7.1), with the arts sector taking a leading role in promoting the area again (cf. Chapters 8 and 9) and inducing regeneration through leisure and residential development alongside the growth in arts activities (cf. Chapters 8 and 11). The low local profile of the Theatre Village is not replicated on a national basis in the arts community, yet even in these fora it cannot be claimed to be high. The flagship can clearly be seen to have failed in its task and, indeed, the private sector vehicle set up to achieve the task, the Westgate Trust, has already been disbanded. However, it is important to consider flagships that have been unsuccessful and this one is particularly interesting for three reasons:

- it was area-based
- it was innovative
- it was initiated by the national business lobby group, the Confederation for British Industry (CBI).

12.2 ECONOMIC BACKGROUND

Newcastle was and is a regional city. Its origins are Roman. Silver, gold and ore trading, plus the local coal for smelting the ore, gave Newcastle its industrial function, and it was also an agricultural market at that time. Its recent wealth was founded on mining and the transportation of coal, while its port function gave rise to a number of other industries and distribution functions. As a port it became a key centre for shipbuilding and repairs. It was also headquarters for the North Eastern Railway.

The Theatre Village area, that was the Westgate district, had grown in population from 3000 in 1830 to 30 000 by 1980. This was the peak of the area and city's prosperity. The city has been experiencing long-term de-cline, the origins dating back to the 1890s when railway transport opened up the city with a consequent loss of regional power and wealth. In 1890, the North Eastern Railway relocated its headquarters to York. The com-petitive edge in the production of photographic dry plates was soon to be lost to Eastman Kodak of America.

The Westgate district had been a major retail centre for the city, remaining a primary function, particularly Lower Clayton Street, until Capital and Counties developed the Eldon Square Shopping Centre on the northern side of the city core. Most of the retailing that remains is important to the functioning of any city, yet is second and third rate in terms of rent and status. It includes second-hand car dealers, bike shops and other retailing which is the subject of temporary planning permissions.

The other primary uses were the textile trade and warehousing, the Co-operative Wholesale Society (CWS) empire owning many of the build-ings. CWS were patrons of architecture, therefore the quality of their designs is high and some are listed buildings. The Roman, Edwardian and Victorian developments have given rise to the Conservation Area status. There are over 100 listed buildings in the area as a whole, 500 residences with 600 people and 2000 jobs.

12.3 CITY POLICY AND CONDITIONS

The conditions in the area were showing marginal improvement. A num-ber of residential developments had taken place since 1980 and the current population of 600 had grown from less than 100 people in 1978. Situated between the centre and some of the poorest areas of the city, for example Cruddas Park, and less than 400 metres from the point where the West End riots started, following a few days after the Meadowell riots, the area contains the 'red light' district and the highest crime figures, especially for car thefts. Over 5% of the area is derelict, that is 17 sites, and over 50% of the building stock is underused or vacant (TNI, 1988). Land was concentrated in the hands of two owners, the City and CWS, the remaining land holdings being highly fragmented. The area was seen as unfocused, without clear entrances or exits, or the pedestrian flows necessary in a street pattern unsuited to car use and parking.

There was no single use or function giving the area a definite image and the environment was adding to the feeling of fragmentation (TNI, 1988). This contrasted with the other areas, where agencies are responsible for image making and providing new foci for the city. The City, Tyne and Wear Urban Development Corporation, the Northern Development Company and other TNI flagships were all contributing at different levels and scales to selling images and parts of Newcastle.[27] The Theatre Village has a number of distinguishing features within its area:

- site line of Hadrian's Wall
- Black Friars Priory
- 13th century town walls and ditch
- Tyne Theatre and Opera House
- Science and Engineering Museum, Tyne and Wear Museum Service, in Blandford House
- Pavilion Theatre
- The Tyne Brewery on the northern fringe.

Any substantial area improvements were blighted by the initiatives for road building. A motorway had been planned through the centre of the area over a decade ago. The proposals have subsequently been downgraded to an east–west distributor, the West Central Route, which is in the Unitary Development Plan.[28] The Department of Transport allocated funds for a public inquiry during 1993 and intend letting the contract in 1994 with completion in 1996, if the proposals proceed.[29] The heritage features and Conservation Area status, plus the blight, have inhibited development, encouraging short-term lets and temporary uses where a market existed (see note 28).

The City had taken steps to encourage revitalization and in that context 160 residential units had been developed in 1980 on the former Crown Hotel site. Restoration of key elements of the medieval city, particularly the former town walls, the ditches and Black Friars Priory had been completed (TNI, 1988). The old theatre had been refurbished. With support from a large number of people under its charitable status, including Placido Domingo and Norma Major, its superb proscenium arch, excellent sight lines and renowned acoustics were brought back into use and it reopened in 1986 under its old name, the Tyne Theatre and Opera House, a year before its 120th anniversary (Tyne Theatre and Opera House, 1987). In addition, the Newcastle Arts Centre and Dance City had been formed in refurbished premises with public sector financial support (Wood and Woodling, 1990).

Therefore, improvements were slowly occurring, despite blight affecting many uses and sites, and this provided a basis for an area flagship concept and the germ of an arts revival.

12.4 THE PARTIES

The City primarily had been involved with the area preceding 1987, but in that year a new initiative was created. Its origins were national. In November 1987 the CBI held its national conference, setting up a task force for business to contribute to the process of urban regeneration. The task force believed that the costs of regeneration would exceed public and charitable funds and needed private funds, direction and local decision making from business leaders. Following the lessons from Glasgow Action, the CBI task force would mobilize local resources, channelling these into a series of flagship projects (CBI, 1987; see also Wood and Woodling, 1990). It was decided to pioneer the approach on Tyneside, the objective being:

> to help establish a local leadership team which could instil a proper sense of purpose and direction in the various local initiatives and help to facilitate a broad measure of agreement about the priority issues facing Newcastle. (CBI, 1988, p.73, quoted from Wood and Woodling, p.2)

The approach was intended to be focused at the local level and based upon networking. Ostensibly, this is very different from the approach of the Urban Development Corporation, which is primarily concerned with the national image of the locale conveyed through marketing, mainly advertising and public relations, to shape perceptions (cf. Ashworth and Voogd, 1990; Robins and Wilkinson, 1990; Wilkinson, 1992).

The piloting of the CBI's task force for Newcastle was set up under the banner of The Newcastle Initiative (TNI). The start up finance was constrained at a figure of £200 000 (Wood and Woodling, 1990). A series of small, tangible, yet various flagships were chosen. The one exception was the Theatre Village – it was considered necessary to provide an independent vehicle for this because of its size and scope. The Westgate Trust was formed to formulate and implement a strategy for the Theatre Village. The other parties concerned were the City plus those individuals and bodies the Westgate Trust involved under TNI.

The creation of the Westgate Trust was itself a part of the policy formulation stage and will therefore be returned to in a subsequent section. It is first necessary to review the market position for the Theatre Village.

12.5 MARKET POSITION

Before coming to the Theatre Village itself, setting out a more comprehensive description of the aims of TNI is helpful. Quoting from the TNI brochure is useful:

> The Newcastle Initiative is a shared vision of the public and private sectors, bringing together influential leaders from business, from central and local government, and the academic world, in a co-ordinated programme of regeneration.
>
> The vision
> - to help develop Newcastle as a vibrant and stylish regional capital
> - to revitalise Newcastle City Centre
> - to stimulate a steady growth in local employment and training
> - an improved urban environment.
>
> Key tasks are contained in a series of flagship schemes designed to bring lasting improvements so that Newcastle meets the mighty challenge of the 21st Century. (TNI, undated, pp.2–3)

Two important points need to be made. The first is that the quotation clearly demonstrates that the approach is top-down, the second that this is not reliant upon the use of statutory or financial power (TNI, undated). Any authority or influence would arise from:

- networking;
- authority of the individuals concerned from other positions held in society;
- respect and trust from the local population, business and other organizations;
- achievements.

This is important for this **G-type** project (see Figures 4.1 and 5.9), for the Theatre Village occupied an **innovative–local** market position. An innovative culture cannot be too top-down, especially in the early stages, in order to work. The absence of statutory powers and financial control was clearly an asset here and the Westgate Trust was endeavouring to pursue the following purposes:

- marketing
- commercial activity
- self-help.

These were pursued primarily from a consumption viewpoint, although many of the local interests did and would embody service provision. Each of these, involving a large number of different interest groups and individuals, could not act within a top-down approach. This is more so for the self-help elements than for the others.

The TNI vehicle, the Westgate Trust, would have to go through a three-stage process of leadership, given the TNI approach and composition:

- encouragement
- exhortation
- enlightenment.

The Trust had two potential starting points within their remit. They could build relationships, using their network, and show leadership by shaping attitudes, or they could act as developers through raising public or private finance to have a demonstration effect. The first involves encouragement, the second is more of an exhorting role by giving direction through actions. Only then could an enlightened response come from others as to how they could contribute, switching the basis for action to a more local and sometimes bottom-up approach (see Figure 5.9). The scope for a bottom-up approach, in the sense of helping the most disadvantaged in the area, was limited because there were few inhabitants in the area and 83% of them were recent newcomers. There are, of course, many disadvantaged people in the surrounding areas who could be helped.

The Westgate Trust envisaged that the Theatre Village would be regenerated through the arts, leisure and residential functions, with the arts leading the way. It is this aspect that added the innovative dimension, and, as shall be seen, the view of the arts in this area was in contrast to the views adopted for the Watershed Complex in Bristol and by Birmingham (see Chapters 8 and 9).

The Westgate Trust also recognized the need to be flexible in the first two years, to maximize the scope for experimentation (Westgate Trust, 1990), yet TNI also needed some quick results in this market position in order to maintain and enhance its credibility (Wood and Woodling, 1990). This takes the analysis into the first policy stage, that of formulation.

12.6 POLICY FORMULATION

TNI first set up a forerunner to the Westgate Trust. West City Regeneration came into being in 1988 in a blaze of publicity, headed by Sir John Hall of Cameron Hall. His company was noted for the development of the Metro Centre in Gateshead, the first British regional shopping centre.

The leadership role that TNI required in the context of their structure and market position can be summarized according to Marshall (1991). He divides the necessary skills into operational and conceptual ones. Concerning operational issues:

They are the abilities and strengths that are essential in management and administration, such as interpersonal skills, experience, judgement, perseverance, analytical and problem solving skills and moral integrity. (p.20)

In essence, these were the requirements for mobilizing, coordinating and marketing through the network. The conceptual tools relate more closely to developing the strategic aims, and are described as follows:

Conceptualizing is the ability to take scattered and sometimes apparently contradictory ideas, phenomena or opinions and build them into a mental image in which each element has a logical and integral relationship with the whole. (Marshall, 1991, p.20–21)

This should be the first task in policy formulation, although networking would be the operational medium for it, conceptual abilities being more important that operational ones, especially for an innovative project of this nature where the local and unsolicited participants were to be asked to embrace a vision and strategy for the area.

This did not occur. Sir John Hall believed that if he showed confidence in the area other people would follow. Announcing a £300m redevelopment of the Westgate Road area (TNI, c. 1990), including the Theatre Village and Chinatown, over a 10-year period was counterproductive. Small-scale entrepreneurs bought some small properties on a speculative basis, and most landowners were determined to hold onto their land on the expectation that land and property prices would rise.[30] Other developers did not follow. The publicity surrounding the launch of the new initiative did not encourage local people to act. If anything, it tended to exclude. Sir John Hall withdrew and the Westgate Trust superseded the first initiative (see note 29).

The Westgate Trust was set up under the Companies Act 1985 to:

- promote a strategy
- provide a forum for discussion
- lobby for additional resources for DoE City Grant funds
- promote the area for the attraction of further resources.

In addition, the Trust had the ability to acquire interests and property, operate a business, enter into partnership agreements, carry out research and promote activities. It could not, however, make a profit (Westgate Trust, 1990). The Board membership included representatives from local business, TNI, the City, Tyneside TEC, Northern Arts, the local Chamber of Commerce and the Tyne and Wear Foundation.

The need was to address the conceptual and operational issues described, despite the damage done to confidence and the economic scope for regeneration. The other parallel policy stream had been conceptual.

The Northumbria branch of the Royal Institute of British Architects (RIBA) was approached to develop concepts for a strategy. This was an innovative idea. Alan Simpson and Prince Charles had visited Pittsburgh in the United States in 1987 to investigate the Regional/Urban Design Assistance Team (R/UDAT) approach to stimulating urban regeneration.[31] By bringing in outside and impartial advice, fresh ideas and renewed visions for an area could be engendered. Alan Simpson was influential in its application to the Theatre Village. The same model was not quite followed in this case as a number of the members of the 4-day brainstorming team were local and did not exclude themselves from accepting commissions within the area (Wood and Woodling, 1990). The team members were able to bring to bear the following skills:

- architecture
- urban design and land use planning
- property management and housing finance
- corporate planning
- traffic planning
- community development
- leisure and cultural expertise
- economic development.

The team focused on the arts sector as the means to give the area an image and focus. They also saw it as a principle object of the micro-economy because the arts and leisure sectors were growing at a rate of 5% per annum at that time (TNI, 1988). The team analysis identified that the arts were not in themselves able to stimulate the urban regeneration process because they were not activities of sufficient individual size or collective critical mass. Something else would have to lead the renewal process, probably property development (TNI, 1988). What the team had really come up with was a twin flagship function:

- economic regeneration through property development;
- image regeneration through the arts.

Property development would kick-start the process, the arts developing in its wake and providing the means by which further investment and property development would occur:

> It is essential that this growth should be fostered and encouraged so that the area becomes internationally recognized for the arts and culture. Successful arts-related activities themselves can lead to wider regeneration of the area. (TNI, 1988, section 4.2c)

There were a number of dimensions to making this process work:

- Property, for example:
  - investment, not grant culture (cf. the Watershed, Chapter 8)
  - major tourism features
  - quality 'gateway' schemes

- Employment:
  - support the image sectors of clothing, arts, Chinatown
  - workshop schemes and support for arts training project
  - tourism as employment generator

- Arts:
  - new concert hall
  - investment in arts productions
  - bottom-up arts strategy development
  - develop electronic media sector

- Village:
  - create sense of place
  - engender local pride
  - improve public space for safety and visual impact.

Catalytic projects were identified to underpin these policy dimensions. They included giving Westgate prominence as a 'gateway' to the area and the old city, and upgrading the High Street by bringing the Pavilion Theatre back into use as a National Centre for Performing Arts Training, linked to the Tyne Theatre and the College of Arts and Technology immediately south of the Village. Increasing the pedestrianization and linking enhanced public squares, and giving the emergent Chinatown area a distinctive look were other proposals. A Business Development Centre, geared to advising the arts community, was also suggested, and an International Youth Arts Summer School and Festival, as well as rekindling the idea for a major concert hall which had been mooted in the past (cf. Symphony Hall, Chapter 9).

This team approach certainly produced a number of ideas for TNI to evaluate and implement through the Westgate Trust. Following Marshall (1991), it satisfied most of the conceptual tasks. In order to make the policy implementable, the concepts had to be made operational, the second leadership need. This could be taken in two directions. The first was top-down, addressing the issue the team left unresolved, namely how funding could be created for arts policy thrust and future projects. Public sector funding was already in use for other arts initiatives, so this would have to come from property development. There would have been two ways to achieve this:

- for the Westgate Trust and the City to require Section 106 agreements on all commercial development in favour of arts facilities and operations;
- for the Westgate Trust to develop directly or in partnership, slicing off part of the rental stream for arts activities.

It would appear that the TNI task force, and subsequently the Westgate Trust, did not perceive the need to be instrumental in these respects. The brainstorming team under the Northumbria RIBA recognized the need for highly commercial development (TNI, 1988). As was shown in Chapters 4 and 5, the ideas were visionary, but this does not mean that developers have to be visionary and innovative. If they are, then there will not be the room for financial manoeuvre necessary to pay for other urban regeneration. 'Traditional'-style buildings would be adequate. Even so, Section 106 agreements are a restraint on development, especially because the costs tend to be incurred early on during development and the rental flows are insufficient without some form of public subsidy. The RIBA team also suggested that TNI set up a development and property investment company (TNI, 1988). The advantage of this process is that costs could be defrayed first, if development is undertaken directly, or an agreed top slice of rental income above a reasonable rate of return taken, if developed under a partnership arrangement. The suggestion of a development company was put to management consultants, Coopers & Lybrand, who recommended that such a company should be established (Coopers & Lybrand, undated). The reasons for doing so were:

- undertaking a lead role
- securing public and private finance
- implementing the strategy (which could be taken to include arts funding)
- promoting the implementation of 'catalyst' projects
- making sites available
- marketing and promotion.

These Development Trusts had proved viable in the United States, successfully cross-subsidizing other activities (Coopers & Lybrand, undated).

This development company option was rejected by TNI and the Westgate Trust. It was believed that the market was the appropriate mechanism for development (see note 30), the underlying concern being conflicts of interest with CBI and local Chamber of Commerce members. Any conflict was more perceived than real, for two reasons:

- it was necessary to unblock supply-side constraints and create the investment climate, hence creating business for members;
- investment in development increases the land and property assets in relation to the level of investment and demand in the local economy (Smyth, 1985).

A development company would thus have been performing a market creation role rather than crude competition for limited opportunities. Overlooking this left a gap in the policy formulation, which would impede any implementation of the vision in a top-down way except by image making alone.

Having neglected the necessary operational issues on a top-down basis, there was opportunity to engender action from the bottom up. This required getting local people and business to 'own' the vision for themselves, and in so doing put together the operational mechanisms to implement the concepts (see Chapter 5). There appeared to be an absence of effort on this front. The financial and staffing support for the Trust were minimal and this certainly reflected a lack of commitment to a large-scale area-based project, and probably a lack of understanding of what was needed to get from the conceptual to the implementation stage.

The Westgate Trust was, by default, left with the following roles (The Westgate Trust, 1990):

- forum for discussion
- lobbying for resources
- advocacy role for attracting development into area
- mediating between interested parties over development proposals.

The other main role adopted was a town and land use planning role (Fox and Healey, 1991). The City planners had produced a Westgate Development Area Strategy in 1989 (TNI, c. 1990), then a Theatre Village and Chinatown Development Strategy in 1991, which was to act as Supplementary Planning Guidance prior to incorporation into the Unitary Development Plan for the city (Fox and Healey, 1991). The planning role was to become the primary one, however, which takes the analysis forward to the implementation stage of the policy process.

12.7 PROJECT IMPLEMENTATION

The first management task for an **innovative–local** project is to provide firm policy and management guidelines (cf. Drucker, 1986). This involves taking the operational issues to a more detailed level (see Figure 5.9). The primary strategic aims were to stimulate economic regeneration through property development and image regeneration through the arts. The former goal had been compromised through avoiding a development role; however, the details of how the property development sector responded will be returned to later, along with the planning aspects.

The arts side of the strategy would require long-term encouragement of the key parties in order to enhance the image in the wake of hoped for development. Therefore a considerable amount of management effort would be needed from the start.

The Theatre Village faced two serious implementation problems at this stage. The first was that the brainstorming team, put together through RIBA, had rather assumed that the arts community was indeed a 'community'. In other words, it assumed a community where everyone knew each other and had shared values and aims. In fact this was far from the case. The arts sector is highly fragmented because different members have different aims. Some were 'purists', others commercial in approach. Artists, in the broadest sense of the term – as that is how the team understood it – work as individuals, in teams, under temporary contracts, and in practices and companies. Their activities are divergent, but even those having activities in common are frequently highly competitive. The notion of a coherent single-voiced community was absent. Thus, the onus was on the Westgate Trust to network, building relationships with all the interest groups in order to create common ground, not only to share the vision, but to engender responses at this stage and advise on what could be implemented and how they might be able to help. Out of this the Business Development Centre, offering commercial advice to the arts sector, would have surely grown.

This was certainly not achieved and, it would seem, hardly started. This was to ensure failure of the implementation stage, for although there was not a critical mass of arts to drive the regeneration, there was a sufficient body from which ideas could come and in which the innovative aspects of this flagship project potentially were located. The arts sector included:

- The Tyne Theatre and Opera House, which had been refurbished under the leadership of Jack Dixon.
- The Newcastle Arts Centre and Dance City had been established and new commercial uses introduced during the 1980s to complement the *avant-garde* approach and increase financial viability (see note 28). However it had a 'cold' image with little presence, and assistance was being sought on creating a more prominent entrance at the rear, facing the city centre (see note 27).
- Dance City had started as English National Dance, having international engagements, but financial problems led to the performance side folding, leaving workshops and studio hiring as the sources of income.
- Projects UK, a photographic, music and multimedia performance organization, which also provided training courses through Enterprise Training policy, is located in the Centre.
- Zone Gallery is another user, which was looking for alternative premises (see note 27).
- The Pavilion Theatre was vacant.
- A number of architecture, design and other professions were located in the area.
- Small businesses that provide the support services were located in Theatre Village.
- Specialist retailing that helps underpin an arts-cum-cultural orientation included antiques and Chinese goods.

In one sense, the easy projects had been completed (see note 28);

however, the purpose of the Westgate Trust was to overcome the difficulties. There was certainly scope for assisting the existing arts operators with the problems they were facing, and building confidence and trust in the organization. There was also criticism from those involved with the arts outside the area because they feared that resources may be siphoned from their activities. Liaison with these groups and interests could have eased concern, helped to alleviate problems and perhaps uncovered new ways of organizing the arts activities to create more financially sound set-ups without compromising the aims of the individuals and organizations.

A new concert hall had been a city aspiration for some time and a site was identified near the Theatre Village and Central Station, a study being undertaken by the City, the Urban Development Corporation and English Estates, who could contribute £10m. However, the remaining £20m was a continuing problem (see note 30). Although the concert hall concept was being copied – from Birmingham, Manchester and Bristol, for example – the financing of a hall was always a problem, yet there was again further scope for exploration and experimentation in relation to the image building around the arts, and through innovation and delivering the substance for the image in Newcastle. Successful innovation does come along with many discarded concepts, yet the full potential was not explored by the Westgate Trust.

In summary, the potential for the regeneration through the arts was present. Failure to achieve much was not the result of discarding ineffectual ideas. It was more a case of the avenues not being explored. This raises the second serious implementation problem. The Westgate Trust was set up with an initial budget of £50 000 per annum for two years to December 1991 (Fox and Healey, 1991), therefore the resources beyond personal commitment to TNI and the Trust were unrealistic for the task involved. Either TNI failed to understand on time the issues for an area project of this size and the additional demands made by an innovative approach or it was felt that these problems could be overruled through a few top-down developments.

The result was that the Westgate Trust essentially concentrated on the land use planning role, indeed Fox and Healey commented, 'It sees itself as an extension to the planning function' (1991, p.7). The way in which this evolved has proved to distinguish the project from many others:

> Many regeneration vehicles work closely with planning authorities to create desirable development, but do not have a direct involvement in the planning process. . . . only Little Germany and Birmingham Heartlands have a strong planning involvement, along with the Westgate Trust. (Fox and Healey, p. 16)

Yet with the inactivity, it was hard to tell what was being planned.

The Tyne and Wear Urban Development Corporation, located in the former dock areas, did not stretch as far as the Theatre Village, so in one sense the area had an uncertain geographical position in relation to inward investment, and this had been exacerbated locally by blight related to the road proposals. The planning function of the Westgate Trust was a useful input and the Trust was recognized by the Department of the Environment when considering City Grant and other funding for projects. The City notionally allocated £25 000 per annum, via the Inner City Partnership, but funds were not released in the absence of suitable schemes being put to the City by the Trust, although £300 000 was channelled into the area between 1988/89 and 1991/92 using funding from the Urban Programme, the Prince's Youth Trust and Northern Arts (see note 29). However, there were problems for the Trust in trying to progress development of the area. The Trust undertook studies to demonstrate that rentals were low and that grant money was needed to ensure that projects proceeded.

There was also a need to assemble land in order to create development opportunities that had some economies of scale and would attract developer interest. The City were prepared to use compulsory purchase orders to acquire sites, but only when a development proposal with a developer had been identified, for the City was not permitted to land-bank sites. The alternative was to take marginal schemes and create profitable or economic development through grants. This could be facilitated by dividing 'one' project into a series of 'smaller' projects so that grants could be attracted for each element. For example, it is believed that £200 000 was raised for 34 Clayton Street, of which finance for the facades came from English Heritage, residential funding from the Housing Corporation and the core funding from Inner City Partnership money. A number of other schemes were funded using conservation grants and Urban Development Grants, for example on Stowell Street by Barratt Homes (see note 28).

Quite how the Westgate Trusts planning function was implemented is difficult to understand. The original RIBA brainstorming in 1988 relied heavily upon City briefing material in its work. Although the City strategy for the area embodied a great deal of the ideas from the brainstorming and through TNI (Newcastle City Council, 1991), many of the ideas may have been fed into the process by the City. In any case, very little has happened on the ground during the life of this flagship project. What did occur may well have occurred anyway.

A number of housing schemes were developed during the 1980s, the first being the 200-unit scheme in Waterloo Street by North British Housing Association on the former hotel site. This scheme was three times over-subscribed, hence there clearly was demand. Indeed, the demand has been present for all accommodation of reasonable standard, so the problems have mainly been on the supply side – notably fragmented land holdings and expectations of higher prices, and vacant units over shops (Newcastle City Council, 1991).

The Theatre Village is a concept that many local people are not aware of, but 'Chinatown' is well known. This grew up during the 1980s into an 'ethnic quarter', populated by restaurants and small Chinese businesses, mainly retailing. A great deal of the finance has come from Hong Kong. The process has been part of a similar process replicated across many world cities, and is market-led. This has been added to by the City, labelling it 'Chinatown' and incorporating Chinese-style artefacts into the street land-scape, which again is a feature of many authorities' policies.

The mixed use of the buildings and the late hours of the shops and restaurants adds a feeling of life to the area, and the City has provided funds for the celebration of the Chinese New Year. The City has accelerated the regeneration through grant aid for conversion.

Regeneration through housing development and in Chinatown would have happened through the market and the funding mechanisms administered through government policies at central and local levels.

During 1992 the City made a bid for City Challenge money in the second round and was successful in securing the money. As part of the bid it was agreed that the Westgate Trust would be wound up. The majority of the City Challenge work is concentrated further to the west of the city in housing estates such as Cruddas Park. However, the Theatre Village comes within the remit of the bid, although it does not feature strongly. TNI has an active role under the City Challenge and has had involvement on housing initiatives.

The role of the Theatre Village as an area flagship has therefore been superseded. Overall there were few signs of urban regeneration:

- having a major impact on the area;
- encouraging investment in development and the arts from external sources.

12.8 POLICY AND PROJECT EVALUATION

Evaluating this project during its implementation stages will depend upon from what stage during the policy formulation process the 'aims and objectives' of the initiators are taken. The research approach, set down in Chapter 3, stated that each project would be evaluated on its own terms. If the analysis were to be based upon the aims and objectives reached at the end of the policy formulation stage, then the project may not have yielded many results, however, the ambitions were not that great and the cost has been minimal.

Given that the CBI's task force originally wished regeneration to be driven by private investment criteria (CBI, 1988), then the few results are a product of the lack of economic opportunities. It has been acknowledged that the Westgate Trust contributed to dialogue and help bring a number of disparate interest groups together for facilitating the economic development and planning process (see note 29). The former Executive Director's comments about the role the Westgate Trust has played were:

- 'We've tried to add value to the system generally'
- 'encouragers'
- 'promotional'
- 'single-minded about the area'
- 'enabling organization' (see note 30).

These statements are reasonable, if the analysis starts where the policy formulation ended. But it is the whole policy process that is under analysis and therefore the aims and objectives from the beginning must be considered, allowing for their evolution and change. The question for this analysis is whether the changes were the product of the market position – market demand and policy supply – or a management problem.

The management of an area-based flagship is certainly a difficult task, and because of all the different interests involved, perhaps impossible from a marketing viewpoint.[32] This does not simply concern those who are, or potentially are, interested parties, such as property owners, business, artists, but also those who affect the image, namely those involved in crime, prostitution and rioting.

An innovative project is also very difficult to manage while ensuring that change is built into the policy formulation stages. Yet Drucker points out the need for firm management of this process, whereby guidelines are used to steer ideas towards a practical outcome in commercial and policy terms (Drucker, 1986).

The arts sector is diverse and integral to the innovative side of this area flagship. Managing the arts is possible and there was a role model for the Theatre Village in Glasgow. In the mid-1980s Glasgow put its proposal to the Office of Arts and Libraries to represent Britain as the Cultural Capital of Europe in 1990. What secured the title was the detailed business plan put up by the artists and their administrators, which had been established through their informal network.

The conclusion of the area-based, the innovation and the arts sector issues is that they all need considerable and sensitive management resources, especially when in combination. The analysis has shown that there was understanding of the need to develop a vision, and TNI realized the benefits of drawing on other resources for this, yet on every other count the management failed to address the necessary issues, either in a top-down or bottom-up fashion, namely:

- resourcing the Trust;
- building relationships through networking;

- getting key individuals and interest groups behind the vision;
- managing the publicity hand in hand with the networking;
- understanding the arts sector in order to operationalize policies;
- taking an active development role;
- involving the local people.

Marketing and selling an **innovative–local** flagship depends upon first 'selling' the concept, envisioning others with the ideas and developing the policy as they feed in their ideas. Managing this process is crucial to producing an innovative set of policies that are implementable (see Figure 5.9). Without this there is no 'product' to sell in the later stages, hence the flagship function fails. TNI and its subsequent vehicle, the Westgate Trust, were unsuccessful in their management efforts for the Theatre Village.

12.9 PROJECT IMPACT

Changes in the area are largely the response to market processes. The regeneration of the Chinatown area was the product of an ethnic grouping seeking a low cost base to operate from and where they felt secure by grouping together. This was accelerated by local authority investment and grant aid. The extent to which this enhanced the informal grouping is difficult to assess. Investment in property was welcomed because the Chinese sought to base their grouping upon property and trading. Whether the 'ethnic' overlay of street furniture in an Chinese style is enhancement depends upon values. On the one hand, it could be seen as patronizing because it is a veneer imposed upon the area. It may be viewed as not directly benefiting the Chinese population, but enhancing the area as a tourist feature, as a place of interest, which in turn benefits the Chinese restaurants and businesses. This 'sense of place' has not arisen from the life of the community but has been grafted onto it. In that way it becomes a part of the spectacle of the urban form and an aestheticization of urban life (Harvey, 1989a). The approach is part of the widespread use of the signs and symbols of heritage, in this case Chinese, that was so common in the urban regeneration of the 1980s (Bianchini, Dawson and Evans, 1990, 1992) and postmodernism in general (Harvey, 1989a).

Another market process at work has been the process of revitalization described by Zukin (1988) in Soho, New York where old warehouse conversions:

- attracted artists, who
- established a lifestyle, which
- was marketed by agents and developers, and
- bought by 'yuppies', resulting in

- prices going up,
- the artists cashing in and being squeezed out.

A similar pattern has emerged in Newcastle on a small scale. It should first be emphasized that this is not involving displacement of an existing population, since the numbers in the Theatre Village were less than 100 at the beginning of the 1980s, but the arts sector, Chinatown and the low cost has made the area popular with Newcastle 'yuppies', that is social workers, teachers and increasingly students.[33] The fragility of this type of 'community' has led to authorities, urban designers and architects giving this marketing image more permanence in the design of the urban landscape. The current penchant for pedestrianization (see also Chapters 8, 9 and 11) has been repeated in the Theatre Village. Whether the plans are implemented remains to be seen, but two points need to be made:

- pedestrian spaces only look interesting and only feel safe if they are well populated;
- they must be through routes.

The problem with pedestrian proposals for the Theatre Village is that they will probably fail to generate sufficient traffic. This may not have been the case if the flagship function had worked because the process of immigration to the area would have continued. But even with this the proposals are suspect, because it is not a through route. Once the proposed distributor route is built, residential areas will be severed from the Village. Traditional footbridges and subways do not overcome this problem. The road would need to be sunk, with wide footpath areas spanning the road (cf. the bridge to Centenary Square, Birmingham in Chapter 9), which is expensive, but necessary.

One of the features of urban regeneration within Newcastle has been the number of different policies and initiatives, which overlap and collide. There are several comments to make about these, for greater coordination and amalgamation may have yielded more results. Each initiative of policy has tended to arise at a different time, but the main issue is that each has arisen for different reasons emanating from a span of operational levels – central government, local government, private and 'independent' organizations. It induces competition for resources and conflicts in managing the policies and projects. On the other hand, many of the same prominent people are influential in managing, advising and overseeing the projects, therefore different approaches and ideas are not forthcoming. This is far from unique to Newcastle.

This leads to a vital point for marketing the city. If each of the initiatives was aimed at an entirely different market position and segments within that position, the different initiatives would be entirely understandable and the overlaps potentially rewarding. However, the thinking is dominated by attracting large-scale inward investment of branch plants and office functions. This aim is achieved through a number of means, from environmental improvement in derelict areas to speculative development with financial and training incentive packages. The result is the same – a concentration on routinized market positions, especially at the national and international scale. Sales efforts are diluted and compete between projects within the same region and city.

For all its shortcomings, and there were many, the Theatre Village concept was exciting, innovative and complementary to the overemphasis upon other approaches in Newcastle. Economic stability and organic growth are far more likely to arise from innovative projects, even though these are more prone to failure, requiring clear and firm management guidelines. However, this approach requires a different understanding of the phrase 'value for money', which has come to mean cost control of inputs. The required meaning is **value of return** on the investment, in other words the output (see Chapter 5). Although costs are important, it is less the cost of inputs that is critical, but the management input.

Another problem with a plethora of policies and initiatives is **governance**. This is a general problem for public agencies in relation to private sector involvement, partnerships or acting in private sector ways because it becomes unclear to whom it is that the authority is accountable and how accountability is achieved. For the public, a multitude of organizations becomes too difficult to understand. It encourages disinterest. Perhaps the public is not particularly interested most of the time. However, in the absence of accountability legitimacy can be lost quickly and the authorities concerned will be unable to monitor the extent and rate of loss. Robinson and Shaw (1991) point out that accountability is poor for many initiatives, such as the Urban Development Corporations (UDCs), but they comment about business leadership teams (BLTs):

> Unlike the UDCs, who are at least accountable in theory, BLTs make no such pretence. Organisations such as The Newcastle Initiative (TNI), The Wearside Opportunity (TWO), or The Bristol Initiative (TBI) are entirely self-appointed, often drawing on the commitment of individuals already involved in urban initiatives under the auspices of such bodies as Business in the Community, The Phoenix Partnership, The Association of British Chambers of Commerce, and the CBI. (p.64)

Governance only works when those in authority are serving the population, rather than pursuing sectional interest and, therefore, political or economic power. Loss of legitimacy is evident when there is political or social upheaval. The problem for those in governance is to know whether real needs are being served and when legitimacy is being eroded.

Social upheaval has been commonplace, the West End riots, which followed a few days after the Meadowell riots, beginning only 400 metres from Theatre Village. These riots concerned a range of issues and tensions in a broader population; however, warning signs were clearly present. An argument can be made that the most powerful images of the Newcastle areas have not come from any of the flagships, including the Theatre Village, which hardly has a profile, but from the rioting and from the British television programmes *Spender* and *Byker Grove*. *Spender* has been the more powerful, reaching audiences of ten million viewers, showing differing aspects of the city, and simultaneously breaking down as well as reinforcing various stereotypes (see note 27). The indirect promotional impact of such programmes has importance, especially as the distinctive features of the culture, factual and mythical, have been emphasized, although the results are more fortuitous that the targeted sales efforts of the Tyne and Wear Development Corporation.

12.10 SUMMARY

The Theatre Village has failed to achieve its original aims and objectives, taking into account the entire policy process. The issues arose out of the area-based nature of the project, the arts emphasis and the innovative aspects. The problems emanating from these issues were TNI's and the Westgate Trust's failure to:

- perceive the management needs, especially for guiding innovation;
- understand the diversity of the arts sector and its interests;
- use its network to build relationships in a bottom-up and top-down way.

These problems arose in the policy formulation stage, and the flagship's failure dates from this time. All the problems are interrelated and concern the operational skills of leadership, which bridge the vision or concept and the implementation stage. Specifically, these were:

- lack of management resources;
- lack of management understanding;
- the decision to avoid developing directly; the demonstration effect plus 'added value';
- failure in getting local people and business to 'own' the vision and hence create opportunities for fostering innovation;
- failure to use the network to 'sell' the idea outside the area, yet create informal accountability within the area.

The role of the Westgate Trust was regulated to a liaison and planning function. The impacts of the flagship are negligible within the area, and it has failed to induce revitalization and further investment in its wake from within the area and from outside.

The idea of an area-based approach for cultural urban regeneration has been adopted elsewhere, for example the Jewellery Quarter in Birmingham (Bianchini, Dawson and Evans, 1990). The scope and economic need for innovative projects, whatever their orientation in terms of market position, is considerable for a successful economy, and few have been tried. Failure rates will be high because many ideas are not operational. This should be assessed under clear and firm management guidelines for the operational aspects in the formulation stage. The Theatre Village flagship project failed because of the absence of this aspect.

Byker Wall

13.1 INTRODUCTION

Located in Newcastle, this residential development is actually called Byker, although the development has become known by the distinctive perimeter block, which came to be called 'Byker Wall'. It is an internationally renowned development because of its design by architect Ralph Erskine and because of the consultation process that evolved in the design and allocation of the units. It has a longer history than the other case studies and is not strictly a flagship development. This is because it predates the flagship development in Britain. Its purpose was to redevelop a 'community' in a sensitive way rather than draw in other investment or consumption activities. It was not located in an area of dereliction, although Byker had a large amount of poor quality building stock. Nor is it located in the centre of the city, although a large proportion of the residents worked in the now defunct docks in the valley it overlooks.

The development was innovative, and would still be considered so today. It was local in orientation, yet has achieved international recognition. As a flagship it would therefore be a **G-type** project in terms of its market position (see Figure 4.1), and had it been developed over the last decade it would surely have been labelled a flagship, and would probably have been scrutinized for application potential to other urban regeneration projects.

There have been few flagship projects that have been purely residential. This is because:

- such developments need to be large enough to have a significant impact upon investment and consumption in a city;
- populations are usually in decline within inner city areas;
- local government is restricted in direct development;
- housing associations have been financially limited for large schemes;
- volume housebuilders tended to prefer:
  - greenfield sites;

- undertaking purely commercial developments rather than strategic investments in order to cultivate future market locations;
- entering partnership arrangements with authorities or housing associations as a means to acquire land and obtain planning permission rather than as a primary business.

There are exceptions, the most notable one being the voluntary scheme developed in phases by the Eldonians in Liverpool. This scheme was bottom-up in policy terms and in opposition to the City Council. The Eldonian initiative was spontaneous, and it is anticipated that this type of response will become increasingly common in its own right or channelled through the voluntary sector. The Byker Wall is interesting because there was a large bottom-up component too, and the way in which that shifted during the policy process is instructive. It has also been top-down, and this interaction is important. It is considered a more useful project for examination, given the policy statements about developing large tracts of urban land for housing, especially the Thames Corridor east of London Docklands.

13.2 BACKGROUND AND CITY POLICY

The economic background for Newcastle has been considered in Chapter 12. A number of supplementary points can be made regarding Byker. Byker was originally a village, largely owned by the Lawson family, who sold plots to developers in the second half of the 19th century as the city grew. The plots were developed in a grid-iron fashion, the 3- and 4-bedroom units densely packed in rows of terraces for the shipyard and engineering workforce. Schools were built on a minimum of site area, and corner shops did not appear until the turn of the century (Newcastle City Council, 1981).

The 1951 City Development Plan introduced a policy to reduce housing densities to 80 people per acre, compared to the 120 people per acre in the 200 acres which Byker covered. In 1953 1175 houses were considered unfit, although slum clearance schemes had higher priority in other areas at the time. By 1959 clearance plans were considered and compulsory purchase orders began to be served in 1963. During this time the Development Plan was reviewed and in 1966 the policy for Byker was clarified. The intention was to clear the entire neighbourhood for redevelopment between 1969 and 1971 (Newcastle City Council, 1981). However, there was also a plan for a new urban motorway (cf. Chapter 12) at the top of Byker and concern about the rehousing of those in its path and the noise generated by traffic. The concern created a pause, out of which the Byker Wall was to emerge over the next 12–15 years.

13.3 THE PARTIES

The City was the developer and ultimate manager of the scheme during all policy stages and in managing the scheme once occupied. It remains the prime owner, despite the growing popularity of 'right to buy' policies during the 1980s. The population of Byker was very influential in shaping the scheme. During the policy pause, cited above, there was disquiet about the form of redevelopment and residents wished to have greater control over their own destinies. This has to be seen in the context of two factors. Firstly, there had been growing dissatisfaction with wholesale slum clearance schemes as neighbourhoods and long-established friendships were broken up, as households were arbitrarily relocated wherever there were available properties. Secondly, the shipyard and industrial workforce were highly organized and were able to transfer this experience into the residential context. It was summarized this way:

> What does make Byker stand out is that its community spirit continued long after other towns had surrendered to modern reserve and indifference. It was this which influenced the City Council in its decision to redevelop the township in such a way as to retain the community (Newcastle City Council, 1981, p.3)

Whether the 'community' was that unique is a moot point. It is more likely that the proposals, coupled with uncertainty about their precise implications for families, had 'got the backs up' of the population:

> A survey undertaken in 1968 showed that there was a positive attitude towards redevelopment – 80 per cent 'approved' of the decision to demolish Byker, of which 91 per cent attributed housing to be the main cause of their view. However, the future of Byker had not been fully decided. Because of the uncertainty, a series of public meetings took place, but these did not answer many questions. Then the clergy and the warden of the Community Centre began liaison meetings with politicians and officers of the Corporation, with the aim of exposing the stress building up in the community as a result of planning blight, the uncertainties people felt about the future and the need to do something positive with the community before it began to disintegrate irreparably. (*Housing Review*, 1974, p.150)

Such unity is difficult to deal with unless a bottom-up approach to policy making is incorporated into the development process. A traditional scheme and approach would be unlikely to carry the day.

Ralph Erskine was British by birth and trained as an architect in Britain, but practised in Sweden. There were close trading links between Newcastle and Scandinavia. In addition, Erskine had been used by a private developer, having won a design competition for some houses near Newcastle in

1967. He was also working on a scheme at Clare Hall, Cambridge, although this had not been completed when he was appointed to master-plan the redevelopment of Byker. He had gained a reputation as Sweden's leading architect for public housing (Amery, undated).

13.4 MARKET POSITION

The set of circumstances had led the City to adopt an innovative approach. This was challenging for a local authority, because the procedural approach is highly routinized in organizational terms, and therefore, the way in which the built environment is managed has tended to be the same. The 1960s and 1970s were even more in this cultural mould, mass consumption markets and rational planning still being dominant. Adopting what could today be characterized as an **innovative–local** market position was a daring step for a local authority developer (see Figures 4.1 and 4.2).

13.5 POLICY FORMULATION

Some of the preliminary policy considerations are outlined above. It had been decided in March 1967 that some form of barrier would be necessary between any new development and the proposed motorway (Newcastle City Council, 1981). Erskine was appointed to address this issue and to investigate ways of redeveloping on a site with a 1:7 gradient, using the preliminary plans and brief prepared by the City. The result was a set of flexible proposals rather than a more rigid masterplan, a Plan of Intent (Erskine, 1970), which was submitted to and approved by the City in 1970. The intent was to develop:

- an integrated built environment for living;
- a low cost in use scheme for residents;
- a scheme implemented through intimate collaboration with the residents;
- a scheme that maintained respect for the surrounding areas;
- an organizational approach that held together the family ties and valued associations among the existing residents;
- a scheme to provide a recognizable physical form that had local individuality;
- on a rolling programme.

The Plan of Intent set down the initial policy goals and was used to gauge the strength of feeling about the concepts both among the population and the City (see Figure 5.9). The City was in favour of the participation in the design process. The concern among the local population was a City problem; however, Erskine and the team assembled for the project were proposing to ease this issue for them. This was a turning point for the City Council. At Byker, it had been the clergy and Community Centre warden who had drawn attention to the local concerns; the same thing was to happen in Liverpool. Father Jim Dunne had drawn the councillors' attention to proposals to demolish the Eldonians housing. In Liverpool, this brought people together to redevelop themselves (Cowan, Hannay and Owens, 1988). However, at Byker, this drew the City into a course of action to incorporate the local population into the process through the architects (cf. Malpass, 1979), if not by policy intention, then by default. This was broadly in line with the recommendations for public participation published in the Skeffington Committee Report (1969) by central government. The architectural team perceived this as an opportunity to maintain fast-eroding self-respect among the local population (Ravetz, 1976). Therefore, the preliminary goals were set, although quite what was being achieved with them was the subject of some contention.

The proposal was to take these outline goals and to test them out through a pilot scheme. This is comparable with the operationalization of concepts used by Marshall (1991); however, instead of the autocratic approach adopted in other innovative projects (see Chapter 12), this was legitimizing the concepts through demonstration (see Figure 5.9). The pilot scheme, Janet Square, a cleared area on the south-east corner of the development, was to be developed to a density of 100 people per acre (compared to 80 people per acre in the 1951 Development Plan). A group of 46 tenants was invited to participate in the formulation of design proposals alongside the architects and the City Housing Department. The tenants had been moved into a neighbourhood seen as having lower social status, and it consequently took the first three meetings to convince the group that the City and the architects were serious. This also demonstrates that Byker was a series of neighbourhoods and neighbourhood perceptions, rather than one single 'community'. As one of the architects wrote:

> It is easy to fall into the trap of thinking of Byker as one tightly knit community, and this was one of several experiences which taught us otherwise. (*Housing Review*, 1974, p.152)

The architects used a questionnaire to gauge the importance of common amenities to the residents and prepared concepts of the house types, which were used to solicit comments on layouts, position and provision of services, storage, work surfaces, glazing, fences and so on. The site plan and layouts were also criticized. Participation was very intensive on this first phase, and gave rise to a highly established and professional tenants' association.[34]

The scheme design was for 46 dwellings of 2- and 3-storey timber framed houses, built at a cost of £197 688, or £5.25 per square foot. They were laid out in a courtyard fashion. The application of low cost and non-traditional materials in a British context was tried. This was to become a hallmark of the scheme in future phases, aiming to give a soft and humane aesthetic to the housing, where people could both overlook each other, yet retain privacy. The scheme was well received and the residents were pleased with the result. However, the architects learnt a great deal from the pilot and were able to make major improvements to the quality of design in sub-sequent phases. The tenants had acted as 'guinea-pigs' and, although they benefited from moving into new accommodation earlier, the quality of the housing was lower than for the remaining phases designed by Erskine.

13.6 PROJECT IMPLEMENTATION

The concept for the main development had grown out of the Plan of Intent and the pilot project. The design turned its back upon the proposed motorway and tried to make the optimum use of the 1:7 gradient, orientat-ing the housing to the south overlooking the city centre and valley. It can be divided conceptually into two parts: the perimeter block, which came to be known as the Byker Wall, labelling the whole scheme in most people's minds, and low rise housing. The Wall wraps around the top end of the site with the majority of the windows and all of its balconies on the south facing elevation, away from the road route. The height of the Wall varies, providing relief to the skyline. It was designed with the elderly tenants in mind, a number of whom expressed to the architects a preference for living above ground level. Each of the floors had a different design to create variety and to ensure that the public areas were easily recognizable (Gracie, 1979).

The low rise is contained in the areas below, linked by fingers of stepped housing which penetrates into the low rise development. Indeed, there was a conscious aim to ensure that the elements 'blurred at the edges' (Gracie, 1979). Six phases of development were envisaged, although only five were built according to the Erskine concept, and these are shown in Table 13.1.

The development consists of twelve separate neighbourhoods, which are pedestrianized, with car parking being confined to peripheral car parks. Major pedestrian routes link the neighbourhoods, and each neighbour-hood is colour-coded. The houses are in informal terrace groupings, with semi-private courtyard spaces for each group. The design included exten-sive hard and soft landscaping. Timber and other cladding materials are used on the housing in addition to brick, and primary colours have been applied. The Wall was constructed of *in situ* cross walls and concrete slabs, metric modular patterned brickwork being used on the outer skin. The link blocks or fingers which rise up to join the wall are served by lifts, stairs and

Table 13.1 Byker Wall

Estate name	Property description	Number of units
Perimeter block: 'Byker Wall'	1-bedroom maisonettes	275
	2-bedroom maisonettes	120
	3-bedroom maisonettes	49
	4-bedroom maisonettes	2
	1-bedroom flats	98
	Bedsits	13
Low rise: 'Byker Estate'	2-bedroom houses	149
	3-bedroom houses	643
	4-bedroom houses	90
	1 bedroom flats	217
	2-bedroom flats	106
	3-bedroom flats	19
	4-bedroom flats	8
	Bedsits	2
	2-bedroom maisonettes	52
	3-bedroom maisonettes	11
	1-bedroom bungalows	18
Sheltered housing: 'Avondale House'	1-bedroom flats	33
Sheltered housing: 'Mount Pleasant'	1-bedroom flats	24
'Tom Collins House'	1-bedroom flats	39
	2-bedroom flats	13

Source: Newcastle City Council (undated).

balcony 'bridges'. Individual houses and units were given privacy, but attempts were made to provide visual contact with the surrounding residents, the high rise elements having balconies. These also give superb views across the city. Some of the lounges were on the first floor, where this enhanced the views. The entire concept was to create a highly textured and informal environment and was revolutionary for public housing schemes in Britain, and in contrast to the austere original Byker estate.

Rough sawn and stained timber was used to reduce vandalism; it is also easily replaceable. Aluminium sheeting was also used as a cladding material. Reclaimed materials from the old development were incorporated into the hard landscaping features. Incidental play areas were provided for children, and these could be overlooked by parents in the houses. Communal facilities were provided in parts, including hobby rooms and the area office, which was used by the architects, so that the detailed design team were constantly on site for the tenants. The office became more of a social and meeting centre for people, rather than a real focus for resident design input.

Corner shops were also provided in the design. The cost of the development grew from £5.25 per square foot to £11.62 per square foot by 1974. Most of the work was undertaken by local contractor Stanley Miller, with Shepherd Construction also carrying out some. Overall, building costs were slightly lower than for other council housing developments in the city (Ravetz, 1976). A district heating system was installed, with power coming from the refuse reclamation power plant and heat station, a backup facility located in Shipley Street, which was the first to come on line.

The design was a radical one for Britain and had extended the ideas Erskine had developed in Scandinavia of design according to context, particularly the micro-climate and development orientation, and concern for the user (Egelius, 1990). This was in stark contrast to the mass and tower block housing of the 1960s, which was the product of social engineering (see, for example, Mellor, 1977).

Resident involvement continued throughout the redevelopment programme through Liaison Committees, chaired in rotation by the tenants. This caused some official concern, because many of the professionals would have preferred a properly constituted association. However, the prospective tenants of the new scheme were not comfortable with that formality (Ravetz, 1976). They were fearful of losing control and the impetus of their actions. Yet it was found that, once rehoused in the new scheme the tenants relapsed into their private ways of living, which Ravetz describes as 'one of the penalties of successful housing' (1976, p.742). This did not mean that they were passive; for example, they did resite some of the landscaping features. They kept an interest in the scheme 'at arm's length'.

This raises the question of the nature of tenant involvement. Undoubtedly Ravetz's comment on successful rehousing is true, as shall be seen from the evaluation, yet looking from the causes leading up to participation, the picture looks different. There had been great concern in Byker about the redevelopment, and community figures had warned the City of the build up of tension. A radical solution was sought in terms of design and process. This was fully developed in the pilot stage. However, the design was clearly Erskine's and while he and his team had always listened to and incorporated suggestions, the basic concept did not emanate from the tenants.

During the implementation phases the nature of participation also changed. The level of consultation and participation was diluted. Although the architect's office was on site to answer queries and act as a meeting point, the change that took place can be described as involvement **with**, as opposed to involvement **of**, the residents. This made the scheme, in one sense, 'no different to any other development' from the City's point of view, for it became a matter of managing the development process with maximum efficiency. Therefore involvement was a 'legitimizing role, as we had to manage it and could speak on behalf of the tenant. It was successful to some extent'.[35]

In other words, the policy formulation stage had focused upon the discontent, and during the implementation stage the concerns were to address fine detail of the development on the one hand, and innovations in allocation policy on the other. Tenants, for the first time, were given six months notice of moving. Although there were construction delays, this did remove uncertainty. Some tenants did choose to move away, and therefore there was not a one-for-one replacement, with people from outside Byker moving in during the last phase.[36]

The level of contact with tenants was increasing nationally at the time in any case because housing managers were being decentralized as part of a trend towards 'generic workers' in local government services, although Byker Wall did not have decentralized management until 1987 (see note 34). However, attitudes were beginning to change, of which the Skeffington Committee Report (1969) and decentralized management were a reflection. Yet the objective had not been to relinquish control, rather of achieving a means to maintain it. Malpass, in his study of Byker, describes it this way:

What we have to comprehend is the political nature of the redevelopment process and the fact that the local authority operated with a hierarchy of policies which gave retention of the community less importance than moving ahead quickly with rebuilding. . . . The policy of retaining the community should itself be seen as the outcome of a prolonged debate, both within the Civic Centre and beyond, as to the best way of dealing with Byker. (1979, p.1012)

Malpass (1979) states that these objectives embodied a desire to retain the 'community'. While this analysis supports the contention that the innovation grew out of political necessity, in other words, containing the response of the 'community', there seems little to support the notion that it was a community of shared values and lives. It is easy to be united **against** something, but much more difficult to be **for** something. The overall conclusion is that the community were only united against the type of threats that redevelopment had introduced into peoples lives elsewhere. The positive things that came out of participation in the implementation stage were:

- some influence on design
- information on progress and allocation of units
- improved understanding among City officials of local needs.

City officials and councillors put a great deal of effort into the process, attending a large number of meetings during out of work hours. This should not be minimized. That said, when the City wished to control the project from the top down, it did so. For example Tom Collins House, named after the chair of the City Housing Committee, was originally designed as a tall block to house youths, but the proposal was overturned without participation to reallocate it for sheltered housing. Some councillors were opposed to the participation, and also feared that it would generate high maintenance costs.

However, the City was to become proud of Byker, as it began to be noticed as an innovative housing scheme around the world. It seemed like a 'reward' for the large personal investment in time that many had already made. There was discussion about managing and further encouraging the interest by setting up a visitor centre, but it was not pursued on grounds of cost, although the development received many visitors who were shown around.

Building continued throughout the 1970s and the last 2000 units were completed around 1982. The final phase of Byker was not developed according to the Erskine design. The Janet Street area was cordoned off for three years because of litigation against the contractors and some of the partly built houses were eventually demolished (see note 36). The City did not have the funds to complete it, although it had wished to do so, despite previous reservations in some quarters. The last two parcels of land, which included part of the demolished area, were developed under license by volume housebuilders in order to introduce private finance into the development along central government guidelines. The City entered into partnership-for-sale schemes with Leech, which is part of Beazer Homes, and Bowey, a local company. The City was able, under the agreement, to have some control over the size, selling price and construction programme allocation. The entire Leech development, Clydesdale, was sold to people nominated by the City, as was 70% of the Bowey scheme, Harbottle, even though the houses went on the open market at the end of a six-week period (Cameron and Thornton, 1986).

This final phase of the Byker redevelopment was imposed upon the City by central government edict and thus compromised the complete implementation of this **innovative–local** project. How the two schemes compare will be considered in the evaluation of this project as a role model and flagship style of development. It is to the evaluation that the analysis now turns.

13.7 POLICY AND PROJECT EVALUATION

The project needs to be evaluated at two levels. Firstly, the overt aims and objectives:

- Management:
  - implementation through intimate collaboration with the residents;
  - redevelopment on a rolling programme.

- Design:
  - an integrated built environment for living;
  - a low cost in use scheme for residents;
  - maintaining respect for the surrounding areas;
  - holding together the family ties and valued associations among the existing residents;
  - providing a recognizable physical form that had local individuality.

Secondly, is the covert objective of maintaining control of the **whole** development process, and in order to do this **some** control over the management and design were relinquished. Power was redistributed in two ways:

- directly to the population;
- indirectly, through the architects, to the population.

The covert objective worked well and was successfully managed. The City had responded to the warning signs conveyed to them by community leaders, and it was from this that a radical solution for its day emerged. One of the main means to achieve social stability, and provide improved communication and facilities for the population, while maintaining City control, was promoting Byker as a solid and united 'community'. Malpass (1979) summarizes the process:

> The constant reiteration of the idea of consensus underlying Byker has been used as a way of engineering a situation in which opposition could be written off as wrongheaded or 'politically motivated'. (p.1013)

The time devoted by officers and councillors to the attendance of meetings and evening surgeries with residents demonstrated the long-term commitment that individuals and the City had for the scheme and its high political priority.[37] There was a constant tension in this for the City, because they did not wish to treat Byker Wall and the people differently, but equally they did not want to lose the uniqueness of the scheme, for it was creating political prestige and was developing its 'role model' image.

A great deal of positive things came out of the process for residents. The scheme, as will be seen, is well liked and much of the uncertainty concerning large-scale redevelopment was alleviated or removed. Nevertheless, the opposition was certainly contained through City management:

> The willingness of officers and councillors to attend meetings with residents over several years has itself reinforced the idea of a co-

operative approach. . . . The paradox of this situation is that consensus is the enemy of participation. (Malpass, 1979, p.1013)

The degree of choice and decision making was not fully in the populations hand. Concerning the offer to tenants of a unit,

> could people turn the offer down once the inevitable pain of redevelopment became apparent? The answer is 'no'. The Byker story is about the management of consensus. There is no room for conflict. (*Architects Journal*, 1979, p.1021)

The covert policy therefore worked and it did so in a two-stage way. The pilot scheme, part of the policy formulation process, involved a high degree of participation, and the implementation stage was more concerned with involvement. The concept of design, even in the pilot stage, came from Erskine. It was his willingness to learn from the population that guided the process, rather than the needs of the residents driving the design (cf. Altman and Chemers, 1984) or the tenants setting out the principles of design (Alexander *et al.*, 1985). During the pilot stage there could have come a point where the residents would have wished to take total control of the project, as had happened with the Eldonians in Liverpool, setting up their own management and ownership structures (Cowan, Hannay and Owens, 1988). This may have produced neither a better nor a worse outcome for the residents, but the point, in Byker's case, is that the original aims remained in the control of the ultimate owner and client, the City. The main difference between the two is that in the case of the Eldonians the innovation emphasized organization, whereas in the Byker case it emphasized design, albeit that design was also used as an instrument of control by the City. The team Erskine formed for the project felt that they learnt a great deal from the participation during the pilot stage.

During the project implementation stage the design consultation was diluted to the level of involvement rather than participation. The design of the Wall itself was carried out without any consultation with the tenants (Ravetz, 1976). This did not dilute the innovativeness of the design – indeed, if anything, it led to its enhancement. Further attempts to induce participation failed (Ravetz, 1976), perhaps because the 'heat' had already been taken out of the situation. The reduction in tenant involvement may not have produced the best user and management solutions for the project once in use, as will be analysed later. However, within the confines of the covert objectives, the process worked and the overt objectives came into play in the two-stage design process to realize the aims and objectives.

The significance for marketing the city is enormous. The absence of a bottom-up process in the Birmingham case studies has been documented (see Chapters 9, 10 and 11), and it has been asserted that this would have helped redistribute the benefits, as well as aiding political legitimacy. In the case of the Byker Wall there has been just such a combination of the top-down and bottom-up processes. However, this chapter clearly demonstrates that this can be managed in a number of ways, and this affects the outcomes for the residents or users. It also shows that the population were moulded in certain ways, in this case in response to tensions rather than invited participation. It underscores the two-edged sword of local people being incorporated into the city 'product' in order to achieve greater benefits.

The design is the lasting benefit, so it needs to be looked at in greater detail, especially with regard to the cost in use objective and the tenants' desire to have an environment that they liked. There are a large number of successful features, as well as a number of aspects that work less well. In some ways, there are familiar council-house solutions designed into the scheme. Firstly, although the Wall varies in storey height, it has high rise features with corridors, link bridges and other common circulation areas, which have proved successful (cf. Coleman, 1990). The ground floor gardens are similar to those of 1930s flats in northern cities, and the low rise dwellings are a variation on the vocabulary of standard housing types (Ravetz, 1976). There were also problems with noise levels from neighbouring tenants, due to design faults. However, most people like the environment, and it has proved a popular development. Tenants were very appreciative of the landscaping at first, which was lush and in dramatic contrast to the old terraced houses and other council house developments of the same period.

The main issue has been management of the development. There is a conflict between the standard approach the City took towards maintenance and the requirements for Byker, which demanded new approaches. This issue was summed up in the sentiment, 'Byker would be really, really brilliant, if only it hadn't been run by the Council' (see note 37). The timber walkways and bridge links needed a non-slip proprietary paint, but this was not used until 1986. The foliage grew quickly – the slope is south facing and the district heating scheme encouraged growth. What was an asset at first became a problem. The trees began to block out light and tenants began to become wary about walking through the pathways between the densely packed buildings where someone could be hiding (see note 37). Crime and levels of attack are low in the Byker Wall, so this was a matter of perception encouraged by the landscape growth (see note 34). The City's solution to this was to cut down a number of the trees and remove some of the shrubs and bushes. They also removed many of the hard landscape features, such as the pergolas, gates, sandpits and fountains because they needed maintenance. Erskine had included murals, which the City painted over. The problem was that there was no planned maintenance programme or a schedule of rates so that a budget could be developed for the maintenance. Therefore, in this case the planting, pruning and thinning were not undertaken and drastic action could have been avoided. This was in part the fault of the design team, who did not communicate the need and details for a maintenance strategy, and partly the fault of the City. Overall, it neglected to take the initiative on maintenance needs and skills, treating the development like any other scheme in some ways. Many of the original drawings and specification details were lost by the City. In other ways, the scheme received a great deal of attention because of the high political profile.[38] In addition, operatives on site had a high regard for the scheme and were both diligent and creative (see note 34). More recently, a planned approach to maintenance has been implemented under contract.

Recently maintenance costs have risen; however, the level of vandalism has been (Ravetz, 1976) and remains low. The Wall, because of the varied design on each level and the predominance of the elderly living in it, has worked very well. This is 'despite all the odds stacked against it' as a high rise development (see note 38). It also works well because the elderly like the district heating scheme, the Neighbourhood Management Office have looked after it well, and the 1- and 2-bedroom flats are above ground level. Residents know that the architects valued them as people, and so they respect the environment too. The increases in costs have mainly arisen because of a maintenance backlog. Costs are less than elsewhere, yet there are particular issues, for example, the use of sawn timber is 'cheap and cheerful' but it is high on maintenance (see note 38).

The timber frame is of high quality, but it has proved difficult to retrofit. Some of the materials are hard to replace, most notably the bricks, which are all metric (see note 34). The district heating scheme has caused a large number of problems. It was installed badly, with pipes going under foundations, and it cannot be regulated within each unit. The cost is also high (see note 38). This was formerly covered under Housing Benefit, but this payment ceased through cuts in 1988. However, in this case, the tenants are contributing towards City waste disposal, although this factor has not been taken into the pricing structure (see note 37). Tenants who live there have to be able to pay for it, which is making it hard to let, especially for young people, even though the price has been fixed since 1985. The district heating pipes are being replaced and run under the car parking areas (see note 38).

Other design problems were the low pitched roofs, in places, and roof fixings, identified by maintenance officers, which led to a survey being undertaken. There was storm damage in 1985. Some parts of the Wall were built without any restraints on the single skin of brickwork. The contractors, Stanley Miller, had a legal action brought against them but went bankrupt during the action. There was a lack of communication between the architects and the contractors, particularly regarding skill transfer for

Scandinavian design and construction detailing. The schools were not rebuilt, and the hobby rooms were converted to stores in some cases as soon as they fell into temporary disuse, or knocked into the neighbouring flat. The shopping at the bottom of the scheme is not thought to be successful, despite remedial security work undertaken in 1985–1986. The link blocks may break up the mass of the scheme, but are themselves the subject of disputes and can be difficult to let. Finally, the pilot scheme has not worn well and there have therefore been social costs associated with this stage of policy formulation.

Other issues relate to use by people. The soft landscaping is seen as creating a security problem for young children. On the other hand, many of the children's play facilities have been removed on maintenance grounds, which has given greater power to older children, who 'control' more of the common areas, thus exacerbating safety issues. Inadequate lighting at night has been a problem. One unforeseen problem has been the growth in car ownership, and some residents drive their cars at speed up the paths to the front doors. This is for convenience and security, but presents a serious hazard to children.

The age profile on the development is also changing. It is difficult to let to many young people because of the costs, especially the heating costs, which cannot be regulated for each unit. However, the proportion of young people on the estate is slowly rising. The main problems of integrating ages is on the high rise. Although the Wall has key access, an entry phone system may become necessary. The low rise works better in this respect. Some young people who have become tenants have caused noise problems for the elderly, and Byker Wall is becoming a destination for young people to spend their time, because of its attractiveness. Glue sniffing and other abuses are on the increase, as is vandalism and harassment. It is easy to get to by both bus and Metro (see note 34). It has become a victim of its own success, within the context of an increase in these social problems across Newcastle and other British cities. Byker is a popular destination; however, it is now firmly 'labelled' among people as council housing **because** of its distinctiveness.

There are disputes between families on the estate, some arising out of changing age profile and design faults, although there have always been some (see note 34), adding further evidence to the notion that Byker has never been an integrated 'community'.

Before looking at the final phase of partnership development, it is worth summarizing the issues arising out of the design and behaviour of the tenants. The main problems were:

- poor communication of design detailing to contractor and the implications for skills and training;
- absence of maintenance budget, planning and skill development;

- high costs for tenants, especially for the district heating;
- a victim of its own success, as Byker becomes 'labelled' and a destination for youth recreation.

Future problems will arise from:

- changing age profiles
- increased voids due to cost
- increased maintenance.

Compared to other schemes, the Byker Wall fairs well. Maintenance costs are no higher than other schemes of the same age. It is in better condition because of the attitude of the residents and the political investment the City has made in it. It still looks different, innovative and a pleasant place to live, although it is beginning to show signs of being 'tired'. Other schemes of the same era have been demolished and those that still exist have more severe problems. For example, Cruddas Park's tower blocks, which were built in the 1960s, have extensive vandalism problems and a large number of units that are difficult to let. It was built to the same cost guidelines as Byker Wall, although it had a different population age profile. Byker Wall has also been the location of the 'respectable working class'; however, the design has helped (see notes 35 and 36).

The popularity of the Byker Wall is high among the tenants. The tenants associations have become vehicles for community work, and, even though the demand for participation died down during the implementation stage, many tenants are very interested in what goes on and wish to contribute to decisions: 'It's still a very, very popular estate, if you compare it to other estates in Newcastle it's extremely popular' (see note 34).

The main problem has undoubtedly been a management one: 'Can a local authority have something unique in its boundaries? I think it is a test for it, (see note 37).

The City has not fulfilled the aim of the architects in the maintenance of the scheme and this aspect will threaten its innovative nature. For all the compromises and control, the tenants have gained a substantial amount through the development, and the next years will determine whether those aspects survive.

In terms of promotion, the City was reactive to the international acclaim. During the early years, two parties each month visited the scheme, many of whom were architects and from overseas. The scheme has acted as a role model and an influence on housing design. It is an indictment of the parochialism of the British housing industry that, as far as those responsible can remember, not one guided tour was made for a volume housebuilder or housing association (see notes 36 and 37).

Nevertheless, the influence of the scheme is apparent in other designs across the city and region. Jane Derbyshire has emerged as a leader in refurbishing social housing. The softer approach of Erskine can clearly be seen in the work of her practice and of those who worked on the Erskine team and contributed to other designs in the city region. Their work is not innovative in the sense that this research defines, but draws on Byker. A large-scale application of the approach could not have occurred in the public sector because of the curtailment of council house building. The lack of vision of the private and housing association sectors is of great concern, given the current problems of housing affordability and cost, the lack of concern for user needs and the investigation of alternative ways of volume housebuilding in other countries, which could threaten the British volume producers in the future. The flagship function is not only within the same locality, but is a national issue. The development has not performed that role, although this was not one of the original aims, since the concerns were local. Therefore, this is not a failure of the City, which was reactive, responding positively to the international acclaim. It has to do with the target groups, the procurers, who have failed to respond in Britain and learn directly from the development as well as being stimulated to try the ideas.

In this context it is interesting to look at the final phase of development, which was a partnership scheme. The developers did not pick up the Erskine design or theme, preferring to use standard house types. The occupants were very similar to the Byker Wall residents. Car ownership levels were low and there was a high frequency of previous council tenants. The main difference was a greater number of young families and white collar workers.

The partnership houses for sale were small and austere in design with small gardens and minimal landscaping. There were complaints about the small rooms in the partnership scheme, the poor levels of equipping and the absence of landscaping. Overall, the residents were happier with the partnership scheme, although a survey showed that people were more content with the features of Byker (see Table 13.2).

Therefore, the satisfaction must have come mainly from the status of buying one's own home and being on the first economic rung of a ladder of future expectations. In fact, less than 5% bought their house because they liked it (Cameron and Thornton, 1986).

13.8 PROJECT IMPACT

What has been the broader impact of this role model project? To what extent have the innovations had a flagship function for other housing projects? The short answer is that the impact has been minimal. Therefore, many opportunities have been lost, for although the scheme has had its critics regarding participation (Malpass, 1979), what has been produced

Table 13.2 Attitudes to housing in Byker

Feature	Level of satisfaction (%)	
	Council	*Build for sale*
Size of rooms	85.5	69.1
Layout of rooms	89.2	90.1
Equipment of house	93.0	80.2
Heating	84.1	93.6
Generally with the house	90.4	92.1
Surroundings of house	76.3	66.2
Living in Byker	87.1	93.3

Source: Cameron and Thornton (1986).

from the tenants' viewpoint is a popular improvement on previous and subsequent public sector developments, yet for no extra cost. If the status and first rung on the ladder arguments are stripped away from owner-occupied housing, then the Byker scheme provides better quality than low cost housing from volume housebuilders, according to people's own judgements (Cameron and Thornton, 1986; cf. Saunders, 1990).

It has also been a scheme that has been ignored in many design and policy debates, for example the issues of 'defensible space' and their application by Coleman (1990). Many of the issues raised by Coleman are broadly supported in the design and findings of Byker Wall, but in a radical way. The Wall itself acts as a barrier, creating semi-private space, which has afforded protection until it recently became a destination for youths to spend their time. The importance of private space is emphasized, but the communal aspects of the development, which helped to reduce vandalism and induce respect, would be an anathema to Coleman. The scheme has created an appreciated environment which flies in the face of her arguments about 1930s-style terraces. Pedestrianization has worked, except where poor landscape maintenance has induced safety issues. In contrast to the other case studies, the pedestrian provision is intimate, and pedestrian flows are concentrated by the exits through the Wall. Lighting and knowing where you are from the visitor's standpoint are the only reservations. This again flies in the face of Coleman's arguments.

Problems have arisen recently within the buildings due to a greater number of young people living on the estate. These might support her arguments in terms of the indicators, yet arise with a change in age profile. While Coleman vigorously denies being an environmental determinist, she believes that environment is a strong influence, yet the Byker Wall would seem to suggest that the problem is more to do with other behavioural characteristics, linked with age and probably other factors too. Creating an environment that people want, like and would have liked to have seen more effectively managed does not solve all issues, but nor does avoiding one particular advocated design solution, that is the 1930s semi-detached house and street pattern, always invoke problems.

The participation exercise, for all its shortcomings, has not been furthered in the British context. Gans (1969) advocated participation in an idealist way, while Goodman (1972) took a more anarchic view. Byker, following the Skeffington Committee Report (1969), incorporated the population into the management process. There has been scope for innovation. Again, the work of Drucker is instructive. His conservative approach recommends investment in innovation and rewarding it. Using Schumpeter's notion of creative destruction, he states 'an innovator's profit is always quite short-lived' (1986, p.110). He also views social responsibility as important for society and for management, thus transferring the profit notion into the social realm – the health of the social order demands innovation. Although Byker has had influence, many of the lessons have yet to be tested to greater limits and 'destroyed' as the ideas are refined into serviced and routinized ways of project implementation (see Chapter 5). Doing this for urban regeneration projects will further test the notion of marketing the city through incorporation of people into the urban 'product'.

The real impact of Byker has yet to come. Combining the organizational strengths of the Eldonians in Liverpool with the design innovations would be a powerful, but low cost, means of fostering social well-being. Such an approach would both challenge the nature of, **and** be within, our society. Such approaches will come from informal groups of people spontaneously erupting into action and from voluntary sector organizations. This would bring the urban 'product' into a self-satisfying form, where the suppliers are also the demand. If a flagship approach was adopted, the urban 'product' would disappear and any development would become a role model, like Byker Wall, but extended to its full.

13.9 SUMMARY

The Byker Wall was an **innovative–local** project in market position. That covers the aims and objectives, yet the full significance of it architecturally has been international and its potential certainly remains national.

The management of the project was successful in maintaining political control through implementing a radical architectural scheme. Despite a number of faults, the development was largely successful in the project formulation and implementation stages. It was the absence of a planned maintenance budget and programme that has and will most threaten the scheme. Indeed, the benefits the tenants have received stand to be eroded as maintenance costs rise for a project that is now 20 years old.

Measured against the hypothesis, this role model has been cost effective, as well as contributing to the social well-being of the population. The full potential of participation in design and management has yet to be fully realized elsewhere. Its radical role has to be measured against past practice, for this need not be the province of socialist principle, as the application of Drucker's work has demonstrated. In the case of the Eldonians in Liverpool, their expression of housing needs was in rebellion against a 'socialist' local government. Given the social instability in society, it is likely that this project at Byker and other innovative residential projects will be of considerable future significance. What cannot be said is how, when and from where new developments that more thoroughly test these notions will spring.

Implications of flagships for urban regeneration and marketing

14

14.1 INTRODUCTION

Assessing the lessons from the case studies needs to be carried out in relation to other flagship and development trends as well as to the rapid pace of policy change. There are a number of comparisons and contrasting points that need to be made from the case analysis. This is commenced by summarizing the main findings, which is the evaluation of their success in terms of the original aims and objectives.

14.2 CASE STUDY FINDINGS

The Watershed Complex, Bristol started as an **H-type** flagship (see Figures 4.1 and 5.10), becoming less innovative and more service-dominated in cultural terms and having a national outlook in geographical terms (see Figure 5.7). It achieved:

- greatest benefit for the City, the aims being achieved by putting the development out to tender;
- attracting developer JT Group, which linked with the Bristol Arts Trust;
- an extremely successful result in terms of image and the marketing of the city;
- a pivotal role in revitalizing the area, confidence among the majority of the population and confidence among inward investors, especially arts- and office-based activities.

It faced serious shortcomings:

- absence of a steering management group for raising capital for the arts side of the project;
- local planning policy thwarted the flagship role, particularly the development of Canon's Marsh;
- lack of funds and poor management of the Watershed Media Centre.

The International Convention Centre, Birmingham is an **F-type** project (see Figures 4.1 and 5.8), having a **service–international** market position. It achieved:

- the repositioning of the city in the **service–international** market;
- attracting office, hotel and arts inward investment;
- stimulating consumption through business tourism and potentially 'traditional' tourism;
- operational success in generating business;
- the user friendly design.

The main criticisms levelled against the project have been:

- a lack of benefits to the most disadvantaged in the local population, although this had not been a primary aim;
- the project management's inability to restrain costs, although many factors were outside the project team's control;
- low level of financial commitment to social programmes;
- role of local government, particularly regarding **governance**.

The Hyatt Regency Hotel in Birmingham was developed on the back of the ICC and depends upon it for a good proportion of its business. It shares the same market position (see Figures 4.1 and 5.8). It has:

- acted in a mutually reinforcing way for the ICC;
- enhanced the sales process of the city.

The shortcomings have been:

- the inability of the initiators to absorb the Department of the Environment's employment objectives, particularly for local disadvantaged people;
- answering questions on city **governance**.

In the cases of the National Indoor Arena and Brindley Place, Birmingham, both are nationally-orientated and service-based, having **E-type** market position (see Figures 4.1 and 5.7).

The overall conclusions are:

- the City became carried away with flagship developments;
- there was a lack of strategic thinking and management behind the National Indoor Arena;
- insufficient resources were put into the National Indoor Arena;

- Brindley Place has failed to date on commercial grounds;
- Brindley Place failed completely as a flagship development when the festival market concept was removed.

The Theatre Village was a **G-type** project for an area of Newcastle. The market aim was to be **innovative–local** (see Figures 4.1 and 5.9). It has failed to:

- achieve its original aims and objectives;
- understand the management and resourcing needs, especially for guiding innovation;
- understand the diversity of the arts sector and its interests;
- use its network to build relationships in a bottom-up and top-down way.

The Byker Wall, Newcastle, was an **innovative–local** project in market position (see Figures 4.1 and 5.9). It proved successful in:

- maintaining political control, through implementing an innovative architectural approach.

It has experienced shortcomings in:

- planned maintenance budget and programmes;
- realizing the full potential of participation in design and management.

It should not be inferred that every scheme had a coherent strategy in terms of the market position. With the exception of the ICC, all the case studies had serious management deficiencies and that in part may result from a lack of understanding of the full role of marketing for a flagship project to stimulate urban regeneration and for marketing the city. In terms of marketing strategy and policy management the ICC is the most successful project, especially given the aims and objectives. If there was a management fault in the approach to the ICC, it was the lack of foresight to include labour market policies to reach the most disadvantaged in the original aims and objectives. The case of the Byker Wall is a useful adjunct for the ICC in terms of its success and potential.

What is clear is the absence of strategic thinking in most cases. Although the size, scale, location and initiators varied greatly, as did the objectives, a number of the major decisions about large commitments of resources were made with scant thought and consideration. This was certainly true of the Theatre Village and, to a large extent, of Brindley Place and the National Indoor Arena. The Watershed Complex, although very carefully thought through in terms of winning the bid, demonstrates that insufficient thought and substance was given to the implementation by all parties regarding funding the arts and planning policies. Thus policies changed and evolved according to circumstances.

The next major lesson is that there is no correlation between the success of a project and the nature of the initiator. The purely private sector, property-led flagships envisaged by central government were in the minority in the examined cases and, indeed, for most flagship developments. Frequently projects were initiated through complex networks and associations. Success therefore did not rely on preferences for, or political leanings towards, one sector or another. Interdependence and intradependence were the prime characteristics of organizational structure and management. Therefore, the notions that the public sector was supporting private sector profit, or that the private sector needed to be bailed out by the public sector, are both crude generalizations. These aspects are worth considering in more detail in the light of other documentation, and doing so will permit a more thorough concluding analysis on the scope and limits for marketing the city, and how this may fit with our visions for future city life.

14.3 IMPACT OF FLAGSHIPS ON URBAN FORM

In looking at some of the more subtle ways of segmenting city markets, and therefore the function of flagship developments, two passages from Jacobs (1965, p.162) and Harvey (1989b, p.14) were compared (see Section 4.6). This took the analysis of segments to a deeper level than the multi-level profile data used for most products, even though this complexity is deeper than current planning methodologies (Ashworth and Voogd, 1990). Jacobs emphasized the urban physical form from the stance of creating a scale and mix of development or uses, which would encourage social and economic diversity. Harvey focused upon the urban form as a spectacle or as the crucible for spectacles which foster social compliance through ephemeral social experience. It is useful to start with the same authors. Jacobs states, 'there is a basic aesthetic limitation on what can be done with cities: **a city cannot be a work of art**' (1965, p.386). She continues:

> Instead of attempting to substitute art for life, city designers should return to a strategy ennobling both to art and to life: a strategy of illuminating and clarifying life and helping to explain to us its meanings and order – in this case, helping to illuminate, clarify, and explain the order of cities. (1965, p.389)

This is very instructive. The concern was to get away from the 'inhumane' architecture and planning of the modern movement. The subsequent postmodern tradition has claimed to articulate meaning through signs and illumination. However, this has not been with an aim of clarifying or creating order, but as an exploration of possibilities and adding new experiences, and hence meanings, to the city and to life. In fact, one underlying trend of postmodernism has been to make cities art and artefacts – the spectacles of which Harvey speaks – and hence mould them by default into products for consumption. Fisher (1991) and Barnett (1991) summarize the 1980s trend of bringing the arts into the city in this way:

> This wider view presupposes a different and more active relationship between people and culture. While the arts are seen to take place solely in theatres, art galleries and concert halls, they can be provided as a gift of an enlightened patron or local authority. Once they are recognized as being part of everyday life, in which all can participate, they begin to grow out of communities rather than being imposed on them. Exciting though the new Symphony Hall in Birmingham is, the beautiful pavement outside it in Centenary Square, designed by the artist Tess Jaray, may well become as much a part of the lives of Birmingham people as the concerts conducted by Simon Rattle inside the Hall. (Fisher, 1991, p.2)

> This is the time for towns and cities to grasp the policy issues raised by new media and exploit the opportunities for access and information, for consultation and therefore greater integration, via a genuinely local media network. . . . These are not necessarily initiatives which would stimulate local economies. But they might stimulate greater involvement in the institutions or organizations that fashion our everyday experiences. (Barnett, 1991, p.171)

These rather naive statements fail to see the links between the city as a commodity and as a work of art. They extol an idealized integration of culture and people in a way which would unite them as a 'product' for the city to 'sell', even though their aims are about enhancing rather than moulding peoples lives. From the point of view of those authors, the actual events are not having the effects they were stating. The case study of the ICC, which includes the Symphony Hall, showed the extent to which the users were consulted in order to provide a relevant building with a competitive edge for its market. In contrast, the artists for the work in the Centre and Centenary Square were chosen by reputation and not according to the needs or wishes of the users, the public. The entire Square has been shown to be rather anodyne and certainly falls far short of enhancing everyday lives, yet it does serve very well the elitist function of business tourism, and so, in this sense, it still becomes part of the city product for a **service–international** market position (see Chapter 9).

The Watershed in Bristol was a pioneer of arts media into urban regeneration and city marketing. It has fared well in the eyes and lives of people living in Bristol. The analysis concurs with Barnett's statement that while such developments may not directly stimulate economic development, the indirect benefits in terms of tourism and encouraging inward investment are important. The Watershed acts at two levels: it genuinely delivers a service locally and nationally, yet it is also a powerful image for

promoting Bristol both nationally and internationally. The integration into
everyday lives in the way Barnett perceives would be an exaggeration, yet
it has contributed to peoples lives and is contributing towards the process
of creating a city 'product'.

Harvey (1989a) supports Jacobs in her analysis that planners tend to fear
diversity and their ability to control it. Postmodernism is ostensibly trying
to create diversity, yet this frequently results in efforts to create a 'sense of
place', a local identity, which squeezes out the most disadvantaged in terms
of labour market opportunities and geographically through planning and
development decisions (see also Chapters 9, 10 and 11; cf. Davis, 1990).
This is the product of wider economic forces in society, namely the
internationalization of business and time–space compression (Harvey,
1989a). The compression comes from increased efficiency in automation,
management, product and service delivery rendering location relatively
less important, yet making the competitive advantage of each location
more pertinent, although less tangible. Therefore the creation of local
identities and 'sense of place' and putting these into a strategic marketing
policy becomes ever more critical:

> the more unified the space, the more important the qualities of
> fragmentations become for social identity and action. (Harvey,
> 1989a, p.271)

The easy solution has been to design buildings and the urban landscape
according to some arbitrary principles. While it may be admirable to
increase pedestrianization and public areas for the pedestrian, it is insufficient to say it is a 'good idea', say on grounds of the environment,
community or safety (cf. Rogers and Fisher, 1992). Pedestrian areas need
to have a dense flow of traffic to 'look alive' and to induce a feeling of being
safe, and, above all, need to be between destinations. Yet the development
of the Lloyds headquarters in Bristol created an anodyne piazza and City
policy undermined pedestrian flows past the Watershed. Birmingham
City Council has encouraged, and is encouraging, pedestrianization in
imaginative ways, yet urban regeneration created a wall of buildings that is
difficult for the pedestrian to 'read' and penetrate, while Centenary Square
ends up as a pleasant monument to civic pride and business tourism, rather
than an inviting space, at least until Brindley Place is built. Having stated
those shortcomings, there is a logic to the Birmingham example, even
though the implementation falls short in the ways described. The Theatre
Village proposals ignore traffic flows and destination needs. The Byker
Wall, on the other hand, is inviting and was designed with the user in mind.
Current problems arise from changing patterns in car ownership without
parallel changes to footpaths, and also to poor maintenance planning. It
worked because the design arose out of a rebellious, and therefore a
political, situation, where the relationships between the parties induced the

design. While design may have had the political role of defusing conflict, it created something according to need rather than arbitrary aesthetics. The Watershed used the postmodern penchant for heritage themes in flagship developments (Bianchini, Dawson and Evans, 1990, 1992), yet in that case it worked, for the public were taken into the vision through the arts interest groups and effective promotion. Indeed, heritage and environment, especially the use of docks, proved popular for urban regeneration generally, for example Liverpool, Gloucester, Chatham and Bristol, as well as London Docklands, which are the homes of a number of flagship developments, not least of which is Canary Wharf.

If users, the local population, business and organizational interests are not taken into account or consulted, then the creation of an identity becomes a concrete image without substance, a packet without the contents. In the entrepreneurial flagship development or the broader marketing of the city:

> we can identify an albeit subterranean but nonetheless vital connection between the rise of urban entrepreneurialism and the postmodern penchant for design of urban fragments rather than comprehensive urban planning, for ephemerality and eclecticism of fashion and style rather than the search for enduring values, for quotation and fiction rather than invention and function, and, finally, for medium over message and image over substance. (Harvey, 1989b, p.13)

Urban space and architectural design, to be effective and durable, has to arise out of the prevailing social relationships between the initiators and the populations and activities within the areas and the immediate surrounding areas. This is the case, whatever the scale of analysis. In the case of the Eldonians in Liverpool, the design emanated from the empowerment of the local population, a bottom-up approach. The social approach was radical, the design conservative, yet appropriate for that set of conditions. In the Byker Wall, the design was radical as the bottom-up threat to the status quo demanded a top-down response, while Hausemann's imperial design for Paris, and the urban regeneration in London Docklands and Birmingham were all top-down. Paris and Birmingham worked on their own terms, for in their different ways both examples were laying down new economic structures and market processes for their cities. London Docklands hangs in the balance.

Urban spaces and building design can be highly charged in power terms. Fascist Germany and Hausemann's Paris concerned political power, Lloyds headquarters in Bristol is about corporate power, while the ICC and the surrounds combine economic and local political power. The 'product' is different in each case, but the social message is clear. On the other hand, some spaces are more neutral or at least ambiguous, such as Times

Square in New York (Harvey, 1991), the areas outside the Pompidou Centre, Paris and Covent Garden in London. For Harvey, the disguise of social relationships is of questionable value. However, it is the interdependence of any social relationship that creates the life in these spaces and renders them ambiguous. It remains unclear which interests get the 'upper hand' for the outworking of that is the dynamic which gives the life. In these cases the life is selling of everything within them – products, events, people, images (Harvey, 1991). This contrasts with the physical, emotional and social needs of the Eldonians, for example those of the pensioners:

> They're looking forward to having no stairs and their own bungalows. They'll be mixed in with the houses, not segregated: I'm living next door to my grandmother. (Cowan, Hannay and Owens, 1988, p.50)

Another example is the public desire for shopping centres that are usable by those with a pushchair or wheelchair, avoid dark oppressive multistorey car parks and have wide well-lit linking corridors and glass lifts (Poole, 1991). Safety is an issue, especially for women, and is in direct conflict with shopping centre design that seeks to minimize costs except where it promotes the retailer, therefore sales, and hence developer rentals.

The developer adage, first quoted by Lord Samuel of Land Securities, that a successful development is based on 'location, location, location' has been revised in the 1980s to 'location, location and design', where design created rental premiums. In future it should become 'location, design and user needs', for if development generally and urban regeneration are to succeed, then **all** these aspects will need to be taken on board. The Birmingham case studies showed clearly how the disadvantaged can be excluded from the aims and objectives, as well as through the creation of a physically segregating 'wall' of development between economic activity and social deprivation. This type of process is likely to fuel pent-up anger and can result in civil disobedience. Failure to take these aspects on board could lead to the next generation of flagship developments or their successors becoming a massive and expensive response to disorder (cf. Berman, 1983).

In concluding this section, flagship developments have an impact upon the urban form, most of which are either ephemeral or negative. The successful forms articulate the social relations of the development, area and city, although the form of those relations and the balance and nature of power within them will vary. In order to reinforce the relationships, design must take into account user needs and these must be built into any marketing strategy for or relating to the flagship or development. Different types of urban spaces engender different possible social encounters by design or by default (Berman, 1983). The importance of this for the design professionals is enormous. Architecture, urban design and the consequent engineering and costing must arise out of the relationships, not out of aesthetics *per se*. 'Function' is too monosyllabic or static, because it is the dynamics that need to be expressed through the form, not as 'signs' and 'collages', but as life in its full tapestry. In the marketing context, the urban form is both the visible part of the 'product' and the 'packaging'. Many of the issues raised concern the wider impact of flagship developments upon surrounding areas and it is to this the analysis turns in greater detail.

14.4 IMPACT OF FLAGSHIPS ON AREAS

Many flagship developments have been grand in scale, requiring a great deal of finance. Harbor Place in Baltimore, Canary Wharf in London Docklands, Broadgate in London, La Defense in Paris and the ICC in Birmingham are all large projects which transform their areas in two ways:

- by their own presence
- through the additional investment and consumption they attract.

This is the purpose of a flagship development – to regenerate an area. There is an important question about the scale of a project or the consequences of a series of flagship developments that **are** the process of further investment and consumption, for example at Harbor Place or the Broad Street area in Birmingham. Scale implies large capital expenditure. One of the issues of this analysis has been whether flagships are expensive in terms of what they deliver towards economic and social well-being. This has been considered for each case study to date. Both the ICC and Byker have met their immediate project objectives and the costs appear to be justified. The remainder have proved costly in relation to their achievements to date, when looking at the returns on capital invested, and the causes of this have been to do with:

- management gaps in policy formulation and implementation;
- finance gaps in providing sufficient funds to ensure the project works in design and management.

These are two important policy pointers, which have a general application to past and future flagship developments. However, this has not specifically addressed the general thrust of large-scale flagship developments and serial developments within an area. Therefore, looking at the supply side, Jacobs voiced concern over large-scale flows of finance into city development in the 1960s, and her comments are pertinent to flagship developments:

Money has its limitations. It cannot buy inherent success for cities where the conditions for inherent success are lacking and where the use of the money fails to supply them. Furthermore, money can only do ultimate harm where it destroys the conditions needed for inherent success. On the other hand, by helping to supply the requirements needed, money can help build inherent success in cities.

Indeed it is indispensable. For these reasons, money is a powerful force both for city decline and for city regeneration. But it must be understood that it is not the mere availability of money, but how it is available, and for what, that is all important. (1965, p.305)

The property development boom of the late 1980s was again fuelled by an availability of capital funding, without discernment among the development industry as to what development was driven by restructuring and what was fuelled by economic growth. The assumption that it was all growth led to the trap, which Jacobs sets out, resulting in oversupply. Yet the issue is more critical than this, especially for flagship developments, for the following reasons:

- such investment can undermine the local economy in the long term;
- such investment can undermine the social structure;
- there is an opportunity cost to such investment.

Yet the situation is not as clear cut as Jacobs suggests, for the prime purpose of 'selling' a flagship and marketing the city is to facilitate the exchange process by encouraging demand within or into an area. Its relevance is that development must take account of demand. This cannot necessarily be done in a 'scientific' way. No market can be predicted with absolute certainty, otherwise marketing would be obsolete, and certainly not in the urban realm, because redevelopment has the effect of reconstituting the area and city 'product' beyond the control and predictions of the developer. Market analysis can be carried out thoroughly (Ashworth and Voogd, 1990) and used to create a strategy in terms of market position, segments and targets. This analysis has shown that few flagship initiators have had coherent strategies, either explicitly or implicitly, and because of this the shortcomings have shown up in the management process, and thus in the end 'product'. For large projects there are the added problems of risk because of the scale in relation to the number of market targets and because of the length of the development process, spanning development cycles, as in the case of Canary Wharf, for example (see Chapter 4). Certainly these problems were met in the Birmingham case studies, especially for Brindley Place, where the latest development plan showed a series of individual developments in order to create more flexible market responses in an area where scale had created high risk rather than a higher turnover of urban regeneration (see Chapter 11).

One other aspect of the demand side is the qualitative benefit of a flagship development, which includes its symbolic importance. This is impossible to quantify and hence can be discounted in financial evaluation, yet these aspects can help recreate new conditions for the inherent success referred to by Jacobs. The symbolic importance is not just the hype or the image making of 'civic boosterism' (see Chapter 2), but depends on whether the expenditure on promotion is backed up by real changes due to development, and whether the development is related to existing market demand or market creation.

Furthermore, what is created must have integrity. This has already been considered in terms of architecture and planning. However, the impact in terms of the activity and related issues must have integrity too. Indeed, appropriate design and planning, it was said, must emanate from the relationships in and around the area. Here we are dealing with the activities that give rise to those relations. One example where there is a lack of integrity is the Wigan Pier Heritage Centre. This £3.5m project was financed by the EEC, the English Tourist Board, the former Greater Manchester Council, the Department of the Environment and by private sector money. The inspiration for the Centre is George Orwell's novel, *The Road to Wigan Pier*, which was about poverty and the hardships of industrial life, yet the purpose of the Centre has been to show Wigan as a place of variety, attractiveness and nostalgia (Bianchini, Dawson and Evans, 1990). This is a particular problem for many heritage attractions, which come to be designed more for enjoyment and for generating consumption than to remain faithful to the historics. This does not preclude making something new. Birmingham successfully repositioned itself as an international city with a service culture (see Chapters 9 and 10), while the Merseyside Development Corporation turned its back on the Toxteth riots and the image of the 'militant' Liverpool City Council to promote the area in North America (*Financial Times*, 1992a). This is fine if there is substance to it.

There is another supply-side issue in this. A commercial flagship may produce income and profit in the short run, yet for the scheme to fulfil its flagship role it must have a positive effect on the locality. Without integrity, it is likely that the long-term viability will be questionable. The National Indoor Arena lacks some integrity towards the user and may thus lose its competitive advantage in the long term (see Chapter 11). Many heritage projects could experience the same future. This may be justifiable, if sufficient investment has been attracted in their wake to create a sustainable social or economic community, however, most are consumption-orientated and rely on the flagship's continued viability.

The demands upon developers to understand the nature of the markets for urban regeneration and flagship developments in particular have proved too great to date. Reliance upon information from surveyors' 'street knowledge', real estate research departments and the specialist property market data agencies has proved inadequate. Most developers produce standard products, based upon a standard delivery system (Smyth, 1991), the scope for niche marketing remaining limited. As a result, most developers began to become wary of inner city development prior to the collapse in the property development market. This was because their flagship developments were not meeting expectations. They were criticizing central government for a lack of investment in infrastructure and were being criticized for their 'central' role in regeneration, the cost of schemes and the failure to create employment opportunities (*Financial Times*, 1992d). This research has shown that the private sector has seldom led development and even in London Docklands planning and tax incentives have provided the economic context. This evidence is supported elsewhere, as most partnership schemes were initiated by the public sector (Fox and Healey, 1991). Success has been shown to be more to do with the marketing strategy and its consequent management than the nature of the initiators. A tentative conclusion would be that the public sector has proved to be better managers than the private sector (cf. Drucker, 1986).

One reason why the public sector may have proved better managers is because of their accountability. However, this has increasingly been eroded in flagship developments. It has been shown that many schemes have been undertaken through **governance**, whereby accountability is indirect, uncertain or absent. Yet, the 'tradition' does alert the initiators to take account of the local population. Those affected by developments are an important part of the supply side for they are **part of** the social relationships within the vicinity. This includes local businesses, organizations as well as residents. It raises again a fundamental question about the nature of the city 'product', but before returning to this, it is necessary to look at the extent of city management in taking a bottom-up approach to flagship development.

It has been claimed that most arts policies have been developed by successful cities from the bottom up (Fisher, 1991). There was some evidence of this in Bristol, led by developer JT, yet the developments in Birmingham and the private sector Theatre Village initiative in Newcastle singularly failed to do so in relation to flagship developments (see Chapters 8, 9 and 11). It has to be realized that any bottom-up successes can also be sold in a top-down form of promotion to attract investment, and indeed, that is one flagship function through the marketing and sales process. Edgar (1991) raises a formula that addresses this dualism. The arts:

- should be priced on a two-tier system for locals and tourists;
- can be publicly funded upon merit and originality rather than reputation and elitism;
- should be seen as separate from the polarization between regeneration and dereliction and blight;
- should not allow a distinction between process and product, animation and social work, arts and therapy, hobby and job.

While this may be fine in the articulation of the lives of individuals, in policy terms it is highly contentious. It is unclear how these pointers could overcome the criticisms of elitism in Glasgow's regeneration programme, which was arts led. Of course, it could be seen as a matter of perception. What this does clearly demonstrate is that the process of regeneration is a highly political one, dilemmas being categorized (Lefebvre, 1991; see also Harvey, 1989a) under the following headings:

- principles of spatial fragmentation as the containers of social power;
- production of space as political and economic phenomena;
- spatial form is dependent upon the social relations in and around it;
- erosion of place through the homogenization of space versus the subservience of space to its political transformation;
- space is conquered through the production of space.

This is articulated in the context of this analysis in Figure 14.1.

Harvey challenges the appropriateness of using public resources for cities to compete against each other in broad terms and specifically to use urban regeneration projects as a means to seek competitive advantage (see note 11). Ashworth and Voogd (1990) demonstrate how there is a growing league table of locations and cities as a means to differentiate competitive advantages, yet the problem is that the investment needed to upgrade the 'product' and effectively promote it contains within it the seeds of foreshortening the product life cycle. This is because the population is being polarized in opportunities, hence in social stability. As any city manager or elected member is well aware, social disorder can spring up in a spontaneous way, undermining flagship developments, images and all the promotion of a city as a desirable location.

The development of flagships has focused upon supply-side issues. It was shown in Chapter 2 that the aim of flagships was related to the urban policy of unblocking the supply side. In this chapter the supply-side focus on financial provision at the expense of overlooking the affected population has been demonstrated. Returning to Jacobs, it has been stated:

> In sum, this money shapes cataclysmic changes in cities. Relatively little of it shapes gradual change. Cataclysmic money pours into an area in concentrated form, producing drastic changes. As an obverse of this behaviour, cataclysmic money sends relatively few trickles into localities not treated to cataclysm. . . . All city building that retains staying power after its novelty has gone, and that preserves the freedom of the streets and upholds citizens' self-management, requires that its locality be able to adapt, keep up to date, keep interesting, keep convenient, and this in turn requires a myriad of gradual, constant, close-grained changes. (1965, p.307)

In the early chapters and case studies it was shown that there was a dilemma for the local population as to whether it should become part of the 'product'. Being separate, as Jacobs states and this analysis confirms, the trickle-down effect is minimal. Becoming part of the 'urban product' allows

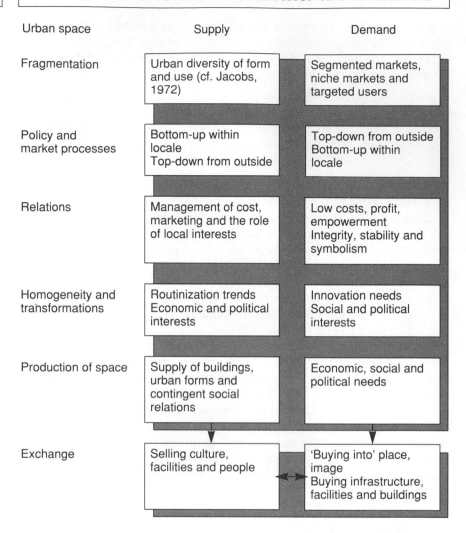

Urban space	Supply	Demand
Fragmentation	Urban diversity of form and use (cf. Jacobs, 1972)	Segmented markets, niche markets and targeted users
Policy and market processes	Bottom-up within locale Top-down from outside	Top-down from outside Bottom-up within locale
Relations	Management of cost, marketing and the role of local interests	Low costs, profit, empowerment Integrity, stability and symbolism
Homogeneity and transformations	Routinization trends Economic and political interests	Innovation needs Social and political interests
Production of space	Supply of buildings, urban forms and contingent social relations	Economic, social and political needs
Exchange	Selling culture, facilities and people	'Buying into' place, image Buying infrastructure, facilities and buildings

Figure 14.1 The dynamics of flagships, spatial production, marketing the city and people

benefits to reach the population, particularly the disadvantaged, in order to minimize social instability and deliver a more comprehensive package to those that 'buy into' the area. This means allowing the population to exert power and shape the product, but it also means that the population is under an implicit obligation, a new type of informal contract, to be ultimately moulded into the form needed to enhance the roles of consumption, investment and command according to the culture and geographical orientation of the market position. The Birmingham case studies are clear demonstrations of 'cataclysmic money', confirming the lack of trickle-down effects and that the more money was poured in, the more the potential of areas such as Ladywood were eroded because of the drain on social resources and the physical boundary created by the 'wall' of regeneration. This has to be viewed as highly significant because of the high degree of success achieved by the City, especially for their first two projects (see Chapters 9, 10 and 11). Even successes can have detrimental consequences, as Jacobs suggested and predicted.

Here a new dilemma is raised, this time, not for the population, but for the project initiators and city management. If smaller scale, phased development is more gradual, then the empowerment process will induce very gradual change. Certainly projects like Coin Street in London have done so, where a local challenge to large-scale office redevelopment took years to be resolved in favour of the expressed needs of the population, and the subsequent development is long-term too. Development at Byker Wall and for the Eldonians has been phased over a long period compared to many volume housebuilders' programmes. This is an anathema to the needs of a developer. Absorbing population needs could create problems in servicing debt charges and will thwart the opportunity cost of capital in creating a sufficient mass and rate of profit. Yet, it is in the short-term interest of the disadvantaged, the long-term interest of society as a whole and, therefore, of developers, to accommodate these needs, as the analysis shows.

However, participation, empowerment and the instruments of bottom-up policy formulation and implementation – on its own account or in tandem with a top-down approach – need not produce a pace of change that is in conflict with the needs of efficiency. It is not a problem of empowerment, not a problem for the population; it is a **management** problem. Empowerment is frequently seen as the province of the 'left' and it frequently is. Yet a conservative, such as Drucker (1986), sees this social responsibility, in a wider context, as the management challenge for the future (see also Section 9.9). Management is responsible for the impacts that its developments have, whether public, private, voluntary, popular or any hybrid. In the case of flagships, they are designed to have an impact, as is the marketing of the city. As Drucker puts it:

Surely business, like anyone else, is responsible for its impacts:

responsibility for one's impact is after all, one of the oldest tenets of the law. And surely business, like anyone else, is in violation of its responsibilities if it allows itself impacts beyond those necessary to, and implicit in, its social purpose, for example producing goods and services. To overstep these limits constitutes a **tort**, that is, a violation. (1986, p.187)

Where a flagship project is developer-led it is almost inconceivable that it should be undertaken without public or voluntary-cum-popular involvement because the impacts do go beyond the organizational competence and purpose of the developer.

The implications of this analysis are enormous for the definition of the urban 'product'. The analysis has already demonstrated that it is difficult for the population not to be included in the 'product', especially if it wishes to benefit from the investment that takes place in urban regeneration and marketing the city. It has also been shown that a 'product' with a long life cycle must have integrity in terms of design of and activities in the development. The integrity flows from the social relations and therefore includes residents, business and organizations in and around the area or city. The analysis has now demonstrated the desirability of, and long-term need for, project initiators to take social responsibility for the impact of their development. By definition, a flagship development aims to have an impact outside itself. This must then draw in the population and its activities. The question that started to ask whether the population could or should become part of the 'product', needs to be recouched to state that it seems almost inconceivable that the population and its activities cannot be part of the 'product'. Any hesitancy about this conclusion arises from two sources:

- the concept of flagship developments and marketing the city is relatively new and is still being tested out in practice;
- the development market, whoever the development initiator, is still very anarchic and these forces can overrule marketing and sales strategies for a project, area or city.

Gradual or incremental change would seem to be the logical urban regeneration strategy, harnessing finance to need:

> The forms in which money is used must be converted to instruments of regeneration – from instruments buying violent cataclysms to instruments buying continual, gradual, complex and gentler change. (Jacobs, 1965, p.331)

At this point the private sector developers may react with two statements. Firstly, they will say that they are not prepared to undertake development through gradual policy formulation and implementation. This is a management question for them and for the other parties in the development process – planners, economic development officers, councillors. They must develop new, effective and rapid techniques to engage with local interests, understand their needs and interpret these in development terms. In any event, the large 'mega' schemes aimed at creating whole new markets take as long and arguably have higher risk factors.

Secondly, they will retort that taking on board the needs of the local population is not in their short-term interests, even if it is in their long-term interest. However, the state of the development market and the changing demands for 'traditional' developments will act as a considerable constraint. On the other hand, traditional development has made a minuscule impact on the totality of urban dereliction and degeneration. New markets are therefore in need of creation. This is one potential new market. Indeed, this new market has parallels with other potential development markets where development management will once again become a large component of activities, reversing the trend of the past forty years since Land Securities introduced the full repairing lease (Smyth, 1985).

Quite how this would or will work in practice brings the analysis back to political issues. According to Harvey:

> The struggle to find a proper representation, a mode of interpretation of an urban society in dramatic transformation . . . is fought from below, but it is also a pressing matter for the ruling classes. The struggle to impose a new set of representations from above can either be waged explicitly . . . or it can be arrived at through the commodification of representation itself. (1991, p.55)

Therefore, the creation of new markets and the involvement of local interests will not be without conflict. While the analysis has stressed all local affected interests, one of the first issues will be to redefine and limit the range of interests. This is self-defeating, yet has been common to many flagship projects to date (see, for example, Bianchini, Dawson and Evans, 1990, 1992; Brownill, 1990; Wishart, 1991; Loftman and Nevin, 1992). Another important aspect to such outworking will be the power of the resultant images derived both from the built environment and in advertising plus other promotions. In specific terms, does this mean that the low self-esteem of the most disadvantaged will induce a psychological barrier to feeling part of the benefits from this development approach? The key will be the extent of successful management of the policy process on both sides, involving those that may be excluded. Five principles of just management and planning need to be addressed from the viewpoint of both formal and informal organizations (developed from Young, 1990):

- minimize exploitation: discover needs
- confront marginalization: develop esteem
- facilitate access to power: engage in self-expression
- avoid cultural assumptions and imposition: articulate needs

- avoid all forms of control and violence: develop empowerment capacity and self-control.

This needs to be undertaken in a frank way and in a forum where different understandings can be shared, inducing mutual respect, leading to developing trust, and finally conceiving a development which meets mutual needs as well as stewarding resources for future generations (cf. Healey, 1992). This proposes a serious challenge to the public sector as well as to the private sector, for authorities have undermined the well-being of their local populations by transferring money away from services to pay for flagship developments (see Chapter 9; McGrath, 1982; Boyle, 1989; Loftman and Nevin, 1992; cf. Barnekov, Boyle and Rich, 1988; Hambleton, 1990). These propositions may be 'idealistic'; however, current development and urban regeneration practice is so far away from it – and even conservative, pro-business management commentators are urging social responsibility – that serious attempts have to made to test the limits to the combination of social responsibility and market creation in this context.

14.5 ROLE OF FLAGSHIPS IN THE ECONOMY

The role of flagship developments in the economy goes well beyond the immediate area; indeed, it has been shown that successful ones can be used to reposition a city in cultural and geographical terms. However, the extent of their success has been seriously curtailed by the ill-defined market positions and attendant strategies and management. The future significance of the successful projects will also depend upon the weight of money that has gone into them and whether this has undermined the organic possibilities for growth in an area or city (cf. Jacobs, 1965). If Jacobs (1972) is correct about the need for diversity and if the economic processes for growth are adhered to, then the major policy element that has been frequently absent – although needed – is innovation. It has been shown that innovation is the most difficult aspect to manage (see Chapters 8, 12 and 13, cf. Figures 4.1, 4.2, 5.9, 5.10 and 5.11).

No less risky – indeed inherently more risky – has been the large-scale project, which was bound to span development cycles and has proved too large for any development company in Britain, if not the world. Canary Wharf and Broadgate are the two most obvious examples. The accounting techniques of limited recourse and off balance sheet finance have not managed to reduce the exposure of developers Rosehaugh and Stanhope in the case of Broadgate, despite its success as a quality development (Goobey, 1992). Olympia and York were not able to ride the development cycle at Canary Wharf, the bankers being concerned not only for the over-expansionist company, but also about the financial commitments for infrastructure development, namely the £400m Jubilee Underground extension (*Guardian*, 1992). This also raises issues about coordinated metropolis development, planning and marketing policies, for the City of London relaxed its planning policies as soon as Canary Wharf was under way, thus creating the potential for competition and oversupply (Goobey, 1992).

Competition is a normal economic process in a market economy. The marketing view of competition is to create and facilitate the market in times of growth, that is to say, competition is positive and contributes to sales of a good product rather than being a question of 'beating the opposition'. Stealing market share is only a significant issue when the market is saturated for that product either because of the stage in the product life cycle or because of recession. There has been concern about competition between cities resulting in a zero sum outcome for flagship projects (Bianchini, Dawson and Evans, 1990, 1992). An example of this has been the growth in the arts sector in Britain and the United States, as well as elsewhere (see Harvey 1989a; Bianchini, Dawson and Evans, 1990, 1992; Fisher, 1991), spawning projects that could be said to raise the stakes between these cities. While 'cultural competition between cities is a serious business' (Fisher, 1991, p.5), it also provides facilities and events for local people as well as tourism. It is not a zero sum game for these people. The second point is not about all the competitor cities that have developed their urban areas and economies to the same level; the issue is about these locations in comparison to those that have not followed suit and are therefore no longer competitors (Barnekov, Boyle and Rich, 1988; Ashworth and Voogd, 1990). The implication of the zero sum criticism is that flagship developments are expensive, often using public funds, and that there are no overall benefits at the end. This clearly is not the case in a growth market and is not even a problem in recessionary times unless there is an oversupply of the types of projects in question. Indeed, the Birmingham case studies would seem to suggest that recessionary conditions are the time to formulate capital projects.

This brings the analysis on to a further common criticism, that is the type of project, and hence its economic function. Many cities have sought urban regeneration through copying other similar projects. Indeed the analysis of project management (see Chapter 5) has shown that adopting and adapting a role model is the usual way of providing a flagship development aimed at the service culture. Furthermore, it has been shown that 'yesterday's innovative project becomes today's service project and tomorrow's routinized one'. Copycat policies and the serialization of the projects is not surprisingly commonplace and is 'understandable' (Harvey, 1989a, p.91).

There are three points to be made about this criticism. The first undermines the criticism for certain sorts of projects. Those of a national or international orientation can benefit from serialization for it helps to facilitate a market, for example annual conventions are not held in the same place and incentive travel encourages organizers to develop a circuit of locations. The ICC in Birmingham is not necessarily competing with the one in Berlin, indeed the Berlin management encouraged the EEC to fund the Birmingham facility to help to develop a European circuit.

The second and third points support the criticism. Serialization can create unnecessary competition for certain facilities. It is important in the market analysis to assess the competition that exists and is in the pipeline, and structure the orientation accordingly. For example, two locally orientated facilities competing in the same local market will face combinations of the following problems:

- dilution of promotional effort;
- leapfrog expenditure to upgrade facilities to secure competitive advantage;
- competing for market share when demand is low;
- redundant capital and opportunity costs.

The same difficulty may occur between two facilities in different towns, both with a national orientation, but in a limited market. The key is to use the geographical orientation to overcome problems of copycat policies and facilities. This can be achieved in the following ways for two flagship projects:

- if competing within the same geographical orientation, ensure the market is large enough for both facilities, even under the worse economic conditions (even though you may think that 'yours' is the better one);
- avoid competition by competing at two different scales, for example one orientated nationally, the other internationally.

If neither option looks secure, then the flagship is in the wrong market, and the developments of the 1980s have frequently fallen into that trap. The other aspect about copycat projects is those that come after the initial project. The strategy for minimizing these risks are twofold:

- invest heavily in the initial project to make it state-of-the-art and form a user point of view, as this will dissuade others from competing for a longer period;
- when competition becomes manifest, have facilities and strategies for changing the market position.

The latter option is not available to an **A-type** project, **routinized–local**, without a tremendous amount of expenditure, and in all cases there may be urban constraints.

The third criticism concerns the copycat designs of projects. There is a tendency for serialization to lead to monotonous and repeated solutions (Boyer, 1988; Harvey, 1989a; cf. Albrechts, 1991). This again has more repercussions for geographical orientation than it does for culture. Living within one locality induces a familiarity on the one hand, and the individual is not always aware of repeat designs and urban solutions in other locations. For example, the Manhattan look of Canary Wharf may not pose a cultural problem for a local resident in Docklands. However, nationally- and internationally-orientated facilities, or local ones that also link into tourism, should avoid repeat solutions. This has been a serious failure of flagship developments for it is the 'sense of place' in the globalization of the world economy which gives one aspect of competitive advantage to flagships, the area and the city for attracting inward investment and consumption. In stating this, an argument for pastiche and heritage-type solutions, so frequently churned out from some postmodern quarters, is not being advocated. It is necessary to return to the issues of integrity, where the history, culture and environmental context can be reflected in an honest or contemporary way. Or it is necessary to have a contrasting design and urban solution where developing a different market position and targeting new types of activities in cultural terms? This will create a new cultural layer of investment and its imprint on the urban form (cf. Massey, 1984). The design must arise out of the social relations of the people and activities of the area, or out of those anticipated in the new market position. However, in any case, the new urban form will reconstitute social relations (Berman, 1983).

There is a strong economic argument in favour of project, and therefore 'product', differentiation. This will enhance competitive advantage and minimize rivalry between city locations, especially where tourism and business tourism are inextricably linked to multi-user locations. Differentiation will of course help in the promotion efforts of public relations and advertising. Differentiation, which arises out of the social relationships within the locality will also help promotion within the city to the local population. A flagship aiming to develop new relationships and economic activities should help stimulate excitement and civic pride among those affected. This is important, especially for projects of a national and international orientation. If local people, businesses and organizations have been excluded from the economic benefits so often, then they have been even more often excluded from the promotion campaigns. Conveying national and international orientations is by far the most difficult, for most people's reaction is that 'it does nothing for us'. This may indeed be true, perhaps necessary, in some cases. Yet for sustenance of the urban economy and future livelihoods, it may also be necessary to first promote the project to the local population. A tentative conclusion of this analysis is that local authorities and initiators fear local reactions, and so try to avoid them. This begins to induce two consequences:

• an inability to listen, understand and respond to local needs, in other words, reinforcing the move away from serving towards political and economic control and power;

- an open invitation to move further towards **governance** and away from government, in other words, away from accountability and towards implicit secrecy.

Involving the local interests in the policy process, and therefore as part of the 'product', does have one potential benefit of recreating greater accountability. This is not ideal and would result in greater politicization of the development process; however, this is the marketing, and therefore the management, challenge for both the private and public sector. This challenge is about:

- maximizing social well-being from flagship developments and consequent regeneration;
- maximizing the economic role of regeneration in the urban economy;
- testing the limits of flagship developments and marketing the city.

One important point that Harvey (1989a) makes is that for those cities experiencing the devaluation of the urban environment through the degeneration process – and property devaluation can be added to this – it is a prerequisite for survival in the national and global traumas of devaluation. This is because of cost competitiveness generally and the increased efficiency derived from restructuring and innovation through flagship developments and the urban regeneration process specifically. Thus, the serious social and economic problems give rise to the possibility of a new efficiency, an element in a new regime of growth. In turn, the new growth requires that the polarized living experiences in such cities will demand the incorporation of the population into the process in order to:

- sustain political legitimacy;
- contribute to that new order of creating and sustaining markets.

Future development and city visions

15.1 LESSONS OF FLAGSHIP DEVELOPMENTS

The main lessons derived from the case studies and analysis from a perspective of marketing the city are:

- flagship developments require an overt marketing strategy;
- flagship developments require management of the policy formulation, implementation and evaluation process;
- the strategy and management may be project-, area- and/or city-based;
- marketing concerns the creation and bringing together of supply and demand factors in an implicit exchange in the urban context;
- success is not contingent upon public versus private finance or initiation;
- design and planning should arise from the social relations – residents, business and organizations – **in** the affected areas and those envisaged **for** the area;
- economic benefits do not trickle down to the disadvantaged;
- all organizations must take responsibility for the impact of their development on others in order to make the market work, as well as for moral reasons;
- political legitimacy and economic necessity will increasingly demand the participation of the local residents and other interests into the policy and development process to help maintain social stability, create a 'saleable' urban 'product' and create new development markets within the urban economy;
- participation may produce benefits for all parties, yet it will be a politicized process, the balance of the benefits being the object of conflict and the outworking of transforming city lives and economies;
- achieving in an efficient way participation of the subjects, transformation of the urban economy and of relations within it is a key management issue;

- management, in this context, concerns identifying techniques and means to facilitate and accelerate the policy and the development process, rather than closing down the process: serving not controlling.

Our analysis of the case studies has shown a repeated lack of full and clearly articulated sets of aims and objectives, especially with regard to marketing. This has had consequential management problems during the implementation stages. These aspects were generally poorly understood, even where large sums of money were involved. The clearest exception was the City's approach to the International Convention Centre (ICC) in Birmingham, although the same clarity was not applied to subsequent flagship developments in the city. This is not to say that the other projects all failed, because common sense came into play during the policy process; however, reliance upon this increases risks dramatically.

15.2 IMPLICATIONS FOR MARKETING AND MANAGING THE CITY

Architecture, urban design and town planning have yet to embrace marketing as part of the development process; indeed, the public and private sectors have been too concerned with supply-side issues, whether it is 'rational' policy, normative policy, aesthetics, financial borrowing, cost as opposed to value, rather than with the nature and extent of demand, competitive advantage, social benefits and what people say they want, even if 'experts' don't like it!

There is a relatively unexplored development market for projects that will facilitate economic and social innovation among users. Innovation is at the forefront of market creation and therefore concerns the internal feeding of the city, as opposed to drawing in consumption and investment activities from outside. This is high risk in the short term, yet, if properly managed, yields greater long-term benefits.

The research commenced by excluding the population and existing local interests from the city 'product' because:

- the product is difficult to define and exchange is frequently implicit, in other words investors and consumers 'buy into' an area rather than come to 'own it';
- people are not subject to a contract, except at work.

Yet just and legitimate management must take responsibility for the consequences of its actions on whomever the impact is felt. Flagships are set up to have an external impact by definition. On the other hand, people wish to benefit from the economic and social opportunities afforded by flagship developments, especially in education and the labour market. It therefore becomes increasingly impossible to exclude people from the 'product', but this means some moulding. It should be moulding by agreement, through open and efficient participation if management and its political overseers are concerned with legitimacy, social development and market creation. Indeed, this type of involvement is the biggest challenge for marketing as a discipline and it involves two aspects:

- creating new markets by developing according to local needs, particularly among the most disadvantaged, in a way that will create internal markets or attract new investment and consumption activities into the area and city;
- selling the urban 'product' to the population and interest groups locally in an iterative way, by integrating the bottom-up approach, as the concepts develop to meet expressed needs.

At present there are not the management tools to achieve this. However, the networking process is surely the means, even if its efficiency is questionable. It requires breaking away from existing conceptions of participation – leaflets and exhibitions of models for development projects that solicit comments, public inquiries and overreliance upon particular views of pressure and lobby groups. Other avenues need to be fully explored, perhaps starting with existing techniques from other fields. Market research does not tell anyone what people want or would like, so it is limited. However, it does inform decision makers of perceptions, existing needs and problems. Qualitative interviews, using semi-structured questions, get around some of the limitations of 'yes–no' answers to very particular market research questions. Multi-level analysis of demographic factors, gender, income, location and other variables can be used too (Ashworth and Voogd, 1990), rather than planners and development units using single sets and asking for comments on draft plans. These and other techniques can all be used in parallel to gain a greater understanding of the issues. However, techniques for involvement in the actual decision making have to be put in place. Options have to be explored. If justice is required maybe a jury system is one option; on the other hand, maybe conflict should be stimulated, giving rise to informal and temporary single-decision 'councils'. This begins to address the problem outlined by Jacobs (1965):

> Big-city government is nothing more than little-city government which has been stretched and adapted in quite conservative fashion to handle bigger jobs. This has had strange results, because big cities pose operational problems that are innately different from those posed by little cities. (p.423)

What this implies is greater intervention from the public sector in the development process. Many may say that this is a welcome reversal of the 1980s, but this would be to misunderstand the events and flagship developments of the 1980s, particularly regarding the increase in intervention during the whole period. The nature of intervention changed and the options multiplied, but partnership schemes, the setting up of private companies to operate public facilities, and private developments within public marketing strategies were all pursued in the case studies, as well as inner city policies and tax incentives aimed at regeneration. All were far more prominent than 'pure' private development. Intervention through networks and facilitation is becoming, or has become, the new norm rather than simple direct development or public sector provision, for example, council house building. The crude analysis of 'privatism' in urban development is dead and policy rhetoric of private property-led urban regeneration hardly lived at all, arguably no more than would have taken place in a property boom without these policies. This whole area of state intervention at the national and local level needs continual re-articulation, endeavouring to get over our 'taken for granted' thinking that the public and private sector are two domains that, *a priori*, work in separate ways in thought, word and deed.

The economy is being driven by financial criteria rather than by production and other activities (Drucker, 1986; Harvey, 1989a). It has become uncoupled from productive activity. In this confusion and chaos it becomes necessary to couple interests at the specific level, to integrate them, taking into account the conflicts. It is interesting that the two contrasting approaches of Drucker and Harvey perceive a common problem, but at this stage of the analysis I wish to stress the conservative viewpoint. Drucker (1986) has stated that the management of corporate capitalism has also uncoupled itself from its employees, from its shareholders and from its financial backers, rendering it only accountable to itself. This has made it extremely vulnerable, for it has no constituency of support when attacked, as takeover battles all too clearly demonstrate. City authorities are in danger of doing the same, and have done so in some cases, which challenges their legitimacy. They need to recouple themselves through the development process to their constituencies. The recoupling can centre around a regeneration project and involve the intrapenetration of public sector and private sector interests, and in the latter individuals and their neighbourhoods are included.

If local authorities need to do this, so does the private sector. In moving towards a network-based approach, society is also moving towards new roles. A mixed economy at the macro-level is simply being changed into mixed endeavours and projects at the micro-level. What we have come to call 'privatization' is no less interventionist than the mixed economy, but in new forms. The distinctions with which we have worked will continue to erode as the private sector increasingly penetrates the public sphere. For some, this reads as crude 'exploitation', yet it is likely to be more subtle than that. Adopting roles goes hand in hand with taking responsibility. Responsibility comes in the wake of financial and ownership decentralization. There is a time lag but the take-up of responsibility is absolutely necessary. This is not a 'radical' statement, but one that concerns legitimacy. As Drucker puts it:

> the major challenges are new ones, and well beyond the field of management as we commonly define it. Indeed, it will be argued that the challenges I have been discussing are not management at all, but belong in political and social theory and public law.

> Precisely. The success of management has not changed the work of management. But it has greatly changed management's meaning. Its success has made management the general, the pervasive function, and the distinct organ of our society of organizations. As such management inevitably has become 'affected with the public interest'. To work out what this means for management theory and management practice will constitute the 'management problems' of the next fifty years. (1986, pp.192–193)

In Drucker's eyes this requires a shift from the military model of management, which is top-down, to an orchestral model, where the conductor is meaningless without the players. The conductor tries, through encouragement, firm leadership and discipline, to get the best out of the players. This is the role of facilitating a bottom-up approach – those who serve lead.

15.3 TRENDS IN POLICY AND PRACTICE

The implications of this for project type will be interesting. Clearly housing will be a popular need and the lessons of Byker Wall and the Eldonians will be important. However, the mix of uses will also be important and it is to be expected that multiple-use buildings will be developed. This simply takes the 'high-tech' approach of an industrial–office mix to its next logical applications.

It is also to be expected that public and private spaces will become less clear as shopping centres are opened for more hours and high streets are managed to protect the town and city retailing 'product' (Rydin, 1990). New organizations and hybrids will be used to experiment, whether it is companies in the mould of Inner City Enterprises, borrowing Community Development Trusts from the United States, charity-based and voluntary sector organizations or popular ones such as the Eldonians. The avenues for exploration can be summarized as:

- new development mixes;
- new development organizations;
- new development uses;

- developments for innovation;
- developments for creating products and services that will speed up the economy.

It has been shown that marketing cannot be divorced from management, the result being that while marketing flagship developments and marketing the city transform the built environment and the activities within it, the management of the process changes the nature of the initiator and of the 'product', for in the urban context marketing is an iterative process.

Policy too is iterative, and marketing could become one of the central tenets of urban policy making and implementation. In fact, the process has already begun in reaction to the property-led and flagship initiatives of regeneration in the 1980s. This has begun in a reactive way.

City Challenge has already begun to create increased dialogue between local organizations, simultaneously, yet covertly, showing the increased intervention into the urban economy. It has encouraged consideration of a wider range of project types and is beginning to integrate education, training and employment initiatives with the development process. This begins to link more closely with the population needs of an area. Theoretically, it can involve the population, although it has not done so to date. This is a serious drawback. Equally serious from a marketing perspective is that tenders are awarded upon the basis of securing private finance for projects and costs. These are supply-side issues and bear no relationship to what may or may not be a successful development in terms of external demands. Indeed, regarding internal demand, the sorts of projects that will genuinely reach the most disadvantaged and create competitive advantage for an area or city are penalized on cost grounds under the bid process.

The smaller scale character of City Challenge projects is more likely to induce gradual and sensitive change, and the implementation may help to evolve new management practices.

The Urban Redevelopment Agency has a number of positive features, particularly the coordination of a range of policy instruments, although it excludes as many as it includes. Again, it is supply side in its approach and has been criticized by the president of the Royal Institution of Chartered Surveyors for being too narrow. It also excludes social infrastructure, such as housing, schools and hospitals (*Financial Times*, 1992d). It is these and other new markets that need to be tapped because it has been shown that even in the property boom years of the 1980s, social conditions became worse in the inner cities (Policy Studies Institute, 1992). Purely spatial and purely supply-side policies are not going to meet the economic, political and social needs in the years ahead.

How long have we got? This rhetorical question has serious implications. Drucker sees new management means as a project for the next fifty years.

Social instability in the city – crime, drugs, violence, homelessness and social disobedience – are all on the increase. Homelessness is steadily growing, while rioting is intermittent and unpredictable. So is the other great growth process, that of city destruction, whether Beirut, Khorramshahr, Kuwait City, Baghdad or Sarajevo. It is the rate of global and societal change that is important, and this has a tendency to accelerate in spurts, so there is no room for complacency.

15.4 URBAN REGENERATION AND CITY VISIONS

The analysis has shown that marketing the city is a potentially powerful trend. Flagship developments have proved to be at the cutting edge of the marketing process, testing the scope and directions in which marketing can be developed. Perhaps the promise and momentum of marketing the city is too powerful to resist or be resisted, but I do not believe that to be an absolute certainty. Yet it cannot be ignored and will become an important part of discovering, debating and developing our visions for the city in the next century.

Determining our vision implies, as Winterson (1991) asserts, finding that city in ourselves. That will develop interactively as we debate with each other our competing views (cf. Healey, 1992). It should continue into practice through the participation process, encouraging others to rediscover their own city (Bianchini, Dawson and Evans, 1990, 1992) and their needs in relation to it (Mayer, 1989). This articulation will need to be grounded in the impact the economy has on urban degeneration and development (cf. Smyth, 1985). The inner city problem and the flagship solution has served to emphasize the nature of the urban 'product'. Just like other products it has a life cycle, both as buildings and in areas. The product life cycle works on a number of levels. For flagship developments the promotional life cycle is short. The life cycle of the users and their activities is longer; however, the life of the building may far exceed that, through new users and change of use.

However, the product life cycle for areas, and indeed for buildings within them, has been shortening rapidly. As the economy has achieved greater efficiency, each successive concentric ring of development has been developed to serve a shorter period of time. Even if this was not consciously considered, then financing development and construction technology has been geared to the production of buildings with a shorter life cycle. The threat is that whole 'rings' of the city will degenerate simultaneously as each development phase has a shorter life.

This poses massive problems because parts of the existing inner cities will be bypassed in favour of development in the next ring. Developments in these outer rings are likely to be of a smaller scale. The land holdings are more fragmented and all the stock will not wear out or fall into disuse simultaneously. The fragmentation of degeneration will perhaps make it easier to recreate a competitive and desirable environment. It will help avoid Jacobs' 'cataclysmic money', which she sees as so harmful. The fragmentation of regeneration need will not demand the same scale of development to create a momentum. Project spend may not emphasize the construction side, but may be used to integrate functions in the way that the 'foyer' housing schemes from France are being piloted to provide the first rung on the housing ladder for the homeless and disadvantaged, with training and counselling services as an integral part of the package.

It is hard to see how marketing the city or any future vision for the city can be conceived without facing up to a massive devaluation of the city stock across certain types of buildings, locations and areas. Addressing this again requires recognition of the dual market: the market outside the city, consisting of inward investors and consumers, and the market within the 'product', in other words those that live in the city. Flagship developments and their successors will have to be more dynamic, more creative and more coherent in strategic marketing and management to face, and overcome, devaluation and degeneration. The closer the concept of marketing the city is examined, the more obvious it becomes that people have to be considered as part of the marketing process. It is a two-edged sword between manipulation, even exploitation, and genuine benefits for the city population, particularly for the most disadvantaged. The challenge for marketing the city is whether this is taken on board and whether it will bring about a better city than those that we experience today.

> If you do away with the yoke of oppression,
> with the pointing finger and malicious talk,
> and if you spend yourselves on behalf of the hungry
> and satisfy the needs of the oppressed,
> then your light will rise in the darkness,
> and your night will become like the noonday. . . .
> Your people will rebuild the ancient ruins
> and will raise up the age-old foundations;
> you will be called Repairer of Broken Walls,
> Restorer of Streets with Dwellings.
>   Isaiah 58:10,12

Notes

1. This includes all expenditure on urban renewal through local authorities and therefore the reductions in construction programmes by local authorities as a result of both changing local management priorities and central government capping.
2. This argument is closely related to the renewed social science interest in biology in general and ecology and evolution in particular. Clearly, diversity is important in natural food chains for the sustaining species. While humans are not apart from nature, one of the natural characteristics of humans is an ability to be creative and stewards of the environment. Whether this stewardship is being carried out with sufficient diligence **is** the current issue. However, it is clear that humans are capable of sustaining life using a few species, the minimal number of cereal crops harvested in bulk being an obvious example. Failure to maintain ecological stability can be viewed as thwarting nature, and thus human existence. It can also be viewed as part of the evolutionary process, which recent thinking has shown to be less of a steady process and more likely to be one of gradual change followed by periods of major change. (Ironically this is more like the economic cycles which economists have tried to eradicate to create greater equilibrium, so as to mirror 'nature' more accurately). The problem with evolutionary theory in a social context, which is being worked out at the level of genes – pools for selectivity, 'selfishness', survival – is that it assumes that genes 'know' or have the capacity to 'know' what is best suited for future survival. For example, how did the genes in Iranians born twenty-five years ago know what would be most suited for a society under an Islamic Revolution, or for the children who were to fight in the Second World War? Nor can it be claimed that the weakest will not reproduce under adverse circumstances because individuals are protected by social conventions thrown up by regimes, by medical advances and by other factors. The weakest will not necessarily die during wars, for example, because of the randomness of military orders and technology for the individuals life chances *vis-à-vis* any inherent ability to fight and survive under war conditions. The continuing problem for the evolutionists is that the significance of the science is derived from Darwin's unproven proposition that human beings evolved from apes. While it would be foolhardy to deny the existence of evolution, the 'missing link' remains; yet the significance, derived from the assumption of its existence, is imported into the

rest of nature. This potentially grossly exaggerates the significance and consequences of evolution. It seems to me that we know something important is going on here, but we really do not know how important it is. Similarly, I would wish to be cautious about its impute into the social and economic realm. We may be, of course, simply dealing with different laws in the social context.

3. There are two important points to be made about sustainable 'covering'. Firstly, the shared values have to come from the population as a whole and therefore will probably form part of a vision. Secondly, there needs to be a mechanism for change to be taken on board, either within the value system or concerning policies. Both these must be a bottom-up as well as a top-down process.

4. The rational planning, derived from positivism, being the most obvious recent example, which remains prevalent in many spheres of activity, especially in natural science and economics.

5. BURA (1991b) set up the following criteria for regeneration projects:

- proven economic viability in their own right;
- making an important contribution to the momentum for sustained regeneration in their area;
- contributing to the pride and cohesion of the local community;
- contributing to an attractive environment.

How each of these criteria is used is up to the individuals and any shared values the committee may discover.

6. However, a degree of interpretation has been made. The research does not claim to be value-free. It reflects the values of the initiators; it also reflects mine, both through interpretation and the use of the marketing matrix for comparing projects. This value issue should not be regarded as unusual; indeed, the focus on the initiators lends considerable weight to the findings, and, brought together with other values, provides opportunities for synthesis.

7. The accountability can be scant. For example UDCs have no local accountability but only through central government (see for example, Robinson and Shaw, 1991), which is judged in electoral terms on a broader basis of policies and action, except where the local population is unprepared to give power to UDCs, civil disorder being the outcome.

8. Excluded are those projects labelled by letting agents as 'flagship' in a pejorative way, for example business park schemes.

9. This matrix only addresses **market** position; social well-being is therefore filtered through this perspective, although the author is well aware of research that places primacy on social well-being as a way of challenging the market. It is possible to explore through the matrix such an approach based upon 'need' as a normative cultural device, and, indeed, subsequent analysis looks at whether this can be separated from the urban product.

10. This integrity need not be one of justice. Nor, therefore, need it be one of honesty concerning just aims and objectives. The integrity springs from the economic laws that give rise to it, which it therefore reflects. In saying this I am somewhat at odds with Clark (1985) and Harvey (1991), who suggests that the 'spectacle' marks the 'dissolution of the city as an affective and knowable community'. 'Community' implies a coherence and cohesion to the organiz-

ation of the city and among its population, respectively, that has never existed.

11. Interview with Professor David Harvey, Halford Mackinder Chair of Geography, University of Oxford, 10 February 1992.

12. Flexibility can be achieved through a number of measures in design, for example putting in infrastructure as plots have prelets against them, designing 'speculative' buildings to permit subdivision and constructing 'speculative' buildings to shell and core only.

13. This could be seen to imply that an innovative project is using service skills. However, what we must clearly distinguish between is the type of project being envisaged, and therefore the market position it occupies, and those responsible for implementation. Those responsible may not, and should not in many cases, occupy the same market position as the project because their function will be particular to the project or part of it.

14. The nature of funded research placed limitations upon the number of case studies that could be resourced. BURA, who commissioned the research with the backing of J Sainsbury, also wished a housing project to be included within the research and it was this requirement that led to the decision to include Byker as a case study, for reasons set out in the chapter text.

15. The Byker Wall was conceived prior to the Watershed and its implementation also began earlier. However, it was completed after the Watershed.

16. Interview with Roger Mortimer, former Director of, and a Consultant to, the JT Group, 21 February 1992.

17. Interview with Martin Heighton, Director of Leisure Services, City of Bristol District Council, 10 March 1992.

18. Interview with Dick Penny, Chief Executive, Watershed Media Centre, 11 February 1992.

19. Interview with Councillor Bernard Zissman, former Chair of the Birmingham City Council International Sub-Committee and former Mayor of Birmingham, 20 March 1992.

20. Interview with John Vergette, Chair of Percy Thomas Partnership, 17 December, 1991.

21. Interview with Luqman Khan, Property Information Officer, Economic Development Unit, Birmingham City Council, 20 February 1992.

22. Interview with Paul Swan, Managing Director, Spectrum Communications Ltd, 7 February 1992.

23. Interview with Gordon Campbell, General Manager, Hyatt Regency Hotel, Birmingham, 9 April 1992.

24. Interview with Alan Chatham, Director, Brindleyplace plc, 20 February 1992.

25. Interview with Alan Chatham, Director, Brindleyplace plc, 1 April 1992.

26. A rights issue is an offer of shares to existing shareholders on a pro rata basis to their existing shareholdings. Confidence in an issue, which essentially dilutes the value of the existing shares held, can be created by the key financial institutions that hold shares guaranteeing to take up their proportion of the shares offered through the rights issue.

27. Interview with Sue Wilkinson and Kevin Robins, Centre for Urban and Regional Development Studies, University of Newcastle, 15 January 1992.

28. Interview with Nigel Perry, former City Planning Officer and employee of architects Fairhursts, 12 February 1992.

29. Interview with John Hume, Economic and Development Division, Development Department, and Ian Hegginbotton, Policy Team, Planning Department, Newcastle City Council, 14 February 1992.

30. Interview with Peter Smith, former Executive Director, Westgate Trust, 11 March 1992.

31. Conversation with Neil Barker, former chair of Northumbria RIBA, 28 January 1992.

32. Interview with Professor Patsy Healey and Barry Wood, Department of Town and Country Planning, University of Newcastle, 14 January 1992.

33. Conversation with David Byrne, Department of Sociology, Durham University, 28 January 1992.

34. Interview with Michelle Hodson, former Neighbourhood Manager of Shield Field Housing, 12 February 1992.

35. Interview with Mike Turnbull, former Area Housing Officer for Byker, Housing Manager, Cruddas Park, 12 February 1992.

36. Interview with Stuart Cameron and Rose Gilroy, Department of Town and Country Planning, University of Newcastle, 15 January 1992.

37. Interview with Paul Keenan, Principal Housing Needs Officer, Housing Department, City of Newcastle, 12 March 1992.

38. Interview with Chris Mills, Housing Renewal Officer, Housing Department, City of Newcastle, 12 February 1992.

References

Albrechts, L. (1991) Changing roles and positions of planners. *Urban Studies*, **28**(1), 123–7.

Alexander, C., Davis, H., Martinez, J. and Corner, D. (1985) *The Production of Houses*, Oxford University Press, New York.

Altman, I. and Chemers, M.M. (1984) *Culture and Environment*, Cambridge University Press, Cambridge.

Amery, C. (undated) Housing, Byker, Newcastle upon Tyne, in *Byker by Erskine*.

Architects Journal (1979) Editor's comment, 16 May.

Architects Journal (1992) Making places: Centenary Square, 5th February.

Architecture Today (1992) Moving experience: the arena comes to Birmingham, no. 24.

Arnolfini Gallery Ltd and Building Partnership (Bristol) Ltd (undated) Life begins at 140: new life for the Bush Warehouse, Bristol.

Arts Business Ltd (1991) The cultural economy of Birmingham.

Ashworth, G.J. and Voogd, H. (1990) *Selling the City: Marketing Approaches in Public Sector Planning*, Belhaven Press, London.

Barnekov, T., Boyle, R. and Rich, D. (1988) *Privatism and Urban Policy in Britain and the United States*, Oxford University Press, Oxford.

Barnekov, T. and Rich, D. (1989) Privatism and the limits of economic development policy. *Urban Affairs Quarterly*, **25**(2), 212–38.

Barnett, S. (1991) Selling us short? Cities, culture and economic development, in *Whose Cities?* (eds M. Fisher and U. Owen), Penguin, Harmondsworth.

BBC (1992) Signs of the city. *Omnibus*, BBC 1, 21 January.

Bell, D. (1976) *The Cultural Contradictions of Capital*, Heinemann, London.

Berman, M. (1983) *All That is Solid Melts into Air*, Verson, London.

Berry, B. (1985) Islands of renewal in seas of decay, in *The New Urban Reality*, (ed. P. Peterson), Brookings Institution, Washington.

Bianchini, F., Dawson, J. and Evans, R. (1990) Flagship projects in urban regeneration. Paper given at Property-led Urban Regeneration Seminar, University of Newcastle, 29–31 March.

Bianchini, F., Dawson, J. and Evans, R. (1992) Flagship projects in urban regeneration, in *Rebuilding the City: Property-led Urban Regeneration*, (eds P. Healey, S. Davoudi, M. O'Toole, S. Tavsanoglu and D. Usher), E&FN Spon, London.

Birmingham City 2000 (1991a) Manchester report highlights Birmingham's strengths. *Communiqué*, no. 4.

Birmingham City 2000 (1991b) Roadshow targets three US cities. *Communiqué*, no. 4.

Birmingham City Council (undated) Birmingham profile.

Birmingham City Council (1989) Poverty in Birmingham: a profile.

Birmingham City Council (1990a) Internal report by the Chief Executive and other department heads on an arts strategy for Birmingham.

Birmingham City Council (1990b) Birmingham annual report and accounts, 1989–90.

Birmingham City Council (1990c) International Convention Centre/National Indoor Arena: Employment impact within the Broad Street corridors. Report of Director of Development to National Exhibition Centre/International Convention Centre Committee, 6 June.

Birmingham City Council (1991a) Facing the challenge in Birmingham, East Birmingham City Challenge.

Birmingham City Council (1991b) Birmingham annual report and accounts, 1990–91.

Birmingham City Council (1992a) Birmingham City Council 1992/93.

Birmingham City Council (1992b) City centre strategy.

Birmingham City Council (1992c) Poverty in Birmingham: City Council strategy.

Bourdieu, P. (1984) *Distinction: A Social Critique of the Judgement of Taste*, Routledge & Kegan Paul, London.

Boyer, M. (1988) The return of aesthetics to city planning. *Society*, **25**(4), 49–56.

Boyle, R. (1989) Partnership in practice. *Local Government Studies*, March/April, 17–28.

Boyle, R. and Meyer, P. (1990) Local economic development in the USA. *Local Economy*, **4**(4), 272–7.

Brindleyplace (undated) The water's edge at Brindleyplace, Birmingham.

Brindleyplace News (undated) Issue 2, Birmingham.

Brownill, S. (1990) *Developing London's Docklands: Another Great Planning Disaster*, Paul Chapman, London.

Building Design (1992) Masterplan submitted, 10 January.

BURA (1991a) The public ownership of land: is it essential for urban regeneration? Briefing note no. 6. BURA, London.

BURA (1991b) BURA announces best practice awards for urban regeneration. *BURA News*, (3).

Burns, R. (1991) The city as not London, in *Whose Cities?* (eds M. Fisher and U. Owen), Penguin, Harmondsworth.

Cameron, S. and Thornton, G. (1986) Build for sale partnerships in Byker. *Housing Review*, **35**(2), 53–7.

Carley, M. (1991) Business in urban regeneration partnerships: a case study of Birmingham. *Local Economy*, **6**(2), 100–15.

Casson Conder and Partners (1972) Bristol City Docks – redevelopment study 1972.

CBI (1987) Initiatives beyond charity, CBI, London.

CBI (1988) Newcastle Task Force, CBI, London.

Champion, A.G. and Townsend, A.R. (1990) *Contemporary Britain: A Geographical Perspective*, Edward Arnold, London.

Clark, T.J. (1985) *The Painting of Modern Life: Paris in the Art of Manet and his*

Followers, Thames and Hudson, London.

Coleman, A. (1990) *Utopia on Trial: Vision and Reality in Planned Housing*, Hilary Shipman, London.

Commission for Racial Equality (1991) Working in hotels, London.

Committee of Public Accounts (1990) Regeneration of the inner cities. 33rd report, Minutes of evidence taken before the Committee, 12 February. HMSO, London.

Communiqué (1991a) ICC and VW–Audi shape future, Winter. ICC, Birmingham.

Communiqué (1991b) So many options available at flexible NIA, Winter. ICC, Birmingham.

Construction Weekly (1992) Special report: Leisure, 26 February.

Convention Centre Partnership (undated) International Convention Centre, Birmingham. Percy Thomas Partnership, Birmingham.

Coopers & Lybrand (undated) Newcastle Theatre Village Development Organisation: West Gate Development Company feasibility study.

Cowan, R., Hannay, P. and Owens, R. (1988) The light on top of the tunnel. *Architects Journal*, 23 March.

Coxe, W., Hartung, N.F., Hochberg, H. *et al.* (1987) *Success Strategies for Design Professionals: Superpositioning for Architecture and Engineering Firms*, McGraw-Hill, New York.

Davis, M. (1990) *City of Quartz: Excavating the Future in Los Angeles*, Verso, London.

Department of Employment (1986) Inner city task forces put people before 'real estate' minister reports, Department of Employment Press Notice 156/86 of speech to Birmingham Chamber of Commerce 23 June.

Department of the Environment (1989) *Review of Derelict Land Policy*, HMSO, London.

DiGaetano, A. and Klemanski, J.S. (1992) Urban regime capacity: a comparison of Birmingham, England and Detroit, Michigan. Paper given at the Annual Meeting of the Urban Affairs Association, Cleveland, Ohio, 29 April–2 May.

Drucker, P.F. (1955) *The Practice of Management*, Heinemann, London.

Drucker, P.F. (1986) *The Frontiers of Management*, Heinemann, London.

Economic Development Office (1992) The Bristol file, City of Bristol District Council.

Economic Development Unit (undated) The Birmingham investment, Birmingham City Council.

Economic Development Unit (1992) Birmingham lifestyle, Birmingham City Council.

Edgar, D. (1991) From Metroland to the Medicis: the cultural politics of the city state, in *Whose Cities?* (eds M. Fisher and U. Owen), Penguin, Harmondsworth.

Edgington, D.W. (1990) New strategies for technology development in Japanese cities and regions. *Town Planning Review*, 60(1), 1–27.

Egelius, M. (1990) Keeping out of the wind. *World Architecture*, 6, 37–41.

Erskine, R. (1970) Report on the Byker redevelopment area.

Financial Times (1991a) Comedy of errors, Bristol Survey, 28 November.

Financial Times (1991b) Untapped visitor appeal, Bristol Survey, 28 November.

Financial Times (1991c) Rosehaugh proposes £250m Birmingham development, 18 December.

Financial Times (1992a) Liverpool steps up to blow its own trumpet, 23 January.

Financial Times (1992b) Trade fairs wooed, Conferences and Exhibitions Survey, 25 February.

Financial Times (1992c) 5 October.

Financial Times (1992d) Partnership in the cities, 14 August.

Fisher, M. (1991) Introduction, in *Whose Cities?* (eds M. Fisher and U. Owen), Penguin, Harmondsworth.

Fox, M. and Healey, P. (1991) Inner city regeneration vehicles. Report for the Westgate Trust, University of Newcastle.

Franks, D. (1983) International Convention Centre Birmingham: feasibility study, Birmingham City Council.

Frieden, B.J. and Sagalyn, L.B. (1989) *Downtown Inc.: How America Rebuilds Cities*, MIT Press, Cambridge, Massachusetts.

Frieden, B.J. (1990) Center city transformed: planners as developers. *Journal of the American Planning Association*, **56**(4), 423–8.

Gann, D.M. (1991) Buildings for the Japanese information economy: neighbourhood and resort offices. *Futures*, **23**(5), 469–81.

Gans, H.J. (1969) Planning for people, not buildings. *Environment and Planning*, **1**(1), 33–46.

Goobey, A.R. (1992) *Bricks and Mortals – The Dream of the 80s and the Nightmare of the 90s: The Inside Story of the Property World*, Century Business, London.

Goodman, R. (1972) *After the Planners*, Penguin, Harmondsworth.

Gracie, V. (1979) Architect's account. *Architects Journal*, 16 May.

Guardian (1992) Too good for Britain, 29 May.

Guiltinan, J.P. and Paul, G.W. (1988) *Marketing Management: Strategies and Programs*, 3rd edn, McGraw-Hill, New York.

Hambleton, R. (1990) Urban government in the 1990s: lessons from the USA. Occasional Paper no. 35, School for Advanced Urban Studies, University of Bristol.

Harvey, D. (1989a) *The Condition of Postmodernity*, Blackwell, Oxford.

Harvey, D. (1989b) From managerialism to entrepreneurialism: the transformation in urban governance in late capitalism. *Georafiska Annaler*, **71**(B/1), 3–17.

Harvey, D. (1989c) *The Urban Experience*, Blackwell, Oxford.

Harvey, D. (1991) The urban face of capitalism, in *Our Changing Cities*, (ed. J. F. Hart), Johns Hopkins University Press, Baltimore and London.

Healey, P. (1990) Urban Regeneration and the Development Industry. Paper given at Property-led Urban Regeneration Seminar, University of Newcastle, 29–31 March.

Healey, P. (1991) Models of the development process: a review. *Journal of Property Research*, **8**(2), 219–38.

Healey, P. (1992) Planning through debate: the communicative turn in planning theory. *Town Planning Review*, **63**(2), 143–62.

HMSO (1977) *Policy for the Inner Cities*, Cmnd 6845, HMSO, London.

Housing Review (1974) Urban redevelopment – the Byker experience, November/December, 149–56.

ICC (1992) Reports, Birmingham.

Independent (1991) Second fiddle hard to find amid a wealth of orchestral talent, 18 December.

Intercity (1991) Birmingham, May.

Jacobs, J. (1965) *The Death and Life of Great American Cities: The Failure of Town Planning*, Penguin, Harmondsworth.

Jacobs, J. (1972) *The Economy of Cities*, Penguin, Harmondsworth.

Jones, B. (1990) All set for take off. Business city of the 1990s. *Birmingham Post/Evening Mail*, 16 January.

JT Group Ltd (undated) Watershed, Bristol.

JT Group Ltd (1991) Watershed, Bristol.

JT Group Ltd and Bristol Arts Centre (undated) Watershed: a new life for E & W Sheds, Bristol.

Kester, G. (1990) A survivor's guide to Baltimore's renaissance. *Architecture Research Criticism*, **1**(2), 18–21.

Leake, J. (1991) School grants go to the ICC instead, *Birmingham Express and Star*, 23 May.

Lefebvre, H. (1991) *The Production of Space*, Blackwell, Oxford.

Leisureweek (1992) Fatboys Diner heads for Birmingham venue, 19 June.

Levitt, T. (1983) *The Marketing Imagination*, The Free Press, Macmillan, New York.

Lister, D. (1991) The transformation of a city: Birmingham, in *Whose Cities?* (eds M. Fisher and U. Owen), Penguin, Harmondsworth.

Loftman, P. and Nevin, B. (1992) Urban regeneration and social equity: a case study of Birmingham. Research paper no. 38, Faculty of the Built Environment, University of Central England, Birmingham.

Malpass, P. (1979) The politics of participation. *Architects Journal*, 16 May.

Marshall, T. (1991) *Understanding Leadership: Fresh Perspectives on the Essentials of New Testament Leadership*, Sovereign World, Chichester.

Massey, D.B. (1984) *Spatial Divisions of Labour*, Macmillan, London.

Mayer, M. (1989) From administration to management. Paper given at the Regulation, Innovation and Spatial Development Symposium, University of Wales, Cardiff, 13–15 September.

McGrath, D. (1982) Who must leave? Alternative images of revitalisation. *Journal of the American Planning Association*, **48**(2), 196–203.

Mellor, J.R. (1977) *Urban Sociology in an Urbanized Society*, Routledge & Kegan Paul, London.

NEC Group (1992) Corporate review, Birmingham.

Newcastle City Council (undated) District 6 – Byker, Newcastle upon Tyne.

Newcastle City Council (1981) The Byker redevelopment, Newcastle upon Tyne.

Newcastle City Council (1991) Theatre Village and Chinatown development strategy, Newcastle upon Tyne.

Policy Studies Institute (1992) Urban Trends, vol. 1, London.

Poole, R. with Donovan, K. (1991) Safer shopping: the identification of opportunities for crime and disorder in covered shopping centres, West Midlands Police, Birmingham and Home Office Police Requirements Support Unit, London.

Quantrill, S. (1991) A city for Europe. *Estates Gazette*, 27 July.

Raban, J. (1974) *Soft City*, Hamilton, London.

Ravetz, A. (1976) Housing at Byker, Newcastle upon Tyne. *Architects Journal*, 14 April.

Robins, K. and Wilkinson, S. (1990) The imaginary institution of the city. Paper given at Property-led Urban Regeneration Seminar, University of Newcastle,

29–31 March.

Robinson, F. and Shaw, K. (1991) Urban regeneration and community involvement. *Local Economy*, **6**(1), 61–73.

Robinson, J. (1964) *Economic Philosophy*, Penguin, Harmondsworth.

Robson, B. (1988) *Those Inner Cities*, Oxford University Press, Oxford.

Rogers, R. and Fisher, M. (1992) *A New London*, Penguin, Harmondsworth.

Rydin, Y. (1990) Demographic change and the retail property market: the relation of use, investment and development markets. Paper given at Property-led Urban Regeneration Seminar, University of Newcastle, 29–31 March.

Saunders, P. (1990) *A Nation of Homeowners*, Unwin Hyman, London.

Skeffington Committee Report (1969) *People and Planning*, HMSO, London.

Smyth, H.J. (1985) *Property Companies and the Construction Industry in Britain*, Cambridge University Press, Cambridge.

Smyth, H.J. (1991) The development process as viewed from the private sector. Paper given at the Development Opportunities in Hungary Seminar, Foreign and Commonwealth Office 'Know How Fund' Programme, Budapest, Hungary, 19–21 July.

Sparks, L. (1991) Changing the image. *Estates Gazette*, July.

Spectrum Communications (1991) The past, present and future, Birmingham City Council.

Squires, G.D. (1991) Partnership and the pursuit of the private city, in *Urban Life in Transition: Urban Affairs Annual Review*, vol. 39, Sage Publications, New York, pp. 196–221.

Stollard, P. (ed.) (1991) *Crime Prevention through Housing Design*, E&FN Spon, London.

Symphony Hall (1991) 2nd season of international concerts, Birmingham.

Three's Company Communications (undated) International Convention Centre Birmingham.

TNI (undated) The Newcastle Initiative, Newcastle upon Tyne.

TNI (1988) Theatre Village and Chinatown, Newcastle upon Tyne.

TNI (c. 1990) Westgate Trust, press release, Newcastle upon Tyne.

The Westgate Trust (1990) Question and answer brief, Newcastle upon Tyne.

Trafalgar House (1992) Report and Accounts.

Tyne Theatre and Opera House (1987) *An Illustrated History of the Tyne Theatre and Opera House*, Newcastle upon Tyne.

Watershed Arts Trust Bristol (1981) Watershed, progress report no. 3, 18 December, Bristol.

Westgate Trust (1990) Memorandum and Articles of Association, Dickinson Dees, Newcastle upon Tyne.

Wildscreen (1988) Wildscreen '88, Bristol.

Wilkinson, S. (1992) Towards a new city? A case study of image-improvement initiatives in Newcastle upon Tyne, in *Rebuilding the City: Property-led Urban Regeneration*, (eds P. Healey, S. Davoudi, M. O'Toole, S. Tavsanoglu and D. Usher), E&FN Spon, London.

Williams, R. (1975) *The Country and the City*, Paladin, London.

Wilson, E. (1991) *The Sphinx in the City: Urban Life, the Control of Disorder, and Women*, Virago, London.

Winterson, J. (1991) Dreams and buildings, in *Whose Cities?* (eds M. Fisher and U.

Owen), Penguin, Harmondsworth.

Wishart, R. (1991) Fashioning the city: Glasgow, in *Whose Cities?* (eds M. Fisher and U. Owen), Penguin, Harmondsworth.

Wood, B. and Woodling, K. (1990) The Newcastle Initiative. Paper given at Property-led Urban Regeneration Seminar, University of Newcastle, 29–31 March.

Worpole, K. (1991) Trading places: the city workshop, in *Whose Cities?* (eds M. Fisher and U. Owen), Penguin, Harmondsworth.

Young, I.M. (1990) *Justice and the Politics of Difference*, Princetown University Press, Princetown, New Jersey.

Zukin, S. (1988) *Loft Living: Culture and Capital in Urban Change*, Radius, London.

Author index

Subject index